EVAN MARSHALL is from N
television there for the last
with Doubleband Films whe
of series for BBC Northern
Northern Ireland Screen's D
that he first saw a Pathé ne
Ireland team. This footage inspired his acclaimed documentary
film, *Spirit of '58*, which he produced and directed. In 2013 he
established his own production company, Clackity Films. He
has written articles for many years on the subjects of music,
sport and television and has contributed to *Record Collector*,
FourFourTwo and the *Belfast Telegraph*. A collection of his writing
can be found at evanrobertmarshall.wordpress.com. He lives in
Belfast with his wife and son.

SPIRIT OF '58

THE INCREDIBLE UNTOLD STORY OF NORTHERN IRELAND'S GREATEST FOOTBALL TEAM

EVAN MARSHALL

·THE· BLACK ·STAFF· PRESS

First published in 2016 by
Blackstaff Press
4D Weavers Court
Linfield Road
Belfast, BT12 5GH

Typeset by KT Designs, Newton-le-Willows, England

Printed and bound by Martins the Printers, Berwick upon Tweed

A CIP catalogue for this book is available from the British Library

ISBN 978 0 85640 957 8

www.blackstaffpress.com

CONTENTS

FOREWORD

Like most Northern Ireland fans today, I wasn't born in time to experience the achievements of the Northern Ireland team in 1958. Football then was very different – the 1958 squad was built against the backdrop of a society coming together in the aftermath of the Second World War. Now, like all competing nations, we have highly professional facilities, structures and preparations in place to give us the best chance of success. There are still, however, similarities between then and now: the selection problems, injuries, the euphoria, success and total togetherness.

The question I probably get asked the most is 'How have you done it?' The answer is team spirit. The 1958 squad also had the kind of true team spirit that will ensure that names – and characters – such as Peter Doherty, Peter McParland, Wilbur Cush, Willie Cunningham and Alf McMichael, along with the likes of Billy Bingham, Danny Blanchflower, Harry Gregg and Derek Dougan, will remain an important part of our history.

Spirit of '58 is full of terrific stories from the era that are sure to resurrect memories for those who were around at the time and will paint a picture of what it was like for those who weren't. The downgrading of a World Cup qualifier against Italy at Windsor Park to that of a friendly because the Hungarian officials failed to show up, and it then becoming anything but friendly. The horrors of the Munich Air Disaster. Northern Ireland's unofficial thirteen-year-old mascot, Bengt Jonasson, the boy who seemed to have taken up permanent residence outside the Halmstad training camp, as an unlikely superfan. Gerry Morgan pouring two bottles of whiskey over goalkeeper Norman Uprichard's injured ankle, enabling him to play on and break his hand … I can hear the quotes included from Dr Malcolm Brodie MBE's copy from the 1950s, read aloud in his voice. All of this and more makes up the story of a squad that stood just one game away from a semi-final in the World Cup against Brazil.

Countless people have congratulated our players, staff and the Irish FA for what we have achieved, and said we've brought the spirit of '82 and '86 back to life. It's something quite remarkable to hear, as I know how those teams inspired a generation and kept people dreaming for thirty years. Billy Bingham and his back room could well have been told the same thing, that they had rekindled the spirit of '58. These memories are precious to so many hundreds of thousands of people, and we're aiming to create some unforgettable times in France this summer – stories to be handed down to another generation.

We want to establish a legacy, to have something for players at all levels to aspire to, and to ensure future managers of Northern Ireland have sustainable foundations to build upon. We all can see that the construction of the National Football Stadium at Windsor Park and its world-class facilities will make a marked contribution to this, and we hope that investment in coaching and player development throughout Northern Ireland will help future generations to realise their dreams.

As Euro 2016 draws closer, our focus is entirely on making these finals an occasion to remember, and to reward the fans who have travelled the length and breadth of Europe and beyond to support us.

This book, *Spirit of '58*, couldn't be coming out at a better time. It shows Northern Ireland football at its typically raw and determined best – and that's something to inspire us all in the months ahead.

Michael O'Neill, Northern Ireland team manager
April 2016

ACKNOWLEDGEMENTS

Many thanks to the team at Blackstaff Press in Belfast for their help and encouragement on the book. In particular, I am grateful to Patsy Horton as editor and Helen Wright as proofreader – both helped to make this a better book. Thanks also go to Jim Meredith and others at Blackstaff for help along the way.

Between 2013 and 2014 I was lucky enough to interview Harry Gregg, Billy Bingham, Jimmy McIlroy, Peter McParland, Billy Simpson and Bengt Jonasson for the documentary, *Spirit of '58* (2015). I have quoted liberally from these interviews in the book and I am especially grateful to those interviewed for giving me such a great sense for what it was like to be involved with the Northern Ireland team in the 1950s. Additional thanks are due to Ben Price who was cameraman and editor on the film and who recorded the interviews for me.

Thanks also go to Dan Morgan, son of Northern Ireland's most famous trainer, Gerry. My conversations with Dan provided yet more stories about his father and his generous gifting of photographs and memorabilia from Sweden has been of immense use in the film and the book.

After *Spirit of '58* was made, I discovered that the historian John Bew had conducted interviews with Bertie Peacock, Norman Uprichard and Malcolm Brodie in 2002 for a possible documentary. I am extremely grateful to John for permission to use the interviews, as well as to Gerry Gregg of Praxis Pictures in Dublin who located and sent the old cassette tapes to me. The Peacock interview was a particularly important source for me as I had no other extensive interview with him on the subject of 1958. The other two interviews were useful for general context.

Further quotes come from a number of media sources. Danny Blanchflower made several appearances on the *Parkinson* series and he was also the subject of an edition of *Desert Island Discs*.

Although incomplete in the archives, his edition did include a segment on the England game in 1957. This fragment, along with many other editions of the series, is available online.

Malcolm Brodie is surely the most famous and most passionate sports writer in Irish journalistic history, with a career spanning over half a century. Shortly before his death he gave an interview to BBC Northern Ireland in which he talked about the Northern Ireland team. Thanks to Declan Doherty of BBC NI for arranging a viewing of the complete rushes of this interview in which Brodie spent a few minutes talking about the Doherty era and his own experiences at the World Cup.

I found a television clip on YouTube that focussed mainly on Northern Ireland's qualification against Italy and the subsequent World Cup. It was of huge interest to me because it featured interviews with Bertie Peacock and the IFA Secretary at the time, Billy Drennan. Despite searches in the archives of BBC NI and UTV no one could find any information on when it was broadcast or by whom, the suspicion being that it had long since been wiped. Although the VHS recording that had been uploaded to YouTube was not of high enough quality to use in the documentary, the interviews proved useful for the book.

Of course the players have written about their experiences at the World Cup and of playing under Doherty. Four of the players I interviewed had written autobiographies that I was able to use to supplement what they told me in interviews – Billy Bingham, *Soccer With the Stars* (1962); Harry Gregg, *Wild About Football* (1961) and, with Roger Anderson, *Harry's Game* (2002); Jimmy McIlroy, *Right Inside Soccer* (1960); and Peter McParland, *Going for Goal* (1960). Several late players had also written autobiographies or football books, and these proved extremely useful too – Danny Blanchflower, *Soccer My Way* (1955), *Danny Blanchflower's Soccer Book* (1959) and *The Double and Before* (1961); Peter Doherty, *Spotlight on Football* (1947); and Norman Uprichard (with Chris Westcott), *Norman 'Black Jake' Uprichard*

(2011). With the exception of Uprichard's, these books are long out of print but second-hand copies are available. They make for interesting reading on a very different and bygone era of football and I recommend all of them without hesitation.

An essential piece of reading for the film *Spirit of '58* was a book on the Doherty years, *The World at Their Feet* (2008), by Ronnie Hanna, a lecturer at Queen's University, Belfast. Ronnie became an important part of the documentary as an interviewee and I greatly enjoyed our discussions on 1950s football during production. Although Ronnie had completed interviews with the surviving players for his book, I wanted to tell my own version of the story so I haven't referenced any of them. Nevertheless, his book is very highly recommended (my own treasured copy is signed by all five living players, Ronnie and Bengt Jonasson) and it is well worth tracking down.

Further useful reading on the 1958 World Cup or individuals connected to the Northern Ireland story can be found in: Dave Bowler, *Danny Blanchflower, A Biography of a Visionary* (1997); Malcolm Brodie, *The History of Irish Soccer* (1963); Malcolm Brodie, *100 Years of Irish Football* (1980); John Camkin, *World Cup 1958* (1958); Steven Gordos and David Harrison, *The Doog: The Incredible Story of Derek Dougan: Football's Most Controversial Figure* (2008); David Tossell, *In Sunshine or in Shadow: A Journey Through the Life of Derek Dougan* (2012).

I would like to thank the always friendly and helpful staff of the Belfast Newspaper Library located at Belfast Central Library who assisted me during my many hours of research for both the film and the book over the last few years. This archive is a little-known national treasure and it has been a joy to lose myself in the newspapers of the period and become distracted by Cold War stories, reports of the Suez Crisis and other world events of the 1950s. The newspapers of the time are mostly kept in bound volumes as opposed to microfilm and it is a pleasure to thumb through them. The *Belfast Telegraph, Northern Whig, Irish News,*

Belfast News-Letter and *Ireland's Saturday Night* have provided a wealth of contemporary comment on events in this book and my account would be much poorer without them.

Some crucial information was accessed from the pages of the *Daily Mirror*. UKPressOnline provide an astonishing service by presenting every single page of the paper from 1903 to 1980. It's not free to use but I've always found it a very useful resource and various other newspapers are also available at the same website.

A number of foreign language publications have helped me in my research: *Herberger's Tapfere Elf* (West Germany, 1958); *Fussball-Weltmeisterschaft 1958* (West Germany, 1958); and *Fotboll-VM i Sverige* (Sweden, 1964). I have also found the following Swedish magazines useful, all from 1958: *All Sport (Nr 5) Fotbolls VM Special*; *All Sport (Nr 6/7) VM Special*; and *Fotbolls-VM 1958*.

Derek Dougan, member of Northern Ireland's World Cup squad, has also written a number of books. While they contain little on the Northern Ireland team in the 1950s, they are valuable for Dougan's intelligent and often prescient thinking on football over the years and for giving such a great sense of the personalities and the period covered in this book. The following are recommended: *Attack!* (1969), *The Sash He Never Wore* (1972, updated version 1997), *On the Spot – Football as a Profession* (1974), *Doog* (1980) and *How Not to Run Football!* (1981).

Two online resources have often been of use to me:

Northern Ireland's Footballing History (which incorporates Today in Our Footballing History) https://northernirelandsfootballinghistory.wordpress.com

Northern Ireland's Footballing Greats http://nifootball.blogspot.co.uk

These sites are invaluable for those interested in the history of Irish football and I am indebted to the people who curate them and contribute to them.

Finally, many thanks to all those who helped with fundraising and financing the film version of *Spirit of '58*. Without the generosity of so many people it would have been impossible to complete the documentary and it is likely that this book would not exist. It's impossible to list all those people here (although we did give them their place in the end credits of the film) but it would be remiss of me not to mention the support shown by the Our Wee Country Facebook page and the heartwarming gesture made by the Amalgamation of Northern Ireland Supporters' Clubs who do such a good job in organising local fandom. Thank you also to Colin Beattie, who shared a chance conversation with me a few years ago and who has been a great help and source of encouragement ever since. His unwavering support of football, rugby, cricket, boxing and athletics in Northern Ireland marks him out as a true sporting polymath. His assistance is always much appreciated while his unbridled passion for sport and its history is both admirable and infectious.

There's always so much more to learn from the past and research should be ongoing. Even when I thought I had written the final sentence for this book and was in the process of signing off on the proofs, one last source of information came to light. I found a lengthy *Belfast Telegraph* supplement for the 1979 Home International series when Danny Blanchflower was manager. It contained a short interview with Peter Doherty in which he made some references to 1958. Gold dust! If I had found this interview even half a day later it wouldn't have made it into the book. I had actually owned this supplement since I was eight years old and had thrown it into my bedside drawer along with other old football memorabilia of the late 1970s and early 1980s when I moved house ten years ago. This priceless interview has been just inches away from me through all my years of research and I had never realised – only finding it by a bizarre accident on the last possible night that I could make use of it. There's always more to find and I hope that this book encourages readers to delve into our sporting history and gain as much enjoyment from it as I have done.

INTRODUCTION

In October 1958 Northern Ireland came off the pitch at Windsor Park following a 3–3 draw with England. Just ten years earlier the game would have been an easy afternoon's work for mighty England, but such had been the transformation in the Northern Ireland team during the fifties that the men in green were now very much their equals. It had been a thrilling game and England was lucky to escape with a draw. That October day Northern Ireland were heroes, newly returned from a stellar performance in the 1958 World Cup, and they received a rapturous reception from the packed stadium. *Spirit of '58* tells the story of the transformation of the Northern Ireland team in the 1950s and their incredible success in the 1958 World Cup.

I grew up during the early 1980s, and was a football fan during that extraordinary decade when Northern Ireland qualified for two successive World Cups, won two British Championships and beat the European Champions, West Germany, home and away. For me the beginning of that great footballing era was the appointment of Billy Bingham as manager in 1980 – that was the start of everything, or so I thought.

Then, about ten years ago, while I was doing research in the Northern Ireland Digital Film Archive, I stumbled on some footage of Northern Ireland's final qualifying game against Italy from January 1958 and it opened up a new chapter of footballing history to me. As I watched the old newsreels and the flickering black and white images of those footballers from half a century ago, a feeling of exhilaration came over me, but it was tinged with sadness. Those players, in the prime of their lives, were at the centre of everything back then and they had lived in extraordinary times. Now they appeared insubstantial, unreal almost. Many of them had already passed away and those that hadn't were old men going about their daily business. Their stories were unknown and, for the most part, forgotten.

I felt a very strong desire to take these figures and make them live again, to bring them out of obscurity. I wanted to turn those black and white images into full colour – to restore Northern Ireland's drab grey shirts to their glorious bright green; to replace the silent cheering of the fans in the newsreels with the roar of tens of thousands of Northern Irish voices booming out around Windsor Park; and to tell the story of those real people, families, fathers with sons tucked in protectively at their sides, all come to lend their collective passion and support to the men on the pitch. Those players weren't ghostly, flickering and insubstantial. These were eleven men carrying the weight of expectation and hope on their young shoulders. They were full of energy and passion for the game and they were proud to be wearing the colours of their country. Agony and ecstasy would unfold on the pitch and in the stands. My aim was to capture the spirit of this time, to follow the incredible journey of a team who during seven magical years in the 1950s went from being regarded as no-hopers to becoming world-beaters.

I immediately set out to find out as much as I could about the team during that period and soon discovered that the 1958 World Cup was, in many ways, the culmination of Northern Ireland's development in that decade from a fairly lacklustre team into one of international renown. It was also a story that took in the Munich Air Disaster and a bizarre civil war within the Irish Football Association about Sunday observance and it brought together a great cast of characters, including football legends Danny Blanchflower and Harry Gregg, as well as team trainer and all-round joker Gerry Morgan, inspirational Northern Ireland manager Peter Doherty – described by sports journalist Malcolm Brodie as 'the father of Irish international football' – and players such as Wilbur Cush, Tommy 'Iron Man' Casey and Norman 'Black Jake' Uprichard, players who with their team-mates helped to put Northern Ireland on the world footballing stage.

I was convinced that the story was a vital part of our sporting history, and that it would make a fascinating documentary. I wanted to capture the fire and passion of that 1950s team and to bring the stories and personalities from that period to a new generation of supporters. The result was the feature-length film *Spirit of '58* which was released in 2015. It was a labour of love for me. I spent months in archives and libraries, trawled through footage from every available source and was lucky enough to be able to interview the surviving players from the 1958 World Cup team – Harry Gregg, Billy Bingham, Jimmy McIlroy, Peter McParland, Billy Simpson. It was a huge delight to track down a film can that had been residing in the BBC archives in London and which should have either been returned to Swedish TV or destroyed back in 1958. Thank goodness it wasn't because not only did it contain new and better footage of Northern Ireland's 1958 World Cup game against France, it also contained the only known recording of Northern Ireland's opening game against Czechoslovakia. This was footage that FIFA had told me did not exist and yet here it was. Being able to present it as part of the film was a great honour.

And yet I always knew that the story of that era was bigger than the documentary allowed. There, we were limited by time and to telling what we could show on screen with footage. Writing this book has allowed me to tell the full story and to give proper place to much of the detail and colour that I just wasn't able to include in the film.

At the time of writing the Northern Ireland team have done the nation proud once more by qualifying for their first major tournament in thirty years and are deep in preparations for the 2016 European Championships in France. Interest in Northern Irish football is reaching heights unseen since I was a boy and the team are garnering many well-deserved plaudits. It therefore seems like the right moment to remind people of the footballing lineage of Northern Ireland and of that great team from the 1950s. It was built upon the pillars of skill, hard work, togetherness and a typical Irish sense of fun which, as you will see, made the team unique. This book attempts to breathe new life into the memories of those heady days and to restore these footballing heroes to their rightful place in Northern Ireland's sporting history.

PETER THE GREAT

The footballing world of the early post-war years was vastly different from today's, but then so too was much of Northern Ireland society. Like many other countries, Northern Ireland was recovering from the Second World War. Belfast had been particularly hard hit – its heavy industry, aircraft and shipbuilding capabilities had made it a target, and many areas of the city had been reduced to rubble by German bombs. However, the people of Belfast were indomitable and, like many other urban populaces that had been particularly affected by war, they were finding their feet again, balancing grief and loss with a new-found sense of hope in the future.

As recovery and rebuilding began, life for Belfast's citizens started to return to normality. Events and activities which had been put on hold during the war – including competitive football, which was much loved in the city – were revived. Windsor Park in south Belfast, the home ground for the Northern Ireland team, had regularly been packed with fifty thousand supporters before war broke out and that same level of support resumed when the war ended. The fans were spurred on as much though by the prospect of seeing the superstars of the English or Scottish game as they were by any hope of Irish victory.

Back in the 1940s and '50s, of course, there was no mass media coverage of the game, only occasional newsreel footage in the cinema, or newspaper articles on matches in Northern Ireland's sports paper *Ireland's Saturday Night* and dailies such as the *Northern Whig* and the *Belfast Telegraph*. Radio programmes often provided commentary on important games but football was all about the live experience on the terraces and it was ingrained within communities – every week, fathers and sons trooped religiously to their local ground. Clubs were more likely to be owned by local butchers or shop owners than by billionaire Russian oligarchs. Footballers, though, were regarded just as much as superstars then as they are now, perhaps even more so as entertainment options were much more limited. They were relatively well paid by the standards of the day, though they earned only a fraction of what the multi-millionaires of today's game command. Their salaries were capped by a maximum wage rule, which many of the players found to be grossly unfair. As a result, their expectations were modest – many of them dreamt of running pubs and B&Bs as a way of earning some income after their retirement from sport.

The game too was very different – player positions such as inside left, wing half or outside right were commonly in use then; the WM formation was pretty much the only school of thought (the 4-4-2, 4-3-3 or 4-5-1 hadn't even been thought of); and defensive tactics were much more primitive, meaning that huge scorelines were commonplace. It was difficult and expensive to travel great distances, so football tended to be a lot less international in flavour and, for a small team like Northern Ireland, it was almost exclusively confined to playing other British teams within the annual British Championship mini-league, fondly remembered as the Home Internationals series. Within the four-team group, Northern Ireland was unquestionably the poor relation – it was the smallest nation and was at a disadvantage when it came to organisation and resources – playing alongside the powerhouse that was England, a Scottish team that was often very good and a Welsh side that, although rarely trophy winners, could usually be relied upon to beat the Irish minnows. By the end of the 1940s, Northern Ireland had only won one Home Internationals series, and that was back in 1914. It was a good year to win, though – due to the hiatus caused by the war, Ireland remained champions until 1920 when the tournament next took place. But this was a high point and there followed a long and dismal run of form.

The partition of Ireland in 1921 had significant consequences for football in Northern Ireland. In rugby, an all-Ireland team continued to compete against the other three home nations under a single governing body. However, the Irish Football Association (IFA) split and it was decided that there should be two football teams, one in Northern Ireland and one in the Irish Free State (later the Republic of Ireland). The governing body in Northern Ireland saw themselves as a direct continuation of the IFA and continued to call themselves by this name and to call their team Ireland. They also continued to select their players on an all-island basis, a practice that continued until 1950. As far as they were concerned, the onus was on their southern counterparts to form a new governing body for their breakaway association and to come up with a new name for their team. That was not how the new Irish state saw things, so bizarrely the two teams continued competing individually but both had the same name.

And so things continued until 1954 when both teams attempted to qualify for the World Cup. Although neither of the two Irelands were serious contenders for qualification, there remained the possibility that they would be drawn together. FIFA, the world governing body, intervened and the teams were obliged to adopt the names Northern Ireland and the Republic of Ireland. However, in domestic competition, Northern Ireland continued to use Ireland, a name they would only start to relinquish in the late 1960s and that would not entirely fall out of use until 1973.

Going into the 1949/50 Home Internationals season the mood was strangely upbeat in the sports sections of the local papers, with the journalist who went under the moniker of 'Ralph the Rover' in the *Belfast Telegraph* proclaiming before the first match: 'Let me say right off that our lads can win. If they can survive that first vital fifteen minutes ... they stand a good chance of pulling off a victory.' Even after Northern Ireland's calamitous 8-2 hammering by Scotland in the opening fixture in October 1949, made all the worse for the match having taken place at home, one local journalist, 'Omar' from the *Northern Whig*, bravely risked his reputation by suggesting that the score had not reflected the game: 'Maybe I will be said to be suffering from an overdose of sour grapes, but nobody will convince me that Scotland were as overwhelmingly superior as the score of 8-2 in their favour seems to indicate.' But there could be no such positive spin the following month when the team travelled to Maine Road in Manchester to play England and lost 9-2. Conceding seventeen goals in two games left the Northern Ireland team nowhere to hide. The Irish Football Association knew that something was badly wrong in the team that needed to be put right quickly.

It is now generally accepted that teams need a single figure in control who will take responsibility for team selection and tactics on the pitch. This was not, however, how things worked at international level – back in the 1950s the teams were managed by committee. Players were chosen by a board of senior officials who had risen up the ranks through their connections to the local clubs – many had never been players themselves, or if they had, they had not been particularly good. In a world before televised matches, even seeing the players in action would have been very difficult for this committee. They were able to evaluate local players easily enough but they had to rely on reports in the press or one of them would have to travel to a game to see contenders in England or Scotland.

England had experimented by appointing a manager, Walter Winterbottom, in 1946 but this was highly unusual. So it came as a surprise when the IFA decided in 1951 that the way to tackle the problems of the team was to recruit a manager. The decision would transform Northern Ireland's fortunes.

'They brought in someone that I respected, and I listened to every word he said. And as a player, he was outstanding. I watched him play as a young boy at Windsor Park. He was my idol – I just looked up to him.' This is Billy Bingham on Peter Doherty, whose name has largely faded from the pages of history. Immediately before the Second World War and shortly afterwards, however, he was one of the most famous names in British football. For the great Irish sports journalist and chief sports writer at the *Belfast Telegraph* Malcolm Brodie, Doherty was 'the father ... of Northern Ireland international football ... second only to George Best. He was magnificent ... Doherty came into it and he had the players there who could back him up. He made people feel tall.'

Doherty was born in Magherafelt in 1913 and joined the ranks of junior football in the north-west coast area before being spotted by Belfast side Glentoran. An outstanding inside forward, he scored one of the goals that secured the team's triumph over Distillery in the 1933 Irish Cup Final. Such was his progress at the east Belfast side that he was soon spotted by scouts from across the Irish Sea and transferred to Second Division Blackpool. It was there that he won the first of his international caps before moving two seasons later to a bigger club, First Division Manchester City, for what was then a large fee of £10,000. In his second year there (1936/37) he finished the season as the top scorer in England with thirty goals, and Manchester City were crowned First Division champions for the first time. Doherty's role in securing the victory had been pivotal as he had scored an incredible eleven goals in the final seven games in the title run-in. The outbreak of the Second World War robbed Doherty of the opportunity to accumulate the medals his talent deserved. He served with the RAF during the war and also turned out for many exhibition and British forces teams, continuing an enviable scoring rate that was not counted in the official record books. Doherty moved to Derby County after the war, where he formed a partnership with another of the great players of the time, Raich Carter. Together they steered Derby to the first FA Cup Final of the post-war period, with Doherty scoring as Derby triumphed 4-1. It was a huge occasion in front of 100,000 supporters and was followed eagerly by fans across the British Isles. Doherty was at the height of his powers but at the age of thirty-three it was also something of a swan song for him. He transferred to struggling Huddersfield as player–manager, helping them to avoid relegation from the First Division, before taking on the same role at lowly Doncaster Rovers whom he helped to win promotion from the Third Division (North) in the 1949/50 season. His growing experience and success as a manager came just at the time when his national team needed him most.

Doherty's appointment as manager of Northern Ireland in 1951 was a huge inspiration to the players. Many of them had been brought up on stories about this local hero and, like Billy Bingham, would have been among the young faces packed into Windsor Park to watch him play for the national team. Jimmy McIlroy remembers the way he and the other players looked up to Doherty. 'When I was a boy Peter was in his prime and he was *the* name in the Irish side. When I made it on to the Irish team I was in awe of him. He really was a superb footballer. He had tremendous energy.'

It's a view echoed by Peter McParland – 'Peter Doherty was the idol of every player in the team. We revered him.' – and by Bertie Peacock, one of the many fine players who would be handed debuts by Doherty over the coming seasons: 'He was a brilliant man, very likeable, good personality, firm: all the attributes that made a good manager.'

For goalkeeper Harry Gregg, who went with Doherty to Doncaster Rovers when he was player-manager at the club, Doherty's appointment as manager was a game-changer. 'The great Bill Shankly played with him in the army teams during the war. He said that Doherty was stopping moves, starting them and scoring them. In fact he said that he never got a bloody kick against him! Now for Doherty to become manager of Northern Ireland was the greatest thing which could have happened to us. He made us. I mean he made us what we were. All he ever talked about was the will to win. The will to accomplish something. That's what he did and I think that's what he helped me do.'

Despite being the most famous Irish player of the time, Doherty had been largely ignored by the selectors for the Northern Irish team, a puzzle that Danny Blanchflower explained in an interview on the *Parkinson* show in 1977: 'They didn't pick him in those days for the Northern Ireland team because he was too good for the others, that's what the selectors said.' It seems like a flippant remark but it is borne out by the facts – Doherty played for his country only sixteen times in his fifteen-year international career.

Doherty played one final international match for Northern Ireland against Scotland in 1950 but from September 1951 he called the shots as manager. The position was only a part-time one, therefore he also continued in his full-time role as player and manager at Doncaster. The panel of selectors remained in place and had the final say on team selection but Doherty was in charge of how the team trained and prepared for games, and of devising their tactics. The IFA were looking to Doherty for some fresh thinking and hoping that he might usher in a new generation of talent.

At the beginning of the 1950s most football teams trained and prepared for matches without actually playing any football, focusing instead on light fitness work. In his autobiography, *The Double and Before*, Danny Blanchflower paints a memorable picture of training in this account of his conversation with the manager of Barnsley, which was the first English team he played in: 'I said I'd like to train with the ball. He said, "No, we don't want you to train with the ball." So I said, "Why not?" He said, "Well, we feel if you don't get it during the week you'll want it all the more on Saturday." I said, "Well, if I don't see it during the week I might not be able to recognise it on Saturday."'

The thinking behind the approach was that you had played with a ball since you were a boy so were unlikely to get any better with it but that your fitness was something that could be improved. This was the approach followed by most teams, including Northern Ireland and other international teams. Again Danny Blanchflower gets to the heart of it in this description of training before Doherty's appointment: 'The training stints were a shambles ... "How about a five-a-side game?" somebody suggested. "We don't want any injuries," one of the two officials with the party shouted, and that knocked on the head any idea we had of a bit of action. We had not prepared much for an international match – but who cared? Nobody had done much, nobody had been hurt and nobody had been responsible.'

Fortunately for Northern Ireland, Peter Doherty believed this approach made no sense at all. And since he had played for Northern Ireland a number of times, he was well aware of the work that needed to be done to improve the team, as he explained in his book *Spotlight on Football*: 'Ireland's weaknesses became apparent to me during my first two international games. There was a complete lack of cohesion about the Irish team.

It was a collection of individuals, each striving to play well, regardless of the performance of the team as a whole. Team spirit was almost non-existent. We were a collection of units, hastily summoned together, and as such we played.'

Doherty was the kind of player who really thought about the game and he began to develop his own philosophy around training: 'It is often said that good footballers are "born, and never made". Similarly, great singers and painters are said to merely acquire their genius at birth. Little account is taken apparently of the part played by hard work and unremitting practice. They "have it in them". I disagree with this general principle, and in so far as football is concerned I know it to be positively untrue. Average ability, plus exceptional keenness and constant practice has pushed more men to the top than has hereditary genius. The remedy lies mostly in our own hands; footballers can be, and generally are "made".' He saw that while the game had evolved both on and off the pitch, attitudes to training had not kept pace: 'Training methods are almost the same as they were twenty years ago. The old monotonous routine of lapping and sprinting ... is still considered the best means of preparing players for a game.' As to the practice of excluding football from training, he was scathing: 'Some club managements believe that too much ball practice makes a player stale. It would be difficult to conceive a more stupid or erroneous idea. Every player, no matter how brilliant he is, has something to learn about ball control; and he can only overcome his difficulties by practising with the ball itself.'

As far as Doherty was concerned there was no reason why Northern Ireland couldn't compete with their British rivals, given the right guidance and foundations to build on: 'Football in Ireland has never been as highly organised as in England and Scotland ... but, in my opinion, one of the chief causes of Ireland's mediocrity in international soccer circles is lack of coaching facilities. There is a love of football in the country which equals the enthusiasm for the game shown in England,

Scotland and Wales. But, by itself, it has never been enough. Guidance and instruction have always been necessary before it could ever hope to become effective.'

Even in 1947, Doherty was aware that a more structured and rigorous approach to training was the means of unlocking success for the Northern Ireland team: 'There are thousands of boys in Ireland who are as keen on the game as I was. From amongst them, a team could eventually be built which would make Ireland a power to be reckoned within international soccer. But organised coaching is the only method by which such a desirable result could be achieved.'

Before he made the move into club management, and while he was still a player, Doherty took the highly unorthodox decision to submit a plan to the IFA for a top-to-bottom reorganisation of the local game along new coaching lines, including the setting up of soccer centres that would train boys and feed into local clubs. It was an idea that was years ahead of its time. Unfortunately, the scheme was deemed too expensive and was shelved, but it served as a marker of the type of radical thought Doherty was capable of and meant that when the IFA hierarchy realised they needed someone to take over as a manager he was an obvious candidate.

A great manager needs a great captain and Doherty found one in Danny Blanchflower, a player who went on to become as famous for his quick wit and intelligence as for his football. Raised in the terraced streets of east Belfast, Blanchflower had followed in the footsteps of his footballing idol Peter Doherty, signing for local team Glentoran. He was spotted by talent scouts of the English League and snapped up by Barnsley when he made his debut for Northern Ireland in their 8-2 demolition by Scotland in 1949. He went on to impress for both club and country in the coming seasons and his commanding performances in the centre of the field as a wing half (a modern-day midfielder) led to him being bought in 1951 by Aston Villa, one of the big clubs of the day. A further transfer to Tottenham Hotspur in 1954 made him one of the most famous and successful footballers in the English game.

Blanchflower didn't know it at the time but the baton between one generation of player and the next was passed on during an international in the autumn of 1950 when, for the first and only time, the aging Peter Doherty took to the field alongside the fresh young talent of Danny Blanchflower.

When Doherty took over as manager of Northern Ireland he and Blanchflower forged a friendship based on a shared understanding of how football should be played and coached. When Doherty eventually appointed him captain in 1954, he gave him free rein and Blanchflower often went well beyond the accepted boundaries of the captain's authority by changing tactics during the course of the game. Blanchflower's argument was that if you were losing late in a game then you might as well try anything to win rather than playing out the tactics that had brought you face to face with defeat.

Having a captain who was able to lead in the way that Blanchflower could – a 'manager on the pitch' – was a great asset at a time when no substitutions were allowed in football. If a player was injured he either played on, possibly injuring himself further, or came off and the team went down to ten men. Today, a maximum of three substitutions are allowed and they are made for tactical as well as injury reasons. Certain managers have gained reputations for being skilful in the art of substitutions and being able to turn a game back in their favour by introducing the right player at the right time. Without this option, managers in the 1950s depended on the captain of the team to influence play and tactics and to make changes and decisions when things were not going to plan. It was vital then that Doherty was able to have complete confidence in Blanchflower.

'He was an intelligent man,' remembers Billy Bingham. 'Without talking just about football, he was intelligent. He was always talking through matches, wanting to win. He was a great passer of a ball. That means left or right side, changing play. He could change the direction of the play just like that.' Jimmy McIlroy too was impressed with Blanchflower's skills: 'I think people forget just how good a player Danny was. With the ball it made him a good player but dealing, working with players and getting the best out of them – I don't think there was anyone better qualified to do that than Danny. He wasn't fast but he was so clever with the ball.' And in an age famed for blood-and-thunder style play Billy Simpson remembers Blanchflower being a different kind of player. 'Danny was a lovely player, you know. He was what we called a delicate player. He didn't ram in with big hard tackles because he didn't need to – he seemed to read the game.'

Harry Gregg particularly remembers Peter and Danny during the team talks in the dressing room. 'Peter would do a team talk and it might go on, it would be explicit and it would be exciting, it would be fire and brimstone. He'd be telling you you're the best and you've got to have the will to win. You'd want to get up and go out and fight now. And then he'd say, "Danny, have you anything to say?" And Danny would talk for the next two days.'

Along with Doherty and Blanchflower, there was one other person who was responsible for bringing new life to the team – trainer Gerry Morgan. Morgan didn't pick the team or advise on tactics but he had a special talent for bringing people together, largely through his distinct brand of humour. Harry Gregg recalls, for example, that Gerry made a point of carrying a comb and a toothbrush in his top pocket, even though he was completely bald and didn't have a tooth in his head. One of the game's great characters, he helped to create a bond between the players in the Irish camp and to convince them that the camaraderie they enjoyed ran deeper and was truer than that of any of the other home nations.

Morgan had been in place long before Doherty took over as manager but his motivational skills had been wasted in a set-up that was lax and aimless. Now, as part of a new regime that was more focussed on training, tactics and self-belief, Morgan's lighter touch became an essential ingredient.

For all his joking, Morgan was a man of great experience. A footballer of some note, he had represented Northern Ireland on a number of occasions, most famously with the team that beat England in 1927. He had been part of the immortal Linfield team that was the first to win all seven domestic trophies in the 1921-22 season and had then been snapped up by Nottingham Forest where he had played for seven seasons before eventually returning home to Belfast and Linfield via several other clubs. Back at Linfield he became team trainer (physio in today's terms) and his love for the club ran so deep that he even slept at the ground in case it was damaged during the Belfast Blitz. What was remarkable was that Gerry was a Catholic working for the country's most staunchly Protestant team. This wasn't the same issue that it might have been during the Troubles, but it was still a highly unusual situation. Gerry's son, Dan, recounts how on one occasion Linfield fans, during a match against their Belfast rivals Glentoran, chanted proudly that they had no Catholics on their team. The Glentoran fans responded with a chant of 'What about Gerry Morgan?' Morgan appeared on the touchline and took off his cap to wave to the stadium, much to the hilarity of the fans.

For Harry Gregg, Gerry was key to the success that Northern Ireland went on to achieve in 1958: 'I think they call them today sports psychologists and things like that. Gerry could have played tig with a fox. He was the most remarkable man. Peter, Danny and Gerry – to me, they made us what we were.'

Morgan generated a tremendous sense of team spirit and great affection in the players. 'He was amusing, amazing and inspirational and yet he was an ordinary man, he hadn't got big words or anything like that but somehow or other he got to you and I loved him,' remembers Billy Bingham. He also generated many many stories. Gregg remembers one in particular: 'Great Britain was playing the Rest of the World and a lad who played for Chelsea, Peter Sillett, was playing right back at Windsor Park. Gerry shouts to a policeman on the side of the pitch, "Officer!" "Gerry, what is it – Be quiet." "Officer! C'mere!" "Gerry, shut up." "C'mere." "What is it Gerry?" "Arrest our right back." "What are you talking about?" "For loitering."' The story illustrates Billy Simpson's point that Morgan 'kept the party happy'. He was 'good fun, which you need, really. You need to be serious on the park but off the park, wee bit of fun. They said he wasn't much of a trainer, physically, to keep players fit, but he was a good jokester!'

Peter McParland calls to mind another humorous incident that occurred when it was announced that Northern Ireland's game against Scotland was going to be televised. Morgan was very keen to appear on TV and wasn't prepared to leave matters to the footballing gods and player injury: 'I said, "I'll get you on Gerry" ... I had a cramp in the second half and Gerry came on. He had a high step thing and he came running out to do the job. And they all thought that I played that, but I didn't, I really had a cramp. I don't know if he was looking at the cameras or not but we said we'd get him on and I got him on.'

Gerry was the perfect foil to the serious and determined Doherty, and to the urbane, witty and philosophical Blanchflower. Together, they would be responsible for turning tiny Northern Ireland into world-beaters. All they needed was the right team.

BUILDING THE TEAM

Peter Doherty's appointment as manager in the early 1950s coincided with an extraordinary flowering of footballing talent in Northern Ireland. One of the best players to emerge was a young goalkeeper that Doherty brought into the professional game at Doncaster Rovers – Harry Gregg. Gregg epitomised everything that Doherty wanted in the Northern Ireland team – an all-consuming desire to win, skill and talent in abundance, and a love for team spirit.

Born in the village of Tobermore near Magherafelt, Gregg was brought up in Coleraine. He started his career at Linfield before moving to his home team of Coleraine where he came to the attention of the IFA selectors. In those days there were many different levels to the international games played between the four home nations. As well as the senior international games, there were also amateur international games and inter-league games. Players for these matches were selected from a country's domestic league and often Northern Ireland couldn't put forward their best team as many of their most talented players were playing in the English leagues. Balancing out a system heavily weighted to the English League team, whose players operated at a professional and much more competitive level than the part-timers in the Irish League, was the fact that the English League would rarely pick all of its best players, probably because they didn't have to. Nevertheless, these were competitive matches in which national pride was at stake and they always received a lot of coverage in the local press. It was for the Irish League that Gregg received his first taste of recognition and his first international call-up, though his initial pride at being selected was short-lived: 'I had the pleasure of playing against the English League at Windsor Park and after the game I didn't go out for at least a month because the score was the Irish League 0, the English League 9. So that was the state of football before I left Ireland and went to England.' Nevertheless, unknown to Gregg, he had attracted an admirer in the shape of Peter Doherty who had first spotted him playing for Linfield. His talent and determination impressed Doherty and he made him an offer to join Doncaster. Gregg had been working as a joiner in Coleraine to supplement his footballing income so he had to take a pay drop to join Doncaster, but the opportunity to work under this idol from his own hometown was too much to resist.

Although he signed Gregg in 1952, Doherty waited until 1954 before selecting him for the national side. There was probably no one better placed than Doherty to know that this was the right time for Gregg to step up to the international scene. Initially, though, Gregg only made sporadic appearances. Norman Uprichard was the regular goalkeeper and he was already well embedded in the team.

Gregg was superbly talented and athletic, and he had a reputation for being uncompromising in his play. As McIlroy remembers, 'He was big, he was powerful and he had great courage. When he jumped with two or three players for the ball, you can bet your life he at least got his fist to it. Sometimes he may have punched the players as hard as he punched the ball, though.'

Billy Simpson also remembers Gregg as a passionate and gifted player. 'Harry was the tops. A great keeper. He commanded the whole six-yard area, sometimes the eighteen-yard area. He used to say, "Hey, you stay out of there, that's my area!" It seemed to work for him. And he was quick-tempered. But you have to be sometimes, you know.'

Bingham is forthright about Gregg's attitude to the game and determination to win. 'Don't run into Harry Gregg – he'll kill you! He was so aggressive in the goals with his punches and his catches, his athleticism. He didn't care if he hit you or not, he just whacked you. I think if I had been a manager I'd have found it hard to handle him. I'm not being naughty saying that but he was strong-minded and stubborn and yet as brave as anything you wanted to name … I wouldn't argue with him too much but he was good-hearted and he wanted to win. He wanted to win badly and if you've got players who want to win badly, you've got a chance.'

In December 1957 Gregg received the seal of approval on his passage from talented rookie to accomplished professional when the legendary manager of Manchester United, Sir Matt Busby, paid what was then a world-record transfer fee for a goalkeeper to take him into his Busby Babes team, the most celebrated English club side of the period.

Gregg wasn't the only Northern Irish player to attract Doherty's attention. Throughout the 1950s, a whole raft of top-notch players emerged and came to prominence, including Jimmy McIlroy. Hailing from Lambeg, just outside Lisburn, McIlroy was one of the many Northern Irish players to pass through the ranks of east Belfast side Glentoran, just as Peter Doherty and Danny Blanchflower had before him. McIlroy was spotted by English First Division side Burnley and, despite initially not taking to the Lancashire town, he soon fell in love with it and its people, and carved out a long-standing and enormously successful career there.

An inside forward, McIlroy gained a reputation as a thinking man's footballer – intelligent in his play, seemingly unruffled by what was going on around him and meticulously turned out. The composed nature of his play made him a natural ally of Blanchflower's. 'Jimmy did everything in his own time, and would play the game in his own time,' explains Peter McParland. 'He was good on the ball and he was very hard to knock off the ball when he got on a run.' The famous number 10 was also a charmer, though a charmer who could run rings around you, as Harry Gregg remembers: 'Jimmy McIlroy? No, you mean Smoothie. What a charmer! Very strong on the ball. Once McIlroy turned to shield the ball from you, you never had any hope of getting it from him. McIlroy could have turned you inside out.'

Billy Bingham rose through the ranks of Glentoran side by side with McIlroy: 'Jimmy McIlroy came up with me from the Co-op Recreation team, Glentoran's fourth team, and he was a young player who like me was picked for youth internationals. He was good on the ball on the ground and had strong legs, a physique that suited him because you could hit him and he'd still carry the ball. He was a great player from midfield to set up passes, to get you movement going forward. Heading the ball, no. Feet, great. Stamina, fantastic, getting up and down, up and down. He had legs on him like an athlete but he couldn't head a ball for tuppence. I'd say, "I'm not crossing the ball for you, Jim, I'm putting it over there." "Don't you trust me?" he asked and I said no.'

Bingham himself was another player who was excelling at club level during this period. An east Belfast man, he came from the same Bloomfield area as the Blanchflower family and knew them quite well from playing football in the street and from local junior teams. Bingham worked as an electrician in the Harland and Wolff shipyard and played for Glentoran part time. He worked his way through the ranks in Glentoran until he was spotted by talent scouts from England. Bingham's father negotiated a deal with Sunderland on his behalf so that he could continue to learn in his trade while playing football. However, it was soon clear that the only tools that Bingham needed were his speedy legs and gifted feet.

Sunderland were known as the 'Bank of England' because they splashed large amounts of cash on highly rated talent. Silverware eluded them, but they were one of the glamour powerhouse teams of the day and the fact that they were prepared to invest in Bingham speaks volumes about his talents.

An outside right (a right winger in today's terms), Bingham's trademark was a surging run followed by a high cross into the box. He was also renowned for coming in off the wing to meet the ball being crossed from the other side of the pitch, and he racked up an impressive tally of goals as a result. McParland remembers Bingham as 'a wee bouncing winger' who 'was always looking to get balls to me on the far post or the near post'. Bingham's crosses from the corner were legendary and the subject of more than a few jokes. 'The fellas who tried to take the mickey out of him would say that his cross disappeared from the television camera because he hit it so high and it took a while to come down,' recalls McIlroy.

Bingham's speed is what stands out for Billy Simpson: 'He was a wee whippet. When he got the ball he was away. He set up a lot of goals.' For Gregg, though, it was the determination to prove himself that set Bingham apart from many of his contemporaries. 'Billy Bingham had what a lot of players with maybe a bit more ability didn't have. He had self-belief. And it's like Peter said, to want to make the game, you've got to have the will to win. Billy had that appetite.'

Doherty was blessed with another star winger in Peter McParland at outside left. McParland was born and brought up in Newry and played for local teams in the area as a youngster, even trying his hand at Gaelic football. He got a break with

League of Ireland club Dundalk, then moved to England to play for one of the country's most famous old clubs, cup specialists Aston Villa. Doherty was impressed with McParland's fighting qualities and quickly spotted the potential of this pacey wide man who liked to move inside and score goals.

'He was a big strong fella and we always said he'd have run through a brick wall. But he could play,' says Simpson. McIlroy also remembers his strength. 'Peter was a powerful lad, a superb header of the ball. He was everything that a manager wanted. If you gave him the responsibility of scoring goals he could score them with his head or his feet.'

Even a hardman like Gregg acknowledges that McParland was a force to be reckoned with. The Northern Ireland players were playing against each other throughout the season when their English clubs met and Gregg had personal experience of opposing McParland. 'You wouldn't want to play against him. Peter wouldn't be my height but he was a big lad for a winger. When Ireland played and Danny Blanchflower or Jimmy McIlroy got the ball in the centre of the field they would always look upfield to the opposition's half and ping the ball out to the wings to either Peter or Bingy.'

As a right-winger Billy Bingham played closely with McParland: 'Peter was fantastic. I could always find him on the far post, he was always looking for a goal. When the play was on the right side, you'd look for Peter because he'd pop up at the near post with a flicked-on header, or at the far post to head it down, or maybe even in the centre forward position to score. I saw him do it so often and I always felt that he would challenge for the ball if I could cross it to him. He wasn't frightened.'

Two other players who came into the team during the 1950s are also worthy of special mention due to their versatility and their ability to play in many different positions around the pitch. These are highly sought-after aptitudes, even in the modern game, but in the 1950s such players were even more prized. Having a player who could change position mid-game to cover for an injured player was highly desirable in those days when there weren't any substitutions, but there was also the fact that international squads were limited in numbers. Often, just eleven players travelled plus a twelfth man in case a player picked up a last-minute injury. Back in the 1950s, club football was much more important than international football and small nations like Northern Ireland often had problems getting players released if their club had important games coming up. A player who was good in several positions was invaluable.

Jackie Blanchflower – Danny's younger brother – had grown up as a contemporary of Billy Bingham in the Bloomfield area of Belfast. Like so many others from this time he found his way to England through his local team, Glentoran. And here at least he outdid his famous elder brother – who seemed to draw so much of the limelight – because he was signed straight away by one of the top English clubs, Manchester United. Billy Bingham gives a revealing insight into the brothers: 'In some ways, Jackie was born in the shadow of Danny. They were from an intelligent family and they were intelligent footballers. Danny for his passing, his inspiration, his lifestyle, because he didn't drink, didn't smoke, looked after himself well, and for his voice and his talk. And I think most people agreed and that's why he went on TV and radio because he had a good speaking voice. Jackie, not so much that way inclined, but very outgoing and, in another way, not in the least in the shadow of Danny because he shone in his own light at Manchester United. Competitive, yes. Probably more competitive than Danny even. Hell of a tackle and he could head it well too. So he was a good all-round player, a good link between the forwards and the defence as a midfield player. And I thought that was his best position.'

Jackie's versatility as a player was one of his major assets.

He started off as an inside forward, then played midfield and eventually become a centre half in defence, which is where he really shone for Northern Ireland. He was even to take over as goalkeeper when on-field injuries necessitated, most famously in the 1957 FA Cup Final.

The other great utility player in the Northern Ireland team was Wilbur Cush, a player who nowadays does not get the recognition he deserves. Small and stocky, he looked anything but a footballer. But looks were deceiving – Cush had incredible speed and was able to out-jump players who were a foot taller than him. Born and brought up in Lurgan, Cush played in the Irish League for his hometown club, Glenavon. After winning Ulster Player of the Year in 1957, he was signed by Leeds United and eventually made captain of that team.

Mostly, Cush's position on the pitch was inside forward but he regularly played in a variety of positions, all of which he excelled at, including centre half, a position normally reserved for tall players as it is the last line of defence before the goalkeeper and the ability to be dominant in the air is of crucial importance.

Cush was also renowned for being one of the hardest players in the game. Billy Simpson remembers bruising encounters with him – 'He didn't draw back. He was a hard wee man.' Wilbur's ability to stamp his authority over opponents was out of all proportion to his size, a fact that Billy Bingham vividly recalls: 'I would say that Wilbur was the nearest thing I've seen to a weightlifter for a halfback. He was that broad and he was small. He had legs like tree trunks. And if he tackled you on a low level you just bounced off him. As hard as nails, tough, wanted to win. And if I was playing against him I'd be very apprehensive, as I did in a few league games when I was younger, because he was strong and he had a will to win which was great because he was always optimistic about what we could do. And if he had to mark someone, God help them. He had these thighs you know and a tackle, a low tackle, low body weight down here – you didn't get up very often.'

'Cush was one of my favourite players,' remembers Jimmy McIlroy fondly. 'He was as good as anything in the country at that time. He was no size you know, but he was built like a battleship. He was as hard as nails, he was quick and he was skilful.'

As the 1950s progressed, Doherty slowly turned Northern Ireland from a losing and downhearted side into a team of players with self-belief and skill. There were hiccups along the way – players who didn't work out – but by 1957 Doherty had assembled a formidable unit. Northern Ireland was still only a small nation with meagre resources so the team didn't have what we now term 'strength in depth' – they couldn't afford too many injuries – but if he could get his first-choice team on to the pitch then Doherty had players with good and established reputations in every position.

One position where they did have good cover was goalkeeper and that cover came in the shape of Norman 'Black Jake' Uprichard. Like Cush, Uprichard had started his career at Glenavon and he had initially played in England for Arsenal before moving to Swindon Town. It was at Portsmouth, though, that he really made his mark and firmly established himself as goalkeeper for his country, relegating Gregg to second choice until the younger man's claim became stronger.

Like Gregg, Uprichard was a brave keeper and picked up quite a number of injuries as he threw himself about the goalmouth. He was something of a character as well, as his rival for the Northern Ireland shirt recalls with a smile: 'They called him Black Jake because when Northern Ireland was playing against Wales and Norman was at Portsmouth, he got a lift in a coal lorry from Portsmouth to Wrexham, and turned up covered in coal dust and then he put in for his expenses.'

Doherty also recruited Belfast's Billy Simpson to the team

to fill a position that had traditionally been problematic for Northern Ireland. Scoring goals had always been an issue for the team and Doherty tried both Billy McAdams of Manchester City and the Irish League's all-time top scorer Jimmy Jones of Glenavon in the front line before he finally found a fit in Simpson. Originally with Linfield, Simpson became a record signing for Rangers in 1950. An old-fashioned centre forward, Billy was tough, good in the air, and eventually managed to translate his high goal ratio from club to international level.

On the other side of Glasgow and playing for Rangers' arch rivals, Celtic, was another player who would become a permanent fixture in the Irish side of the 1950s – Bertie Peacock. The Coleraine man had come through the Glentoran route like many of his national team colleagues but he was to truly flourish in the Celtic team. A tenacious left half in midfield, Peacock provided the hard tackling that allowed Danny Blanchflower the time and space for his more composed style of play. 'He was very aware of the people around him,' recalls Billy Bingham. 'He was a bloody good tackler and that left foot – hard as nails. Underneath Bertie was the sweetest guy you could meet, but on the field he was a tiger.'

Gregg believes that the move to Celtic was the best thing that could have happened to Peacock: 'Bertie was a great passer of the ball but not a flying machine. But if you've got intelligence, you can do without the pace thing. Bertie was a very, very good player and a good wing half.'

The remainder of the Northern Ireland squad was made up of a trio of footballers from one of the most glamorous teams of the period, Newcastle United, who won three FA Cups during the 1950s. Two of these would form the lynchpin of the Northern Irish defence as the left- and right-sided fullbacks and their careers followed a similar trajectory – they were both born in Belfast, started off at Linfield and moved to Newcastle United. The older of the two, Alf McMichael, was a veteran of the pre-Doherty side and was the captain before Blanchflower took on the role. The other was Dick Keith, and although he was considered too young and inexperienced during the early years of Doherty's term as manger, by the time he made the move to Newcastle in 1956 he quickly drew attention to himself and went on to to carve out a place as a key figure in the Northern Irish team.

The final member of the trio was another great utility man and, like Wilbur Cush, a hard-tackling player – Tommy 'Iron Man' Casey. Originally from Comber, Casey began his career at Bangor then moved to Leeds United before eventually winding up at Newcastle with his two Irish teammates. Gregg remembers his toughness on the field: '… in a football battle or any battle, I'd want Casey in my side'.

Willie Cunningham from Newtownabbey was the last of the noted regulars of this period who would make the journey to Sweden and the World Cup. He had first moved into Scottish football at St Mirren but then went on to spend six productive seasons with Leicester City. Naturally a right back, he eventually played centre half in the Northern Ireland team.

With the exception of Keith, who made his debut a year later, this was the team Doherty had in place by 1956. It had taken him five years, but now the players had gelled as a team and Northern Ireland was ready to start raising its ambitions. Glory years lay ahead but, in the same way that it takes time to turn a heavy oil tanker in the sea, Doherty would need some time yet to transform the nation's footballing fortunes.

TURNING THE TIDE

Northern Ireland's final game before Doherty took over as manager was a highly credible and most unexpected 2-2 draw in a home friendly against France. Games against teams from outside the British Isles were very unusual for Northern Ireland at the time and to come away with a respectable result hinted at better times ahead. In particular, the growing potential of Danny Blanchflower and the explosive debut of the young Sunderland winger, Billy Bingham, were worthy of note. Bingham had been in inspired form that day and the press were relishing the prospect of further impressive displays.

The press build-up to Doherty's first game in charge against Scotland in October 1951 signalled that confidence was running high in the Northern Ireland camp. Much was made of Doherty's appointment and of the talent of the young players emerging at this time. 'Ralph the Rover' of the *Belfast Telegraph* caught the feeling of optimism when he wrote, 'The appointment of "Peter the Great" as team manager has given birth to high hopes among fans that he will impart some of the secrets of his success at Doncaster.' The journalist went on to report rigorous training and a happy atmosphere in the camp and predicted in his final pre-game column that Northern Ireland would win – an optimistic note that hadn't been heard for some time.

The trio of new caps that Doherty handed out for the Scotland game was a clear indication that a new man was in charge. Although the selectors were still heavily involved in choosing the team Doherty had the freedom to introduce raw talent. Norman Uprichard was brought in as goalkeeper after impressing in the lowly English Division Three (South) with Swindon Town, while Bertie Peacock of Scottish giants Celtic was also given a chance. Both players were still youngsters at only twenty-three years of age. But the real marker of Doherty's new regime was his choice of Jimmy McIlroy of Burnley, just seventeen when he stepped out on to the pitch against Scotland. It was clear that age was no barrier to selection under Doherty, as long as the talent was in evidence.

Doherty's final words to the press before the match suggested that Northern Ireland had, at the very least, regained some semblance of team spirit and self-belief: 'Every player will be out on the Windsor pitch doing his best for victory. The match itself means so much to me – more than others. I'll be very disappointed if the trail of defeats is not broken. The boys are in the best of spirits. They are not over-confident – just quietly optimistic. That's the way I feel too.' In the end, though, despite the talk of how much Doherty had inspired the players and Windsor Park being packed with excited fans who had quickly snapped up their tickets, Northern Ireland suffered a 3-0 defeat.

Regardless of the result, Northern Ireland, captained by the veteran Jack Vernon, was showered with praise in the press. Journalists had seen Irish teams being mauled in recent years and going down without any attempt at a fight. The feeling after this defeat was that the first green shoots of recovery were present. The *Belfast Telegraph* highlighted the positive effect of Doherty as manager and singled out the performances of Bingham and Uprichard as being especially commendable alongside those of Alf McMichael and Len Graham at the back.

The following month Northern Ireland travelled to Birmingham to play England. Doherty emphasised that from now on he wanted as much continuity within the team as possible, a stark contrast to the panicked changes that had followed previous defeats. For Doherty the secret of success rested in players becoming familiar with the game of their colleagues, and training and playing together as often as they could. Nevertheless, he was a realist and knew that he had only started to change the thinking in the team. In England, Northern Ireland would be facing one of the world's best teams. As he told the press, 'No miracle can be expected.' The memory of the last away trip to England, two years previously, and the 9-2 thumping that came with it must surely have been on his mind.

In the end, Northern Ireland lost the game 2-0 but the second goal came late in the game and the *Belfast Telegraph* was full of admiration for Doherty's men: 'England were distinctly flattered by their two-nil win over Ireland at Villa Park here today. The Irish team gave a magnificent display, particularly in the first half, but they just could not get the goals. They fully bore out the promise shown in the Scottish game. Indeed there was not a weakness in the side.' And then came high praise indeed, given that the press usually called for most of the team to be dropped after each abject performance: 'If there was another game to be played within a reasonable time I would say they would probably all be retained.'

Northern Ireland were judged to have matched England throughout much of the game until they tired near the end. They even had a chance to level the game in the second half when Eddie McMorran hit the post with a thirty-yard drive. The *Belfast Telegraph* was so impressed with the performance that they ran another column the day after their match report in which they continued to pay tribute to the players, with Uprichard, McMichael and the young Jimmy McIlroy all singled out. Just two games into the new regime and already Northern Ireland's prospects were looking much more favourable.

Following the winter recess, Northern Ireland travelled to face their final opponents of the tournament, Wales. Some changes were made to the squad after all and stalwart Jack Vernon was discharged to make way for young players such as Danny Blanchflower, who was making his first appearance under Doherty. Alf McMichael took the captain's armband from Vernon. The Welsh team that Northern Ireland were up against were trying to win that year's title but in their report on the match the *Belfast Telegraph* commented that 'Ireland played as if they were fighting for the championship, not Wales'. In spite of the 3-0 scoreline, it is clear that Northern Ireland had once more performed admirably but had fallen short in front of goal. For the second game in a row, McMorran had hit the post when the game had been in the balance and if better luck had prevailed then the result could have been very different. Another piece of bad luck was that Wales had been awarded a penalty, from which they scored, when it was clear that the foul had been committed outside the penalty area.

The result meant that Northern Ireland had finished the campaign with three straight defeats and without scoring a goal so had once more claimed the wooden spoon at the bottom of the table. However, it was clear that this was a team in transition and that they had potential. The *Belfast Telegraph* enthused, 'What I liked about them, too, was their fight. They started the battle the way they ended up – fighting for every ball.' Praise was also forthcoming from Wales, with captain Wally Barnes claiming they were 'the greatest Irish side I have ever played against'.

On the face of it, three straight losses don't seem the most auspicious of starts for Doherty. But he had significantly narrowed the scorelines – the demolitions from two seasons earlier had been followed up in 1950/51 with 6-1 and 4-1 thrashings in the same fixtures against Scotland and England – and was getting better performances from the players. There was a sense of what might be achieved going forward. Ralph the Rover declared strongly in his favour: 'The appointment of Doherty was surely the greatest stroke of business the IFA have done for years. He has instilled wonderful discipline and team spirit into the side without being unduly rigid.'

The next season saw Northern Ireland begin to deliver on that potential. In the opening game of the campaign in October 1952 they welcomed England, led by the great Tom Finney, to Windsor Park. It must have seemed like business as usual when England took the lead during the first minute of the game. However, Northern Ireland were soon level thanks to Celtic's outside left Charlie Tully. Early in the second half Tully scored again to put Ireland in the lead and on the brink of an incredible upset. Despite being reduced to ten men while McMorran was in the dressing room having stitches to a wound, Northern Ireland looked as though they would hold on for a shock victory. However, it wasn't to be – England broke Irish hearts by forcing an equaliser in the ninetieth minute. Nevertheless it was only the second time that Northern Ireland had avoided defeat against England since 1927 and the country saluted its heroes. As the *Belfast Telegraph* reported, 'Every Irish soccer fan, irrespective of club partisanship, is proud of you. Today, in offices, in works, everywhere, your efforts were talking point number one.'

It might have been easy to write off the result against England as a one-off freak result. However the Northern Ireland team, now brimming with confidence, produced another heroic display the following month in Scotland. Once more Northern Ireland were holding their own against superior opposition. Then, veteran inside forward Seamus 'Jimmy' D'Arcy scored with just nine minutes remaining and it seemed as though the first win of the Doherty era was within Northern Ireland's grasp. Unfortunately, the bad luck of the England game struck again. Scotland redoubled their efforts and snatched a draw in the last minute with a header that took a cruel deflection to evade the Irish keeper. There wasn't enough time to even centre the ball again. The result was particularly hard on Uprichard who had enjoyed a magnificent game in goal, pulling off some superlative saves. Indeed, the manager of First Division Portsmouth was so impressed by Uprichard's performance that he immediately signed him, catapulting him into the top tier of English football.

There was almost no time for Northern Ireland to celebrate this positive start to the British Championship campaign before they set off to France for a friendly a week later. This was their very first international game outside of the British Isles. On the face of it, the 3-1 defeat they suffered speaks of a team unfamiliar with travelling abroad and playing against top-class opposition. However, a reading of the contemporary match reports tells a different story. Once more, Northern Ireland held strong against a better team and were only defeated through some atrocious refereeing errors. In the first half they ended up a goal down though the French actually had twelve players on the pitch after a temporary substitute (allowed in the rules of the friendly) failed to come off when the injured player returned. Despite protests, the referee allowed the goal to stand. Shortly afterwards, he allowed a second goal when a pass by the French international Strappe to his team-mate Kopa was made from a position so far offside that Northern Ireland had actually stopped playing. Northern Ireland had pulled a goal back before half-time and it was only in the final minutes that France had scored the third goal to kill the game.

For the third match in succession Northern Ireland had competed strongly only to be undone by bad luck. Against Wales in April 1953 McMorran finally came good with two goals but the game finished 3-2 in favour of the visitors. With two draws and a narrow defeat, the curve of improvement was clear and the words embarrassment, humiliation and demoralisation had been removed from the lexicon of Northern Ireland reviews.

At the end of the 1952/53 season Northern Ireland embarked upon something very novel for them – a tour of North America. It was usual for English and Scottish club sides to go on tour at the conclusion of the long season as a means of winding down, but Northern Ireland did not usually follow suit. The team sailed to Montreal in Canada and took some time to relax there before embarking on a busy five-week tour that took in eleven games in all, some of which were against English and continental club sides who were also touring, but mainly against amateur local sides. None of the matches counted as international fixtures, or are detailed in the record books and none of the players taking part were awarded caps for international appearances.

While it wasn't exactly a first-choice Northern Ireland squad that went on tour – some key players, and even Peter Doherty, were unavailable due to commitments to club tours – a number of talented players were present, including McMichael, Blanchflower, Uprichard, McMorran and Casey. Their results were extremely mixed – the team lost their opening game 4-0 to Liverpool and in their closing game they took a 4-1 hammering from Berne Young Boys of Switzerland. In between, they managed some impressive victories but the patchy tour performances of a makeshift Irish side played without their observant and inspirational manager were of little benefit, other than to further foster camaraderie between the players and officials.

The team's hopes of turning their improving form into victory now rested on the 1953/54 Home International season. Unfortunately, Northern Ireland didn't have a full-strength team – goalkeeper Norman Uprichard was going to be out for the whole season due to a serious hand injury – though they did welcome back Wilbur Cush of Glenavon, who was making his first appearance under Doherty.

The campaign did not begin well – two 3-1 defeats by Scotland and England. Contemporary reports, however, again suggest a more nuanced and complex game than the scorelines indicate. The *Northern Whig* was particularly frustrated following the opening defeat to Scotland, leading their analysis with, 'It gets monotonous writing, at least once a season, "Ireland had the most of the play but could not get the goals", but until we develop a couple of target-shooting forwards of the old type we are going to remain in the international "dog-house" for many years to come.' The journalist went on to state that the scoreline should actually have been reversed and that it was 'a travesty of a result'.

The following month the paper made a similar argument – England 'won by three goals to one at Goodison Park, Liverpool, yesterday, but any resemblance between their football and the margin of victory is purely coincidental'. England scored after just thirty seconds following a horrendous mistake from stand-in goalkeeper Billy Smyth. In the past, Northern Ireland would have folded after a blow like this, but not any more. They remained focussed and took control of the game, scoring an equaliser in the second half. In the end England managed two further goals but the *Northern Whig* was in no doubt that if Northern Ireland had been in possession of a better goalkeeper and a striker capable of taking chances up front, 'we would fear no country'. Cush and Blanchflower were deemed to have controlled the centre of the pitch and the latter was singled out for praise – 'he has not got much physique to boast of, but he is all brain. He set a pattern of skilful play which was sheer soccer poetry.' Indeed, the paper considered that Northern Ireland's performance, orchestrated by Blanchflower, had been, 'a feast of football fare which has probably not been bettered by an Irish team in three decades or more'.

Two games into the season and Northern Ireland had only two bad defeats to show for it. But the style of play and the promise of what the team could go on to achieve, if only they could find the final few missing ingredients, must surely have counted in Doherty's favour against those in the IFA who noted that he was yet to produce a single victory after almost three seasons in charge. Northern Ireland were producing impressive displays and outplaying the world-class talents of England in all but one regard – their ability to convert their chances into goals.

Sending out a very youthful team and selecting four new caps for the next fixture against Wales may have been a final throw of the die from Doherty, conscious there was only one remaining match that season and in need of a victory. Whatever the reason, his selection produced some striking results. Twenty-one-year-olds Harry Gregg of Doncaster Rovers and Jackie Blanchflower of Manchester United, twenty-year-old Billy McAdams of Manchester City, and nineteen-year-old Peter McParland of Aston Villa all made first appearances in the match against Wales and, even taking into account two more experienced players like Alf McMichael (29) and Bill Dickson (31), the average age of the team was an incredibly youthful twenty-three. In one further change, the impressive Blanchflower was given the captain's armband, taking over the duties from McMichael. Doherty was no doubt hoping that his star player would inspire the rest of the team.

Two of the new caps were actually old adversaries from their younger days, as Harry Gregg recalls: 'Peter McParland and I played in a summer competition down in Enniskillen. In those days you caught the ball and the centre forward came charging in and you either hit him or you avoided him and I bounced the ball and kicked it away because this man had gone past me. And then all of a sudden I got such a kick up the back of my leg. And I remember running after him to the halfway line but I couldn't get him. Then when I was picked for my first international against Wales at Wrexham this fella came into the hotel, was introduced, and I said, "You're the so-and-so that kicked me!"'

Any remaining animosity was, however, quickly forgotten, especially when McParland took the match by storm, scoring with his very first touch. As McParland remembers, 'The first ball knocked out to me was after only seconds. I controlled it, whipped it into the middle as soon as possible to get them under pressure and with that first kick it was in the back of the net. It was a bit of an achievement that. I'm not sure if there's that many people have done that with their first kick in an international debut. That was something nice but it was a bit of a fluke I suppose because I didn't mean to score, I had meant to get the ball into the middle and let the centre forward Billy McAdams go in after it, but it was nice.' Even nicer was a second goal for the nineteen-year-old in the second half. 'That was a good football goal. We footballed our way in and scored the second one. I did miss one, though. I was unlucky in that I could have had a hat trick, which would have been nice in my first international.'

Northern Ireland ran out 2-1 winners in the end with Wales' only consolation coming from a goal by the great John Charles late in the game. Charles was one of the stars of the British game, a six-foot-two-inch mountain of muscle who was equally at home playing at the back as a centre half as he was playing up front as a centre forward. At Leeds United he was fondly known as King John Charles and his impressive physique and aerial skills made him a handful for any experienced goalkeeper, let alone a young rookie in his first international. The fact that Gregg won this crunching duel earned him almost as many plaudits as McParland received for his goals.

The significance for Northern Ireland of this victory over Wales in March 1954 cannot be underestimated. It was their first international win since they beat Scotland 2-0 in October 1947 and, even more importantly, it was a victory won by a wave of new talent. In Belfast, the press were quick to praise the team and their tactics. The *Belfast Telegraph* proclaimed 'Ireland international policy pays', while the *Northern Whig* highlighted the magnificent performances of both Blanchflower and Peacock in the halfback line. For Peacock, it was a welcome return to the side – since debuting in the very first Doherty-led international back in 1951, he had only played in the friendly against France. After the Wales match, he was to become an almost permanent fixture in the team.

Of course, with the core of the team being so young, they still had a lot to learn and it took time for them to mature into fully formed players for both club and country. That there was still work to be done was in evidence the following season when the team failed to win a game. A home defeat to England in October 1954 was dissected by the press and there were the usual observations that the Irishmen had controlled the game but failed to capitalise upon their superiority, a feeling summed up in the *Northern Whig*'s headline: 'Ireland were artists, but England got the goals.' If Northern Ireland had only managed to find a deadly strike force then this mid-fifties period could have been a memorable one. As it was, Doherty's players were unable to turn their impressive performances into victories.

A match the following month in Scotland produced a similar hard-luck story. Bingham in particular had an outstanding game and Blanchflower and Peacock were dependably dominant in midfield. However, despite being 2-1 up at half-time and the better team, Northern Ireland allowed their lead to slip and Scotland scored an equaliser towards the end. The reporter known as 'Omar' in the *Northern Whig* opened by apologising to his readers for the monotony of his reports before going on to say, 'Again we played the better football and again we were thwarted in not winning outright.'

When the season's Home Internationals concluded the following spring Northern Ireland completed a hat trick of hard luck stories when they were edged out 3-2 in a home defeat to Wales. The Northern Ireland story continued to be one of what might have been – the fans, the press and the players all knew that they were incredibly close to having a great team.

Victory over Scotland at Windsor Park in October 1955 gave the Irish home fans their first taste of success on Irish soil since the same fixture in 1947. They had only been able to read about the Northern Ireland win against Wales. Ironically, after all the bad luck of previous seasons, the *Belfast News-Letter* proclaimed in its headline that the Irish had been lucky to hold on to victory, thanks to the heroics of Norman Uprichard in goal and goals from Jackie Blanchflower and Billy Bingham. The 2-1 victory was an excellent start to the campaign but in November they faced a far greater challenge – a match against England at Wembley.

Northern Ireland had never played a single game at the English home ground, largely because they weren't regarded as a big enough team to play there. International games at Wembley were reserved for grudge games against the old rivals, Scotland, and for prestige games against foreign opposition. Northern Ireland and Wales games against England on English soil were rotated around English club stadiums such as Everton's Goodison Park, Manchester City's Maine Road or Sunderland's Roker Park. However, Wales were given the step-up to full Wembley honours in 1952, leaving the England v. Northern Ireland fixture as the only Home Internationals game not to be played at a side's home ground. It was a sign of the team's growing prestige when Northern Ireland were finally invited to play at the most famous football ground in the UK.

It's no surprise that Northern Ireland lost the Wembley fixture 3-0 – a one hundred thousand capacity stadium (albeit with only sixty thousand of the tickets sold) would have been a daunting prospect for almost every member of the team. Nevertheless,

Northern Ireland held what was deemed to be a very lively England team to nil-nil until half-time, provided periods of excellent play, and certainly didn't disgrace themselves.

Despite the heavy defeat, Northern Ireland entered the final game of that season against Wales knowing that victory could win them the British Championship if the England–Scotland fixture played out as a draw. The Irish League forward, Jimmy Jones of Glenavon, was given a first cap after scoring an impressive fifty goals that season. He rewarded the faith shown in him with a goal at the start of the second half, helping Northern Ireland to recover from being a goal down after a poor first-half showing. In the end, they had to be satisfied with a 1-1 draw. One of the main pluses of the match was the successful experiment of playing Jackie Blanchflower, an inside forward, at centre half – his position for Northern Ireland from this point onwards.

Three days after the game against Wales the final match in that year's championship was played. England snatched a last-minute equaliser to draw against Scotland, stopping them from clinching the title and resulting – for the first time ever – in all four teams finishing level on points. As goal average was not used to decide the rankings, it meant that Northern Ireland shared the championship with the other three nations, with each of them keeping the trophy for three months. It was the first time Northern Ireland had helped themselves to even a share of the trophy since they were crowned outright champions in 1914.

While it had been a mixed campaign for Northern Ireland, there had been clear progress for the team. Key to that was the influence of Peter Doherty. For Jimmy McIlroy Doherty was the only reason for the turnaround in the team's fortunes. 'This is where I give Peter all the credit. Everything he said to us made sense. At the beginning of the fifties Peter joined the Irish team and from that moment it seemed as if the team took off and year after year with Peter there he inspired us. He came at the right time to the Irish team, and luckily for him, there were enough quality players in that squad to do as much as they eventually did.'

For McParland, that improvement was most visible in Northern Ireland's matches against England: 'We had the basics of a team and we built up from there. We had a problem beating England but we did get close to them. At times we outplayed England and lost. We realised that England were the chopping block for the teams, that they just took them apart here and there but we were able to hold our own. Instead of going into the four, five and six we were holding them to a goal and giving a good account of ourselves.'

That progress was also brought about by a growing sense of team spirit, an aim at the heart of Doherty's revolution, as forward Billy Simpson makes clear. 'We were kind of the underdogs in those days. Wales were just above us, England and Scotland were the top dogs. But we kept improving over the years. The whole Northern Ireland team were close and they played for each other, you know. We hadn't the resources really and we hadn't much to pick from in Northern Ireland so every player went out to play for the ol' country. That's what we had to do. Give double the effort.'

Effort, passion, togetherness, spirit, desire: those were the watchwords of a new Northern Ireland and all they could achieve. Doherty had already accomplished the near impossible task of transforming Northern Ireland from being the joke of the British Championship to becoming serious contenders that even England struggled against. Now he was ready to take them into territory far beyond their dreams and on to the world stage.

THE QUALIFYING ROUNDS

The draw for the European qualifying rounds of the 1958 World Cup took place on Friday 27 April 1956. When British teams had entered the 1950 and 1954 competitions they had simply used the preceding season's Home Internationals as the qualifying group instead of playing qualifying fixtures against continental opposition. This arrangement saved them from having to play additional fixtures and it also guaranteed a British presence at the World Cup since the top two teams went through. However, for the 1958 World Cup, the system changed. This time, each of the four home nations sent a team into qualifying groups with other teams from Europe, leaving open the possibility that the United Kingdom could end up with all four countries qualifying … or none.

It was typical of the lower level of interest in World Cups prior to 1958 that the reporting of the draw was hidden away in the columns of the sports sections of the national press, receiving far less attention than domestic club football matches that week. Even in the local press, as Northern Ireland embarked on an historic first qualifying round against continental opposition, the draw only merited a few sentences – England's draw in a group with the Republic of Ireland and Denmark actually gained greater attention.

The lack of local coverage was perhaps a reflection of the fact that many people weren't hopeful about Northern Ireland's chances. Billy Bingham remembers that optimism was in short supply:"The papers were saying it was a hard group and it was going to be difficult. Of course, it was a challenge for us – you're playing against better players, better teams, teams that have gone the distance in many competitions.'

You didn't have to look far for reasons to be pessimistic. Although there were only three teams in each qualifying group, Northern Ireland were up against the very capable Portugal and the two-time World Champions, Italy. The Italians were perhaps the most fanatical footballing nation in the world – they had played in every World Cup and could call on players from the most illustrious clubs. Being up against foreign opposition in competitive matches for the first time was daunting enough, but to be up against the very best teams in the world was an almost unthinkable challenge.

But things had begun to change within the Northern Ireland team and there was now both belief and talent. Harry Gregg remembers that, in spite of the pessimism around them, the team felt they could perform well in qualifying: 'The people who believed were Doherty, Blanchflower, Gerry Morgan. They believed and the players all believed.' Familiarity and the bonds of friendship, vastly improved footballing skills and growing confidence meant that it was a very able team indeed that began the season in which their qualifying campaign would commence.

In October 1956 England visited Windsor Park and were given a torrid time. By then, Gregg had claimed the Number 1 jersey from Uprichard and Willie Cunningham had cemented his place in the starting line-up. The two Blanchflowers, McIlroy,

McParland and Bingham had long been automatic inclusions and with added steel from Tommy Casey, the team was a confident one, even against a world-renowned team such as England. The final result was 1-1 but England was considered exceptionally fortunate to have escaped with a draw. There was a particularly colourful account from 'Omar' in the *Northern Whig* under the headline 'Confident English eat humble pie. Ireland richly deserved victory – only bad luck prevented it.' He described how England's 'grin became wider than that of a Cheshire cat, wider even than the smile flaunted by Liberace to his adoring fans, when a Stan Matthews goal two minutes in sent them off on a glorious rampage which had Ireland floundering and ready for burial in the heavy soil of Windsor Park'. The tables turned, however, after Jimmy McIlroy's first international goal and 'right from this moment the English victory smile deteriorated into nothing more than a sickly grin as Ireland took over command and held the whip-hand right to the end'.

In November Northern Ireland took on Scotland at Hampden Park. They lost 1-0 but were extremely unfortunate not to do better – a draw would have been a fairer reflection of the game. The gap between them and their Scottish and English neighbours was closing fast. What had seemed like a yawning chasm just seven years before with those 8-2 and 9-2 defeats had now been reduced to an incredibly narrow margin.

A few months later, in January 1957, the Northern Ireland team prepared to fly out for the first qualifying game against Portugal. The team was in good shape but other elements of the team organisation now seem gloriously naive. Much of the attention in the *Belfast Telegraph* focussed on the advice given to the team by their doctor, Dr George Scarlett, as this headline makes clear: 'Irish team are told to watch diet. British meals only until after game.'

Despite only bringing twelve players with them to Portugal, with others apparently on standby to catch a flight in the event of any of the travelling party injuring themselves, confidence was running high. Peter Doherty told the *Belfast Telegraph*, 'We are looking forward to the trip and hoping to win.' The night before he had gathered his squad together and told them, 'You have a tremendous task confronting you. There must be no let-up in preparations. We go out to fight for the honour of Northern Ireland and for the glittering prize of a place in the World Cup final sixteen. Remember we are ambassadors for our country.'

The match with Portugal was due to be played at the famous Estádio José Alvalade in Lisbon, capable of holding a crowd of sixty thousand. Even before the match began, there was a good save by the Portuguese footballing association. They had originally contacted the Irish embassy to request the Republic of Ireland national anthem, not realising that Northern Ireland was a separate country. Fortunately, they noticed their error before the match, preventing a lot of embarrassment all round. They had less luck with the programmes, though, where they had gone too far in the other direction and used a Union Jack to represent Northern Ireland on the cover, rather than the Celtic cross which was their badge at that time.

Sunday was the usual day for playing international matches in Portugal but the IFA had refused to play on that day of the week for religious reasons, and the match had been switched to midweek. Kick off was scheduled for 9.45 p.m. local time, meaning that the match would not finish until nearly midnight and that it would be the first-ever international match to be played under floodlights in Portugal. The extremely late kick off was unusual but the Irishmen welcomed the opportunity to play in cooler temperatures. As Doherty was quoted saying, 'The crowd and the small pitch will not favour us but the night air definitely will.'

On the day itself, the match ended up being further delayed. As Peter McParland recalls, 'They played funny games with us. They left us standing in the tunnel for about three quarters of an hour. They were celebrating a Portuguese man winning a marathon and he was running round the track and we were standing waiting. So that made us more determined and Peter was giving us inspiration in the tunnel about that, "Look what they've done to us, let's get out there."'

The team that took to the field for Northern Ireland was a strong line-up. Wilbur Cush had been recalled to the side – despite having been impressive in his two previous games for Doherty back in 1953, the selection committee had waited four years to recall him. Fay Coyle of Coleraine at centre forward was perhaps a surprise inclusion ahead of Billy Simpson of Rangers, but the only other area of debate was the decision to leave out Bertie Peacock, who travelled as the unused twelfth man, in favour of Newcastle's Tommy Casey. However, Cush and Casey provided a tough tackling combination that would have intimidated many opponents and Doherty perhaps had one eye on countering some expected roughhouse tactics from their continental opponents.

The teams were as follows:

NORTHERN IRELAND: Gregg; Cunningham; McMichael; D. Blanchflower; J. Blanchflower; Casey; Bingham; McIlroy; Coyle; Cush; McParland

PORTUGAL: Gomes; Virgilio; Angelo; Pedroto; Passos; Monteiro Da Costa; Hernâni; Vasques; Águas; Coluna; Perdigão

When the match did eventually kick off it was a dream start for Northern Ireland. From a Peter McParland corner the ball fell to Bingham who placed it just under the bar to give Northern Ireland the lead after just five minutes. Soon afterwards Bingham almost scored again when a speculative shot struck the crossbar and Peter McParland also shook the frame of the goal. With Jackie Blanchflower having a superb game against the Portuguese danger man, Águas, and with Cush and Casey taking care of matters in midfield it looked as though Northern Ireland's introduction to international World Cup qualifiers would be a very happy one – until disaster struck just before half-time. The Portuguese whipped a corner into the box and the ball ended up in the net courtesy of Vasques, with Gregg seemingly having done very little to stop it. Recriminations were swift. Gregg defended himself, saying that he couldn't see because of the lights: 'Casey would have fought King Kong. He didn't take prisoners. I'm saying, "The lights are bad" and Casey said to me, "You're the only effing one can't see" and I said, "You what?" So he started to run and I ran after him.' It seems that even Iron Man Casey knew that having enraged Gregg it was advisable to get away as quickly as possible, but he was perhaps unprepared for Gregg running up the field after him, angrily pulling off his shirt and offering it to him, while roaring that he could go into goal if he thought he could do any better.

Tempers soon cooled though and as Jimmy McIlroy says, 'I think only an Irish team could produce a move like that. Harry came charging out and I thought for a moment or two they were going to be at each other but common sense won through in the end. I think that was the only time I can remember an argument or a row amongst the team.' Who knows what the Portuguese players and fans made of team members fighting with each other and it was a disappointed Northern Ireland that left the field at half-time knowing that they had squandered a lead.

In the second half of the game the Portuguese became much more tenacious in their tackles. 'The right back didn't hold back,' recalls Peter McParland. 'I had a few tussles with him and there was one particular tussle where I thought I've got him here, he's coming at the right time, I'm going to pass him but I'm going to give him a crack as well when I'm getting past. But I missed him, although he lay rolling on the deck anyway and the crowd were chucking the cushions from the concrete seats at me. He also had a high tackle on me after that which got me. I didn't play after that when I got back to England. The Portuguese opened our eyes as to what these continental teams would do to us.'

McParland was rugby tackled during the match, without any punishment for the offender, and Fay Coyle was blatantly kicked at one point, but the Northern Ireland team pushed hard to win. Gomes pulled off fine saves from Cush and McIlroy but, at the end of the match, the scores remained level. Still, there was a sense of a job well done for Northern Ireland – they had come through a tough first match unbeaten and now had the measure of this side for the return fixture later in the year. What was more, the team was not overawed by the occasion and, despite having no pedigree in such matches, they had taken it in their stride. The new more optimistic mood was apparent in the headline in the *Northern Whig* in January 1957: 'Ireland's World Cup hopes now brighter'. It looked like this minnow nation was now suddenly a contender.

Northern Ireland next saw action in a trio of matches played between 10 April and 1 May 1957: one marked the end of the British Championship and the next two were qualifying games for the World Cup. While England had an agreement that those selected for international duty would be automatically released by their clubs, no such agreement was in place for Northern Ireland players. Club versus country has always been a battlefield – clubs pay salaries and stand to lose out if a player is injured on international duty. Today, the top division takes a break during international fixtures so that clubs aren't deprived of their best players. In 1957, however, there was no break and the clubs had to continue without their star performers. While the clubs were prepared to accept this sacrifice to ensure England did well on the international stage, they were less concerned about Northern Ireland's fortunes and weren't prepared to lose additional players unnecessarily if they had an important match coming up. In the

Harry Gregg flies into action for Manchester United against Tottenham Hotspur.

Peter Doherty in his playing days, one of the most celebrated inside forwards of his time.

Jackie Blanchflower of Manchester United.

Billy Bingham taking on Scotland in Peter Doherty's first game in charge.

Jimmy McIlroy at Burnley where he was to become a legendary player.

Doherty and his inspirational captain, Danny Blanchflower.

The team against Wales in 1954. Back row, left to right: Morgan (Trainer), Blanchflower, Graham, Gregg, Blanchflower, Dickson, Peacock. Front row: McAdams, Bingham, McMichael, McIlroy, McParland.

Peter McParland scoring against Wales on his debut.

Harry Gregg in action against Italy at the Stadio Olimpico in Rome.

Peter McParland rushes in on Manchester United's keeper, Ray Wood, in the 1957 FA Cup Final.

Harry Gregg is hoisted aloft by the celebrating Irish fans at Wembley in November 1957.

The Italian captain, Rino Ferrario, is attacked by fans at the Battle of Windsor, December 1957.

Wilbur Cush scoring the crucial goal against Italy at Windsor Park in January 1958.

The great 'Busby Babes' line up for the final time against Red Star Belgrade in the European Cup, February 1958.

The team against Wales in 1958. Back row, left to right: McParland, Cunningham, Gregg, McMichael, Keith, Peacock. Front row: Cush, McIlroy, Blanchflower, Bingham, Simpson.

Northern Ireland find themselves in a challenging group at the World Cup Draw in Stockholm.

On the runway in London preparing to carry the nation's hopes to the World Cup in Sweden.

spring of 1957 just such an important match was looming.

Matt Busby's famous Manchester United team of Busby Babes had made it to the FA Cup Final and there was a very real possibility that they could become the first team that century to win the holy grail of the league and cup double. Their opponents in the final were Aston Villa. Northern Ireland had two key players – Jackie Blanchflower and Peter McParland – who played for Manchester United and Aston Villa respectively. Since the FA Cup Final was scheduled for 4 May, the clubs refused to release Blanchflower and McParland to Northern Ireland for the Portugal game at Windsor Park on 1 May. Less easy to understand is their refusal to release them for the Italy game in Rome on 25 April, a whole ten days before the Cup Final. McParland still rues missing the game. 'We had two games coming up, Italy in Rome and Portugal coming to Windsor Park and we're in the Cup Final and all of a sudden, which I was annoyed about, I saw the Irish team picked and I wasn't in. The chairman of Aston Villa said, "No, he's not going, he's not being released, it's ten days 'til the Cup Final." So I was annoyed about that and if I had had a wee bit more savvy about me I'd have said, "Look, I'm playing for Ireland in this game."'

At least Aston Villa released McParland to play in the Home International against Wales on 10 April – Blanchflower was not released by United for the same game. Jackie Blanchflower had become a hugely important figure for Northern Ireland, dropping back into defence and doing a wonderful job there, so much so that Manchester United had even started employing him in this position. His absence was a massive blow and Peter Doherty took the brave decision to place the smallest man in the team, Wilbur Cush, in this role. That Cush was to be employed against the giant that was John Charles initially seemed a mismatch but by the end of the game it was clear that the gamble had paid off and Northern Ireland had solved the problem of who was going to fill the centre half position for the crucial game in Rome.

Other than the success with Cush, the match against Wales was a disappointment for the Northern Ireland team. A tame nil-nil draw, it highlighted the problem they had up front and their inability to put chances away. Billy Simpson had been recalled to the team following Fay Coyle's unimpressive performance in Portugal but unfortunately he injured himself during training and Jimmy Jones was drafted in as a last-minute replacement. Jones had had an excellent season for Glenavon in the Irish League but he failed to impress against Wales and the Irish were aware that this was the one position on the field where they didn't have an automatic first-choice player. For the two crunch qualifying games Simpson was match-fit again and Doherty gave him another chance to prove himself as a convincing centre forward.

The Northern Ireland match against Italy was due to take place in the impressive 100,000-capacity Stadio Olimpico. Unlike the game in Portugal, where only 30,000 of the 60,000 seats were sold, there was a brisk trade in tickets among the football-hungry Romans who anticipated getting their campaign off to an easy start. As Gregg put it: 'We were wonderfully well received in Rome because they expected us to get a hammering!'

There were huge differences in the preparation that both teams had been able to undertake. While Italy had been training together in the mountains for the two weeks prior to the game, the Irish team had not spent any time together at all and the players had just come from a gruelling domestic club programme. It was the norm for English clubs to cram together a number of fixtures over the Easter holiday period, just as they did over Christmas. This meant that almost all the Northern Ireland players had been playing games on Good Friday, on the Saturday and then again on Easter Monday. So, most of the Northern Ireland team had had to endure three games in just four days before facing a five-hour flight to Rome to play a team who had had two weeks off in preparation.

The Italian press were suspicious when they were told of the multiple fixtures that the Northern Ireland players had played before their arrival. And they were even more suspicious when it was announced that the diminutive Wilbur Cush would be playing at centre half with Bertie Peacock playing out of position as McParland's replacement on the wing. They thought the IFA were playing mind games with them, lulling them into a false sense of security. Danny Blanchflower remembers it well: '[The Italians] saw something sinister in our approach and our team selection. They were reluctant to believe that we had all played three League matches in the previous four days. And why had we chosen a small inside right at centre half and a regular left half at outside left? The Italian pressmen were agitated with desire to discover our deadly plot. They asked Peter Doherty. "The selectors pick the team," he told them, "and your guess is as good as mine as to why they did it." And he smiled at the thought of it. Of course they wouldn't have this. It was the devil himself leading them up the garden path and smiling at the thought of his own devious work. So they asked me about it. I laughed occasionally because I was amused by them. Of course they thought I was too glib and that I was obviously in on the plot. Then some of them asked Gerry Morgan. They were not to know what a practical joker he was and were intently impressed when he laid before them some wild scheme of a tactical plot of his own making. He gave them what they wanted.'

When match day arrived Northern Ireland acquired an unusual mascot. Cork-born Leslie Nicholl had moved to Northern Ireland aged ten and had become a huge fan of his adopted homeland, travelling to away matches as part of a tiny contingent of such fans at a time when it would have been both exceptionally difficult and expensive to do so. Leslie had made his way to Rome to support his team. As Danny Blanchflower recalled, 'He booked himself into an apartment room and made himself a tall cardboard hat, covering it with green and white crepe paper and a triangular Union Jack. He also decorated a long stick and walked into the team's posh hotel. Peter Doherty thought Leslie was Saint Patrick himself and insisted that Leslie lead out the team – which he did.'

It wasn't the only unusual thing about Northern Ireland's appearance before the packed stadium, as Jack Milligan of the *Daily Mirror* reported: 'The crowd roared with approval as the Italian skipper handed Danny a gigantic cellophane-wrapped bouquet of roses. It would have been an embarrassing moment for most Britishers, who do not believe in such fripperies on the soccer field. But not for Danny boy. He grinned and accepted the gift with a gracious courtly bow. Then he did something of which only Blanchflower could think. As the players took up their positions and the referee waited to start the game, he raced over to the running track and, cavalierly, tossed the bouquet to one of a group of raven-haired beauties. It was a spontaneous gesture that captured the imagination of the sentimental Italians – and immediately Ireland had made 90,000 new friends.'

The teams then were as follows:

ITALY: Lovati; Magnini; Cervato; Chiapella; Orzan; Segato; Muccinelli; Galli; Firmani; Gratton; Frignani

NORTHERN IRELAND: Gregg; Cunningham; McMichael; Blanchflower; Cush; Casey; Bingham; McIlroy; Simpson; McMorran; Peacock

The Italian team was largely built around the formidable Fiorentina side who were performing so well in the European Cup at that time, giving them an even bigger advantage in terms of familiarity with each other's play in the run-up to the game.

The day of the match was blisteringly hot and Doherty suggested to Gerry Morgan that they fill a bucket with a mixture of eau de cologne and cold water which the Irish players could use to sponge their faces during the game. The suspicious Italians were very interested in what was in the mysterious bucket! Within minutes of the start, however, the Northern Ireland team received a very cold slap in the face indeed.

Having conceded a free kick outside the box, Northern Ireland formed a defensive wall under Bingham's supervision. The referee intervened and moved the wall further back until it had reached the designated ten yards. While this was going on, the Italian player Cervato tried a cute piece of gamesmanship, lifting the ball and placing it several yards to the side of the wall and, without waiting for the referee's permission to take the kick, struck a shot which was now able to sail freely past an outstretched Gregg who had not been ready for the kick to be taken. It was a goal that should never have stood but the referee allowed it to be counted and the jubilant Italians were one goal up after just three minutes.

Even today Bingham is dismayed by the unfairness of that moment. 'I remember that gamesmanship and we were very upset because the referee didn't spot it, nor the linesman. It was very clever, but they got away with it. It should have been disallowed. I don't know why it wasn't. Maybe he didn't see it. You give him the benefit of the doubt, but we were quite upset.'

The remaining eighty-seven minutes of the game that stretched ahead of them in the oppressive heat must have seemed like an impossible endurance task for the Northern Irish players. However, from somewhere deep within, they found new reserves of strength and determination and much of the rest of the game, incredibly, was played on their terms as they gave their illustrious opposition a lesson in what teamwork and belief could achieve.

From about halfway through the first half Northern Ireland began to exert their influence, stopping the Italian threat on goal and actually taking the game to their opponents. Up until then Gregg had been equal to anything Italy had thrown at him with a string of magnificent saves. Towards the end of the match though, it was all Northern Ireland and, with the second half of the match being broadcast live on television back in the UK, it must have been agony for their fans who had to endure the woodwork being struck no fewer than three times in a frantic last ten minutes. It was terrible luck for Northern Ireland – first, Danny Blanchflower hit the crossbar and then Jimmy McIlroy and Eddie McMorran both struck the post. With Italy riding their luck as the clock ticked down to the final whistle no one could argue against a draw being a much fairer result and a truer reflection of the match. As the teams left the pitch the Italian fans left their team in no doubt as to how they felt about the narrow margin of victory and the fact that they had been outplayed by a team they had expected to roll over. A chorus of boos rang out and seat cushions were hurled on to the pitch in frustration.

Wilbur Cush had once again performed magnificently at the centre of defence with the *Northern Whig* describing him as, 'a defensive giant in every sense of the term'. The man he marked, Eddie Firmani, told Jimmy McIlroy after the game, 'He was like a brick wall. I couldn't go through him.' Blanchflower also had a superb game, pulling the strings in the centre of the pitch, with the *Whig*'s Steve Ireland noting that, 'Danny Blanchflower was as cultured as ever. He worked like a Trojan in the broiling sun. Blanchflower's display was attacking wing half at its best and this was one of his best ever games for Ireland.'

The greatest plaudits were reserved for Harry Gregg and with this game he marked his presence at an international level. Back home he may well have still been toiling in the Second Division with Doncaster Rovers but now his skills had been brought to the attention of a much wider audience. As Gregg remembers, 'The Italian fans gave me an amazing reception coming off the pitch and their generosity continued when I went to a sports shop in the city. The shop owner handed me a pair of new boots and said: "For you, Mr Gregg, take them."' The Italian press and public alike were certainly impressed and there was talk of the Italian club side, Genoa, being interested in signing him. Of course, Peter Doherty was also Gregg's club manager and wasn't prepared to lose the services of this maturing talent just yet. He informed Gregg on the flight home that he would be going nowhere and that when he did it would be to a club that was both right for him and worthy of him.

In the end, however, despite the praise for Northern Ireland's performance and the acclaim for certain individuals, and despite both Doherty and Blanchflower being quoted as saying that they were happy with the result, Northern Ireland had only won one point in their first two matches. Qualification for the World Cup was going to be an uphill struggle and it looked as though they would need to win their two remaining fixtures to be in with a chance. It was a sobering reminder that, despite all the improvements under Doherty so far, Northern Ireland had won just two games out of seventeen over five seasons. There was a long way to go.

Six days after the Rome fixture, Doherty named an unchanged line-up for the next qualifying match against Portugal on home soil in Belfast.

The full line-up of both teams for the match was:

NORTHERN IRELAND: Greg; Cunningham; McMichael; Blanchflower; Cush; Casey; Bingham; McIlroy; Simpson; McMorran; Peacock

PORTUGAL: Gomes; Virgilio; Pires; Pedroto; Graça; Cabrita; Hernâni; Vasques; Águas; Salvador; Cavém

The local press believed that they had seen enough over the two previous games to suggest that Northern Ireland were more than capable of beating Portugal. The *Northern Whig* urged the team to go for an all-out attack. Malcolm Brodie in the *Belfast Telegraph* despaired that Northern Ireland's performances had so often been brilliant in recent years but had been let down by poor finishing from the forward line.

It would seem that perhaps these comments were taken on board because it was a Northern Ireland team in an attacking frame of mind that took to the pitch on the Wednesday evening. Billy Simpson had the ball in the net as early as the fifth minute, only for it to be ruled out as offside. However, after twenty-two minutes Northern Ireland scored again, legitimately this time, with Casey thundering in a low shot from twenty-five yards out. McMorran tested the Portuguese keeper twice in quick succession with on-target efforts forcing him into saves. Gregg, meanwhile, was once more in inspired form, flinging himself about with great agility to push away a number of dangerous shots when the Portuguese managed forays into the Northern Ireland half.

In the second half Simpson again had the ball in the net and was again ruled offside. It was a tough decision on the Rangers man who had scored a superb overhead kick. Just reward was to come in the sixtieth minute when Willie Cunningham's free kick into the box was powered into the net by Simpson to double the Northern Irish lead and give them some breathing space. Ten minutes later, with the Portuguese keeper lying injured on the goal line, a header from McMorran was on its way to crossing the line for a third goal when Cabrita handled the ball to stop it. A penalty was the only possible outcome and it was then that Northern Ireland tried an unusual move that was to cause something of a stir.

The art of penalty-taking is straightforward – blast the ball into the net from twelve yards out while the keeper dives despairingly, gambling on the correct side. Putting the ball high and into the corner makes it almost impossible for the keeper to save the penalty but also carries the most risk of sending the ball wide of the net or over the bar. On that night McIlroy and Blanchflower conspired to do something that would stack the odds in their favour and which no one in the crowd had witnessed before. Instead of kicking the ball hard towards the net Blanchflower pushed it out wide for McIlroy to run in and shoot in his place. With the keeper already committed to diving he was powerless to change his course and McIlroy's shot easily found its way into the net. The sheer audacity of a move like this was breathtaking. As Gregg recalls: 'The referee didn't know what happened. Nobody knew what had happened. Typical Blanchflower.'

Bingham suggests that the manoeuvre was something that the two players had been working on together in secret. 'They probably did it in practice on the quiet because I don't remember them doing it. But Danny and Jimmy were quite close as pals and they respected each other, so I can imagine them designing that. If it didn't go in, though, what would we have said? Silly buggers! But when it goes in you're a hero.' In all likelihood Blanchflower and McIlroy had probably got the idea for the 'two-touch' penalty from their idol, Peter Doherty. He is credited with having created the unusual move alongside his great strike partner at Derby County, Raich Carter.

As it turned out, the goal did not count. Some suggested that the referee panicked when confronted with something he hadn't seen before and ordered it retaken, unable to work out if it was in the rules or not. However, the footage captured by British Movietone shows that McIlroy fractionally mistimed his run from behind Blanchflower, encroaching into the penalty box just a heartbeat before Blanchflower touched the ball to the side and into his path. It's still possible that the referee ordered it retaken for the wrong reasons, but it turned out to be the correct decision, even if only by accident. It was a shame that such original thinking wasn't to be rewarded with a goal but the penalty was taken again and this time McIlroy made no mistake, blasting the ball into the net in the traditional way.

Northern Ireland missed opportunities to further extend

their lead towards the end of the match and the press all agreed that the final scoreline could have been even more emphatic. Nevertheless, the 3-0 score was the first time in twenty-one years – not since a match against Wales in 1936 – that Northern Ireland had scored three goals in a game.

The victory against Portugal put Northern Ireland at the top of their group, though they had played more games than their two rivals. A month later, Italy travelled to Lisbon for the first of two matches against Portugal. Italy's hopes must have been high having seen the Portuguese beaten badly by Northern Ireland a few weeks before but they were soon reeling with shock. Portugal had impressively lifted themselves after their Windsor Park defeat and turned on the style to inflict a defeat by the same scoreline over the Italians. It had blown the group wide open.

After four games, and with just two more to play, all three teams knew they could still qualify. Next up was Northern Ireland against Italy in November in Belfast before the final showdown between Portugal and Italy in Milan. Northern Ireland knew that if they beat Italy they would be at least guaranteed a play-off against Portugal. They were still in with a chance and there was now a growing belief that they were capable of taking it.

	Played	Won	Drawn	Lost	Points
Northern Ireland	3	1	1	1	3
Portugal	3	1	1	1	3
Italy	2	1	0	1	2

TAKING ON ENGLAND AT WEMBLEY

The 1956/57 season had ended in triumph for Northern Ireland – the team had come away from Rome with many plaudits and then thrashed the Portuguese at Windsor Park. In addition, they had also conceded only two goals in that year's British Championship. It was true that they had failed to win their matches, notching up two draws and a narrow 1-0 defeat but all great teams are built on a solid defence and it was clear that Northern Ireland now had that. The 3-0 win over Portugal was also a solid indication that perhaps Northern Ireland's perennial problems with scoring were coming to an end.

It is perhaps not surprising that the team were having a better run of results given how much the players themselves had improved over the previous few years. Two players in particular had been shielded from the potential injuries of playing in international football so they could shine in that season's domestic football showpiece – the English FA Cup Final. Jackie Blanchflower and Peter McParland played in the match that was watched by one hundred thousand fans at Wembley and eagerly followed on radio sets across the country, and arguably they were the two most talked about players on the day.

Jackie Blanchflower's Manchester United had already won the First Division title that season, impressively retaining it from the year before. They had also become the first English team to enter what was then the fledgling European Cup, annihilating Anderlecht of Belgium in an early round with an incredible scoreline of 10–0 and only narrowly losing in the semi-final to the eventual champions, Real Madrid. In addition, United had reached the FA Cup Final and were aiming to become the first English team to win a League and FA Cup double that century. It was good news indeed for Northern Ireland to have a player holding his own in such an illustrious team.

Aston Villa were a team in decline but with a proud history, especially in the FA Cup, though it had been a long thirty-seven years since they had won the coveted trophy. McParland, however, was to write the team a new chapter of glory in May 1957, guaranteeing Aston Villa, himself and Jackie Blanchflower a place in FA Cup folklore.

Just six minutes into the match, McParland charged in hard to challenge the United goalkeeper, Ray Wood. Looking at the footage today it is difficult to see it as anything other than a rather hefty foul. However, in 1957, shoulder charges were still a legal part of the game. Both players went down, hurt by the force of the collision, but it was Ray Wood who came off worse and he had to be taken off the pitch for treatment. Since substitutions were not allowed, one of the United outfield players had to take over Wood's role. Step forward, Jackie Blanchflower.

Wood later returned to the pitch, but ended up playing out on the wing. Blanchflower, meanwhile, distinguished himself in goal, and at half-time he had held off Aston Villa to keep a clean sheet, despite United now being down to just ten effective players and having to reshuffle their team. To those who knew Blanchflower well his performance came as no surprise, especially not to Harry Gregg who had known Blanchflower since they played at youth level together. 'Jackie Blanchflower was so gifted, even as a schoolboy. People watched Jackie Blanchflower when Ray Wood got injured in the Cup Final ... they watched Jackie Blanchflower in goals. I saw that when we were fourteen. Jackie Blanchflower could keep goals as well as me.'

As the game progressed through the second half and reached the hour mark it was still possible that Manchester United could take the coveted Double and that the younger Blanchflower would eclipse his more famous brother. However, in the sixty-eighth minute of the game, McParland, the villain of the piece for United fans, became the Aston Villa hero when he planted a bullet of a header past Blanchflower. Just five minutes later McParland took advantage of a rebounding shot that had struck the United crossbar and reached his leg round to volley it high into the net and bring his team to the brink of glory.

United pulled back a goal and Wood retook his position as keeper for the last few minutes to allow Blanchflower back into play in the hope he would score an equaliser, but it was to no avail. Villa had won the Cup and McParland's two goals had made him a hero. His involvement in the Wood injury only increased his fame – the rights and wrongs of the incident were debated in pubs everywhere.

The FA Cup had also been a happy hunting ground for some of the Newcastle United players within the Northern Ireland squad. Alf McMichael had joined Newcastle in 1950 and reached his first final with them in 1951. Unfortunately injury prevented him representing them in the final. This was a particular setback as there were no winner medals in those days for anyone other than the team on the day, regardless of your role in earlier rounds. Nevertheless, McMichael had certainly contributed to the team's success and they ran out 2-0 winners with the great Jackie Milburn scoring both goals against Stanley Matthews' famous Blackpool team. The very next year Newcastle returned to the final and this time McMichael played his part, receiving his richly deserved medal as they triumphed 1-0 over Arsenal.

In 1955 Newcastle were back in the final against Manchester City. McMichael didn't make the starting selection this time but another player from Northern Ireland did – Tommy Casey, who had joined Newcastle after their triumph in 1952. A 3-1 scoreline in Newcastle's favour ensured that another Irishman would savour the long walk of victory up the Wembley steps to collect the trophy. A third Irish player, Dick Keith, only joined Newcastle in 1956 but he had already enjoyed personal success by being Ulster Player of the Year in the 1955/56 season.

Ulster Player of the Year was won by another member of the Northern Ireland team, Wilbur Cush, in 1957. As it had been for Keith, the award was a springboard to bigger and brighter things – he transferred to Leeds United in 1957 and was made captain of the club. His towering performances against Wales, Italy and Portugal in 1957 are even more impressive given that they took place before his transfer – he was still only playing Irish League football at that time.

In Scotland, Billy Simpson closed the 1956/57 season with his second straight Scottish League Championship title with Rangers, having also been part of their triumphant team in 1953. He had also famously scored the winning goal in the replay of the 1953 Scottish Cup Final and his two goals in a famous New Year's Day – 'Ne'erday' – fixture against old rivals Celtic had been immortalised in the song, 'I took a trip to Ibrox', which is still sung to this day. Bertie Peacock, meanwhile, had tasted success with Celtic, winning both the league title and Scottish Cup in 1954 to add to the Scottish Cup he had won in 1951. He would add two more finals in 1955 and 1956 to make it three in a row, although Celtic failed to lift the title on either occasion in the two later years.

Both Sunderland and Portsmouth, home to Billy Bingham and Norman Uprichard respectively, were struggling by 1957.

However, Bingham and Uprichard had enjoyed the thrill of challenging strongly for the English title in 1954 as Portsmouth finished third and Sunderland fourth, just a few points behind that season's champions, Chelsea. Bingham had also gone tantalisingly close to reaching the FA Cup Final, suffering the heartbreak of exiting at the semi-final stage two seasons in a row, 1954 and 1955.

Other players were enjoying great personal success, even if their teams were not. Doncaster Rovers were a Second Division English team but it was clear that Harry Gregg would not be lining up in the second level of the English League for much longer. His performances were beginning to attract a lot of attention from top-rank English clubs. Like Gregg, Jimmy McIlroy had been receiving attention from Italian teams but he was happy at Burnley.

One player who had made a big-money move during the 1950s was the Northern Ireland captain, Danny Blanchflower. In 1954, he had become the most expensive midfielder in Britain when Tottenham Hotspur paid the record fee of £30,000 for him to transfer from Aston Villa. By the summer of 1957 Blanchflower was one of the most famous faces in British football, appearing on television and radio and penning newspaper columns with his strongly held opinions on how the game should be both played and organised. Eloquent, charming and armed with an endless supply of witty one-liners, Blanchflower was a completely new breed of footballer on a crusade to modernise the game he loved, and he was prepared to use all forms of media at his disposal to communicate his thoughts on the matter.

One person not impressed by Blanchflower was his manager at Spurs, Jimmy Anderson, who in 1955 replaced Arthur Rowe, the man who had signed the Irish captain. Blanchflower had also been made captain of Spurs but his relationship with Anderson was never as good as with Rowe and Blanchflower's ideas about being the 'manager on the field' brought him into conflict with

Anderson; a conflict which boiled over after a 1956 FA Cup semi-final. With the team losing 1-0, Blanchflower decided to take matters into his own hands and change the team around to try to find the equaliser that would keep alive their hopes of a dream appearance in the final at Wembley. However, the equaliser did not happen and, following a very heated post-match argument, Anderson dropped him from the team for their next match – a crunch relegation game against Cardiff. The official line was that Blanchflower had been injured but he made the truth known in the *Evening News*, in which he also wrote a column, when he was directly asked. This only angered Anderson further and for the final game of the season Blanchflower was stripped of the captaincy.

Despite the disharmony with his manager, Blanchflower was very much in love with the club, its history and its style of football. Many players in his position would have asked to be put on the transfer list but Blanchflower was happy to stay and to help push Spurs from the bottom end of the league table back up to the top. The team launched a title campaign the next season and, having only narrowly survived relegation in 1955/56, they found themselves genuine contenders in 1956/57, finishing second only to the great team of the time, Manchester United. At the beginning of the summer break Blanchflower cemented his position as one of the most influential wing half footballers in Britain and his media work ensured that he was well known even to those who weren't ardent followers of the game.

Willie Cunningham was one of the few regulars on the international team not playing for a top-level club. He had been transferred a few seasons before from St Mirren in Scotland to the English Second Division side of Leicester City. However, even he could boast a vintage year as Leicester had won the Second Division and he was now looking forward to a new season in which he would at last be able to play at the very highest level in England in the First Division.

By the summer of 1957, then, the Northern Ireland team had matured into a cohesive unit, boasting players of talent and skill. The football cards swapped in playgrounds featured the faces of many Northern Ireland players. They weren't makeweights any more, they were genuine stars supported by a second rank of solid performers. As Northern Ireland looked towards the next season, there was a sense that the team had hit its stride. As Billy Bingham says, 'We had a nice combination of players and they all came to a peak at a certain time ... It seemed to permeate through the team, that we were all just at our best, and that's why we got the results.'

The Northern Ireland team were running high on confidence when they met up in Belfast for their first game of the new Home International series against Scotland in October 1957. The 1-1 draw in which Billy Bingham scored Northern Ireland's goal was another of those nearly games that had haunted the team in recent seasons. They would definitely need to raise their game for their next match, against England at Wembley.

It was only the second time that Northern Ireland had played at Wembley. Doherty had graced the arena as a player in the 1946 FA Cup Final and three of Northern Ireland's starting line-up in November 1957 had played finals there, Jackie Blanchflower and Peter McParland just six months earlier. However, none of the Northern Ireland team played regularly at a stadium of this size – the English team would have been familiar with it both through club and international games. At times such as these, Gerry Morgan was a useful card to have up your sleeve, as Harry Gregg makes clear: 'We're walking round Wembley, eleven players, the manager, Gerry Morgan and twenty-seven selectors, saying isn't it great wee Ireland playing at Wembley and Gerry says, "Great my arse, sure the greyhounds have been running here for a hundred years." That was typical of Gerry. He brought it all down to that wonderful Irish level.'

Northern Ireland had come very close to beating England under Peter Doherty. They had lost games that really should have been a draw and they had drawn in games that they really should have won. However, Wembley was a different prospect and the statistics did not make for pleasant reading for Irish players and fans. England, with a nucleus of players from the exceptional Manchester United team, had been unbeaten for sixteen consecutive internationals, twelve of which they had won. This was staggeringly impressive, especially since those wins had included games against Spain, Brazil and the World Champions, West Germany. While Northern Ireland was facing a must-win game against Italy in a few weeks time to keep their World Cup qualification hopes alive, England had already qualified with ease, scoring either four or five goals in each of the three games they had played. This wasn't just an England team that carried a reputation based on name alone, it was one of the great England teams on a long run of good results and blessed with exceptional talent.

England's recent record would have been intimidating enough but then there was Northern Ireland's record against England to consider. They hadn't beaten England since 1927 when Gerry Morgan had been playing, and they had only beaten England once away from home, in 1914. Thirty years since a win against England and forty-three years since a win on English soil. The omens were not good.

Harry Gregg returned to the team for the 6 November game and Dick Keith replaced the injured Willie Cunningham at right fullback. The only other change from the team that had drawn with Scotland the previous month was a surprise one up front. Billy McAdams was dropped – the Northern Ireland selectors were still unhappy about the general lack of goals being scored – and in his place came Sam McCrory from English Third Division (South) side Southend United. McCrory had never played for Northern Ireland before but he was having an excellent season for Southend and would end up as the joint-top scorer in the division that year. However, it was highly unusual to be winning your first cap at the age of thirty-three, especially considering the enormous step-up in the quality of the opposition that McCrory would be facing. One of the oldest players on the field, McCrory joined Billy Simpson and Jimmy McIlroy as the spearhead of Northern Ireland's attack.

The teams that day were:

NORTHERN IRELAND: Gregg; Keith; McMichael; D. Blanchflower; J. Blanchflower; Peacock; Bingham; McCrory; Simpson; McIlroy; McParland

ENGLAND: Hopkinson; Howe; Byrne; Clayton; Wright; Edwards; Douglas; Haynes; Taylor; Kevan; A'Court

It was England who held sway for most of the first half of the game. Both Simpson and McCrory looked well off the pace and the English wingers were proving extremely successful at pushing the Irish back and creating plenty of chances for their forwards. McMichael, Peacock and Jackie Blanchflower had to provide a number of last-ditch tackles to keep England at bay and when they couldn't, it was left to Gregg, who had another inspired game as he dived bravely and leapt acrobatically to push away any danger.

Then, in the thirty-first minute, just as it seemed as if Northern Ireland was going to be fighting a rearguard action for the rest of the match and desperately hanging on for a draw, there was an unexpected breakthrough. Simpson played a clever flick through into the penalty box and as McIlroy raced in to collect it, Billy Wright was forced into fouling him in order to prevent him having a close-range shot. McIlroy himself took the resulting penalty which hit the inside of the post before coming back across the goalmouth, rebounding off the body of the outstretched England keeper, Eddie Hopkinson, and bouncing over the line to give the Irish a 1-0 lead.

England were shocked but they soon gathered their resolve and were on the attack again. They were unlucky not to equalise shortly after when Blackburn's Bryan Douglas tried a cross-cum-shot from the wing that hit the crossbar. They were quickly out of the blocks in the second half, testing Northern Ireland over and over, and Gregg in particular had to raise his game to keep them at bay. However, in the fifty-eighth minute England finally got the goal the run of play demanded when Alan A'Court of Liverpool dribbled through the Irish defence and loosed a shot that Gregg could do nothing about.

Instead of being downhearted at conceding the equaliser Northern Ireland simply redoubled their efforts and their passion. Bingham – who had been receiving a fair amount of criticism in recent games, to the point where the press suspected this game might be his last in a Northern Ireland shirt for a while – was playing well and was making good progress with tormenting the man defending against him on the wing, no less than Roger Byrne, the Manchester United captain. McParland was also having some success on the other wing and Danny Blanchflower and Peacock were beginning to effectively pull the strings in midfield with Jimmy McIlroy dropping off the attack to latch on to their passes.

What really changed for Northern Ireland in the second half, though, was that Simpson and McCrory suddenly began to work well off each other up front and in the sixty-seventh minute Sam McCrory found himself living in the pages of a fairy tale. Peacock had started a move that involved first McParland, then McIlroy, then Simpson and finally McCrory, who shot the ball into the English net to restore Northern Ireland's lead. The English supporters most likely had never heard of McCrory before the match. Perhaps even some of the Northern Ireland supporters weren't familiar with him. They all knew him now.

Within five minutes the Northern Ireland fans, made up mostly of ex-pats working in London, had even greater cause to celebrate. McCrory passed to Bingham on the wing who squared the ball for Simpson to launch himself forward and head the ball low into the net to put the visitors 3-1 up. Two goals up and with less than twenty minutes left to play, this looked like being Northern Ireland's moment. Ten minutes later, however, England struck back with a powerful shot that hugged the grass all the way into the net. The new 3-2 scoreline energised England even further and they bombarded the goalmouth of the visitors in pursuit of the equaliser. It looked as if England might yet again escape defeat by the Irish.

Peter McParland recalls the tense finish: 'Duncan Edwards hit a daisy cutter to make it 3-2 and we were under the cosh then. But we battled and fought and we were able to hold on to it.' The Northern Ireland defence was a strong green line with the yellow-jerseyed Gregg marshalling them from the goal line in his terrifyingly effective manner. Anything that got past the outstretched legs of the defenders met an immovable wall in the form of Gregg. This time Northern Ireland stood firm.

When the final whistle sounded the Northern Ireland fans invaded the Wembley turf. They hoisted their heroes on to their shoulders and chaired them around the pitch. Jimmy McIlroy savoured the moment. 'On that day nobody gave us any chance of winning but the team clicked. It was a wonderful feeling. I think it was one of the greatest feelings I can remember regarding a match in my career. To come off at Wembley after beating mighty England was something special.' Billy Simpson took particular pride as the scorer of the winning goal. 'Scoring at Wembley against England was the Number One. I think some of the English players thought, "Ach we'll whip these boys." But it turned out the other way. We were always the whipping dogs and more so at Wembley. England were nearly unbeatable there. Some of the England players weren't very pleased with us at the end of the game. But Billy Wright, he was a gentleman and after the game he went round the whole lot of us and congratulated us, "Well played, lads, you deserved to win."'

The graciousness of the England captain in defeat wasn't completely shared by their manager, Walter Winterbottom. As Harry Gregg recalls, 'Walter Winterbottom went on television and said good luck to Ireland but he felt on the day they were a very lucky team. And who appeared next on television? The great Danny Blanchflower. He said. "I've just heard what Walter's said but my answer's that if that is so I would rather be a lucky team than a good team." Blanchy, bless him, he always had an answer.'

Of course, Winterbottom's remark that luck had played a part in proceedings airbrushed from history the fact that England themselves had been very fortunate to avoid being defeated on other occasions by Northern Ireland during the Doherty years. The victory for Northern Ireland had been borne of hard work and had been on the cards for a number of years. It was a victory that was savoured by Irish football fans and that would be remembered fondly and with pride for many more years to come. As Harry Gregg says, 'That victory, to this day, means so much to me in my time, the people of my time, as much even as the World Cup. Little Ireland playing at Wembley. They weren't little Ireland that day, no, they were not indeed.'

Blanchflower's wit was very much in evidence again when he spoke about the match a few years later on the BBC's long-running radio series *Desert Island Discs*. Blanchflower referenced the fact that for years Northern Ireland had taken solace in claiming something from defeats and draws. 'All our success has been built on failure, really. We are the greatest moral victors in the world. When we get defeated it's a moral victory for us. We try to change it into one. This was one of the blackspots when we sort of defeated ourselves by winning.'

Having defeated one of football's great powers away from

home, Northern Ireland now began to believe that beating Italy in front of a passionate home crowd was more than possible. The victory also put them in prime position to take that season's British Championship, something they hadn't achieved since 1914. And they were scoring goals thick and fast, something that had always eluded them. When they had beaten Portugal a few months earlier, they had notched up three goals, the first time they had managed this number of goals in a game in twenty-one years. Little did they realise that two matches later, they would do it again. That must-win game against Italy suddenly presented a real chance of qualifying for the World Cup.

THE BATTLE OF WINDSOR

With the final World Cup qualifying match against Italy just around the corner, there was almost no time to revel in the victory against England. Northern Ireland had returned from Rome in April knowing that for long periods during the game against Italy, they had matched their opponents. The victory over England, arguably a team as good as, if not better than, Italy had shown Northern Ireland that they should no longer be content with the 'moral victories' they had prided themselves on but could now provide real competition for the finest nations in the world. The Italians must have been reassessing their opinion of Northern Ireland, who would have seemed like the easiest of their qualifying opponents when the draw had been made. While the upcoming match was not a must-win for the Italians in the way it was for Northern Ireland, and qualification for them could still be achieved with a draw, it would still have been a slightly more wary Italian squad that travelled to Belfast than the one that welcomed Doherty's squad to Rome eight months earlier. A sign of how seriously they took the Northern Irish threat is the fact that they flew out two English League clubs, Luton Town and Charlton Athletic, for hastily arranged friendly games in Milan in the belief that it would give them an indication of the kind of football played by Northern Ireland.

Despite the recent run of good results and the gelling of a fine team of players, Northern Ireland approached the game with a degree of trepidation. The only team ever to have won consecutive World Cups at this point, Italy also had an enviable record in terms of qualification, and had never failed to make it to the World Cup finals. Perhaps most worryingly of all, though, was the fact that not only did Italy have a glittering array of superstars from the Italian Serie A League – perhaps the most prestigious league in all of Europe where players commanded wages far in excess of what was on offer at the English League clubs – but also had some of the best players from Uruguay, the team that had won the World Cup in 1950.

Nowadays, we are used to footballers playing for nations that they may not necessarily belong to but for which they qualify because their parents or grandparents claimed that nationality. In the 1950s, the rules were even more relaxed. Italy and Spain, for example, often fielded players from other countries who came to play in their lucrative domestic leagues and then qualified to play for the country through naturalised citizenship. Incredibly, you could, in effect, transfer from one country to another – having represented one nation was not a bar to switching your national allegiance to another. In this way, Italy came to acquire the services of two Uruguayans from the 1950 World Cup-winning side – Alcides Ghiggia and Juan Alberto Schiaffino, who were credited with silencing 200,000 supporters in the famous Maracanã Stadium in Brazil in the final game of the World Cup in 1950. Brazil clearly expected to win the game against Uruguay, especially since they were playing on home ground, but it was not to be. Uruguay cancelled out Brazil's lead with a goal from Schiaffino and famously won the game 2-1 with a goal eleven minutes from time by little Ghiggia who became famous as the man who broke a nation's heart. Alongside the two Uruguayan players, Italy had the Argentinian Miguel Ángel Montuori who was plying his trade with the illustrious Fiorentina club side. This wasn't just Italy that Northern Ireland was facing. It was Italy plus some of the best footballers from around the world that they had harvested and incorporated into their ranks.

Despite a good and credible campaign from Northern Ireland, the stark reality of the group table was clear to everyone. Northern Ireland topped the group alongside Portugal – both teams were on three points, having played three games. However, with two games left to play and sitting on two points, the Italians were very much the favourites. Northern Ireland were also in the unenviable position of knowing that beating the Italians might not even be good enough. If Portugal beat Italy in the final game then they would finish tied on points with Northern Ireland, and the two nations would face each other in a play-off on neutral territory.

Unfortunately for Northern Ireland, their preparations were dealt a blow when their first choice centre forward, Billy Simpson, was ruled out through an injury he sustained playing in the European Cup for Rangers. No other injuries were reported, however, and, unlike the first game in Rome, Northern Ireland did not lose any players due to club duty. With the addition of Billy McAdams of Manchester City in place of Simpson, this was a Northern Ireland team at full strength and eager to rise to the occasion. Writing in *Ireland's Saturday Night*, the week before the game, Doherty was alert to the possibilities presented to them: 'After beating England at Wembley this month, we should be confident of getting through against the Italians, and so we are. But it must be confidence harnessed to sanity. I believe it will require all the spirit, strength and ability of every Irishman on the field at Belfast next week to take us to Sweden.' Tickets were eagerly snapped up for the match at Windsor Park. Working men travelled from across the country, many of them losing a day's pay to do so.

Newsreel footage shows the Italian team out and about around Belfast on shopping trips and relaxing the day before the game. They had arrived in good time to soak up the feel of the city and to prepare themselves for the match, using Cliftonville's Solitude ground for training. Helping to sustain their good humour and focus was the promise of a generous bonus of £100 per man if they won the match.

The run-up to the match wasn't quite so relaxed for István Zsolt, a highly respected referee and head of the Hungarian officials appointed to referee the game. Their travel arrangements for the match involved a gruelling journey across Europe on four separate aircraft, changing in Prague, Brussels and London before finally touching down at Nutts Corner airport. With such complicated arrangements, there was plenty of scope for something to go wrong – and that is exactly what happened when heavy fog stopped the Hungarians from landing at the correct airport in time to connect to the final stage of the journey.

Still, this delay wasn't immediately a problem as Zsolt was due to arrive the night before the game. The hope was that he would simply be able to reschedule for the following morning and still arrive well in advance of kick off. Unfortunately, the fog had other ideas. As the seconds ticked inexorably closer to match time, the IFA realised that they had a major problem on their hands. A last gasp plan to drive Zsolt to Birmingham so he could fly from there was also defeated by the weather. Billy Drennan, the IFA secretary, tried to recruit the English referee Arthur Ellis to take charge of the game. This, however, did not meet with the approval of the Italian officials from their governing body, the FIGC. As far as the Italians were concerned he was a British referee officiating in a game involving a British team and therefore they questioned his neutrality. While Northern Ireland

and England played as two separate nations at international level, they were both part of the United Kingdom and ten out of the eleven Northern Ireland players in the line-up that day played in the English First Division.

With Ellis ruled out, the IFA made a desperate attempt to have the match refereed by a local official, but not surprisingly this suggestion was also rejected by the Italians. Italy, meanwhile, proposed postponing the match until the evening and playing under floodlights in a bid to buy some more time for Zsolt. In the end, however, it became obvious that the Hungarian party was not going to make it to Northern Ireland at all and that any alternatives to Zsolt would, quite understandably, be vetoed by the Italians. With the possibility of the Italians refusing to play the match at all, and with fans arriving in Belfast from all over Northern Ireland, there was only one course left open to the IFA, although they knew it would be immensely unpopular.

A provisional decision was made to employ a local referee after all – Tommy Mitchell from Lurgan – but on the proviso that the match would only be a friendly with the Italians agreeing to a return friendly in Rome. The all-important World Cup qualifying match would have to be postponed. An agreement to this effect was witnessed by the Lord Mayor of Belfast, and the scene was set for what became one of the unfriendliest friendly matches in the history of international football.

For the Northern Ireland players, it was a disappointing decision, heightened by the fact that they only found out about the reduced status of the match shortly before kick off. As Peter McParland recalls, 'We were in the dressing room getting ready and we're all geed up for a World Cup match. Then at 2.40 p.m. Peter Doherty walked in and said, "I want to tell you something, lads. You're going to play a friendly, the ref hasn't turned up." That was a bit of a sinker but then he said, "Right, let's go out and beat this lot."'

While the players were disappointed to find out that the

game was now merely a friendly, it was as nothing compared to the misery felt by the fans. Fifty thousand of them were packed into Windsor Park that afternoon. In the previous day's *Belfast Telegraph*, Billy Drennan had urged them to arrive at the ground as early as possible to help with crowd congestion and many of the fans had been in the stadium for quite some time, unaware that there was any problem and eagerly anticipating the match. An initial announcement had been made over the Tannoy at 2 p.m. informing the crowd that the Hungarian officials had not arrived and, although rumours began to circulate, it was only a later announcement by Drennan, just a few minutes before kick off, that confirmed that the match had been relegated to that of a friendly.

For the thousands of men who were losing pay to attend the match this was a bitter blow. A chorus of boos broke out around the ground and when the teams took to the field the Italians bore the brunt of the discontent of the crowd. It was well known that the Italians had been playing hardball for some months on a number of issues such as the original choice of referee and that the IFA had been forced to give in to their refusal to play the game on a Saturday or in the evening under floodlights. According to Jimmy McIlroy, 'The Italian players had my sympathy as a wave of booing accompanied the playing of their national anthem. The Irish spectators knew full well that the real culprit was the fog, which had delayed the referee. But fog could not be booed. The Italians could. And they were – most brutally.'

It was undoubtedly this bad feeling from the crowd that set the tone for the match that followed. The Italians would have seen themselves as victims of circumstance, just as much as the Northern Irish team or their fans, and quite justified in turning down what were quite clearly non-neutral alternatives for a replacement referee. One can only imagine that the disrespect shown towards their national anthem influenced their play once

Tommy Mitchell blew his whistle to start the match.

The teams for this infamous game were:

NORTHERN IRELAND: Gregg; Keith; McMichael; D.
Blanchflower; J. Blanchflower; Peacock; Bingham; McIlroy;
McAdams; Cush; McParland

ITALY: Bugatti; Corradi; Cervato; Chiapella; Ferrario;
Segato; Ghiggia; Schiaffino; Bean; Gratton; Montuori

Very quickly, the game descended to brutal levels – there
was a catalogue of violent encounters that would have left
any modern-day referee reaching repeatedly for the red card.
Tommy Mitchell, thrust on to the stage so late in the day, seemed
completely out of his depth and was unable to establish his
authority. With horrific challenges left unpunished, the players
became even more savage, which in turn fed the black mood of
the crowd who became even angrier with the Italians – it was
a vicious circle. Billy Bingham remembers: 'We were kicking
the shit out of each other … I was getting whacked all the
time. It was the unfriendliest friendly I played in. I knew the
left back was whacking me. So I whacked him back.' Bingham
also recalls that the Irish, once on the receiving end of the foul
play, were keen to get even, egged on by the crowd: 'It must
have been a frightening experience for the Italians. They were
all heroes in their own right. But they brought it on themselves
unfortunately and they met a team that would have a go with
the Irish temperament. Don't kick me or I'll kick you twice. We
never let people away with kicking us at Windsor Park. No, you
didn't get away with it. You were always going to get it back.'

Early exchanges saw Billy McAdams go in hard on the Italian
keeper, Bugatti. In response, the Italians unleashed a series of
shocking tackles upon their Northern Irish opponents. Billy
Bingham came in for particular physical abuse from Cervato
and Wilbur Cush received such a hard tackle from Schiaffino

that his shin pad was broken and the stuffing started to come out of it. Cush was quick to take revenge. 'All over the pitch there were verbals, sly punches and kicks. It was war,' remembers Harry Gregg. Danny Blanchflower was a victim of one of these punches, from Chiapella, but even worse was to come.

The game had descended into chaos. At one point, when Northern Ireland was awarded a free kick in front of the Italian goal, the Italians simply refused to retreat the required ten yards from the ball. Frustrated, Bingham paced out the ten yards and tried to move the Italians back. Their reaction was simply to lift him and throw him out of the way – watched by a helpless referee who was no longer prepared to enforce the rules and was allowing the Italians to do what they liked. To avoid any further trouble, Danny Blanchflower ended up just taking the free kick as it was.

Bingham recalls perhaps the most blatant foul in the whole match: 'McIlroy and I took up position near the far post, and as soon as McParland put his foot to the corner kick, Ferrario, the Italian centre half, let out a Tarzan yell and jumped at both of us with his feet. For this offence we were given an indirect free kick!' There could be no possible justification for Ferrario remaining on the pitch after an act of violence such as this but Mitchell, whether from fear of making the situation worse or perhaps from trying to show the Italians that he was neutral, had lost all command of the game. When he finally did act, following a similar launched tackle through the air, it was much too late, with only two minutes of the game remaining.

Northern Ireland's tough outside left, Peter McParland, carried something of a reputation for being slightly rough with goalkeepers following his infamous shoulder charge on Ray Woods during the 1957 FA Cup Final seven months earlier. He was a skilled exponent of using the manoeuvre to get under the skin of goalkeepers and shake their confidence, and it was one such challenge from McParland that sparked off the final melee of the game: 'I went in and shook the goalkeeper up a bit and they were up in arms over it. I knew that I'd better not turn round because the Italians were coming to me. I kept walking behind the goal at the Railway End at Windsor Park. I kept walking without turning round and Billy McAdams came in and pushed a guy who was in mid-air. He was going to dig his boots into my back and Billy was my saviour. He pushed him out of the way in flight.'

McAdams himself wasn't so lucky. Incensed by McParland's treatment of the Italian goalkeeper, Chiapello had raced twenty yards to get involved, launching himself through the air with his studs up but taking out McAdams rather than McParland. This time there was no option, even for the reticent Mitchell, and Chiapello was ordered off the pitch. Even then Chiapello looked as though he might refuse to leave and eventually had to be persuaded by the Italian FA officials to do so.

And yet, even in the middle of all this trouble, an enthralling game of football was played. In newsreel footage of the game, almost all the violent play has been edited out for cinema audiences of the day. A few strong challenges on the goalkeepers are all that remain, along with some pushing and shoving resulting from Chiapello's antics at the end. For the most part, though, this was a pulsating game, full of attacking verve and providing chance after chance for both sides. Twice the Italians took the lead: in the first half, through a ball from their Argentinian-Italian Montuori to their Uruguayan-Italian Ghiggia and in the second half through a goal from Montuori himself. On both occasions they were pulled back level by goals finished off by Wilbur Cush, the diminutive player who had shocked the Italians by playing at centre half in Rome, and now back in his more accustomed role of inside forward.

Sadly, however, despite skilful play, brilliant attacking football and superb goalkeeping from both Gregg and Bugatti, the game will always be remembered for its atmosphere. By the time the final whistle was blown, the match had already fully earned the title 'The Battle of Windsor' but the events that took place as the teams attempted to leave the pitch made it doubly applicable. Danny Blanchflower had an inkling that the crowd might attempt to take their anger out on the visitors as they left the pitch and thought it would be a good idea for the home side each to take one of the Italians and escort him safely to the dressing rooms. It was a magnanimous gesture given the bad feeling during the game and some of the acts of aggression perpetrated by the Italians. Billy Bingham paired himself up with Cervato who had been one of the first to start the trouble on Bingham himself early in the match. Blanchflower, meanwhile, sought out Ferrario who had jumped at both Bingham and Cush for no reason. As they were exchanging the traditional handshakes and beginning to head for safety, the fans began to pour on to the pitch and it was instantly clear that they were not coming on to give the usual friendly slap on the back.

Bingham managed to run off the pitch, grabbing Cervato by the hand to guide him away from the crowd while 'ducking punches and jinking round kicks'. Dick Keith attempted to use his hands to sign to an Italian player to leave the pitch and to ignore the crowd who were shouting abuse at him. Unfortunately, the Italian misunderstood and ended up aiming a punch at Keith that narrowly missed him. Elsewhere, Blanchflower was guiding Ferrario when the Italian suddenly screamed out in pain. It appeared that he had been punched by a spectator, or mistaken some contact from a spectator as being an attack, and he turned on the fan he thought was responsible. As Blanchflower recalls in his book, *The Double and Before*, 'he [Ferrario] punched the overcoated figure in the stomach and as it doubled up he struck it to the ground with a fierce blow on the head. Then he belted into the crumpled figure with both fists giving it a real hiding.' A policeman arrived and continued to hit the prone spectator with his truncheon and the crowd around him became even angrier. Blanchflower only just managed to get Ferrario away before anything worse could happen.

Gregg, meanwhile, found himself stranded on the pitch in the face of an angry mob. 'The crowd rushed the field. I saw them giving Bean, an Italian player, a kicking and I gave one or two of them a clip. Gave one or two of them more than a clip as well. I eventually got him [Bean] off and up the tunnel, got him into their dressing room and they were terrified. There I was caught with this fella and they thought it was me that had done it to him and I had to get the hell out of there as well. It wasn't pleasant.'

Sitting on the Italian bench that day was a player familiar to crowds in England, Eddie Firmani, who had played for Charlton Athletic during the 1950s but was now back in Italy playing for Sampdoria. Jimmy McIlroy remembers Firmani approaching him after the tumultuous scenes: 'It was impossible to suppress a laugh when he showed me his "shiner" and complained, "I wasn't even playing in the so-and-so match!"'

As was traditional in those days, the players all convened for the post-match banquet. It seems almost unthinkable that following such naked aggression on the pitch and a full-scale invasion by the fans afterwards, resulting in several Italians being punched and attacked, that the players could then sit down to a meal together. But that's simply what happened in 1950s football. Blanchflower recalled that, 'At the banquet the Italian players were genuinely friendly. They had lost their tempers as we had done, in the misunderstanding of the moment, and now they were repentant. Big Ferrario was a charming, friendly giant who loved soccer, was highly respected and liked by all who knew him.' Even more incredible is that the socialising didn't end with the banquet but continued at a pre-arranged dance that was held at Belfast's Floral Hall. This event had been organised by a group who ran a local amateur football team for Italian ex-pats called Lazio, named after the famous side based in Rome.

Despite the fact that the players shook hands and set the whole episode to one side immediately following the game, and despite Italian FA President, Dr Ottorino Barassi, stating that it would be no problem for the team to return to Belfast for the rescheduled World Cup qualifier, feelings ran much deeper in Italy and with other members of the Italian football party. The furore even reached the floor of the Italian Senate with representatives from across the political spectrum, including the Socialist Party and the Christian Democrats, asking the premier if he intended to raise the lack of protection for their players with the government of Northern Ireland. One senator, Andrea Negrari, head of the group of senators with special concern for sport, even went as far as demanding that the planned qualifying game be played at a neutral venue.

These speeches were critical but showed diplomatic restraint. The Italian press, however, pulled no punches and described the scenes in Belfast in an extremely colourful and angry fashion, and took a very one-sided view of events. The famous *Gazzetta dello Sport* claimed that, 'An atmosphere of prejudice hung over Windsor Park. The scenes were wild and disgraceful.' *Il Messaggero* went for: 'These people, incited by some newspapers, descended to the levels of barbarians of a primitive epoch. It was a scene of savagery and unbelievable cowardice.' The Communist newspaper *L'Unità* claimed that, 'It was a scene of collective hysteria. Scenes of unchained fury.' And *Gazzetta del Popolo* described the Windsor Park match as 'the most disgusting ever recorded in football history', suggesting that if the next game was to be played in Belfast then it should be behind closed doors and that the fans should be banned.

The press in Northern Ireland reported some unusual remarks from the Italian trainer: 'I don't believe that the Irish are cannibals, but it is certain that they have no spirit.' He went on to give a somewhat surreal account of the foul play: 'From the very beginning they went for our men's ankles deliberately.

I examined all our players' legs at the end of the game and they were all bruised and slashed with kicks. One thing is certain, we will never come to Belfast again.' The *Belfast Telegraph* reported that the Secretary of the Italian FA, Vincezo Biancone, said, 'In thirty years of football I have never seen anything like what happened in Belfast. They even spat in our faces as we went on to the field.'

The press within the British Isles were also quick off the mark to attack the Irish supporters and FA with Donald Saunders of the *Daily Telegraph* commenting that, 'It was one of the dirtiest, nastiest matches I have seen.' The *Irish Independent* meanwhile blamed the IFA for not having the referee in place days before the game and suggested that the responsibility for all the subsequent violence should be laid at their door first and foremost, then at the door of the supporters, then with an Italian player who should have been sent off and finally with two Irish players who should also have been sent off. This seems a particularly unfair appraisal, ignoring some of the wilder Italian tackles altogether and placing the blame on the IFA for events outside their jurisdiction – the responsibility for scheduling the arrival of the refereeing party lay with FIFA and they had informed Zsolt only on the Saturday before the match that he would be refereeing it. In fact, Drennan and the IFA tried to help FIFA by putting pressure on the British Consulate in Budapest to speed up the visa application process for the three officials when they discovered that they still didn't have any of the necessary paperwork on Monday, two days before the game.

The whole affair was a dark moment in the IFA's history with opponents around the British Isles and on the continent openly criticising Irish football. While everyone had wanted to pat them on the back just one month earlier at Wembley and Irishmen everywhere had wanted to be associated with them, the opposite was now true. The attaché to the Éire Legation in Rome issued a statement distancing his entire nation from the events at Windsor Park: 'Belfast has no political connection with us. It is the principal city of Northern Ireland which is part of Britain. The team which played against Italy represented only Northern Ireland, and not the Irish Republic.'

Yet despite all the histrionics of the press, who managed to ignore equally bad-tempered matches in England and Italy, as well as crowd trouble in both of those countries, it was clear that for the players themselves the matter of the Battle of Windsor was closed. While harsh words may have been spoken in the heat of the moment and there was plenty of speculation in the media about possible sanctions against Northern Ireland, the Italian FA never seriously considered refusing to return to Belfast. Ferrario was even presented with a bouquet of flowers by Irish fans before he left Belfast.

This spirit was embraced by two Northern Irish citizens of Italian descent who wrote a letter to several newspapers in Italy to try and set the record straight and to encourage forgiveness in both camps. Published in the *Belfast News-Letter* on 10 December, the letter described the disappointment of the spectators who had lost a day's wages for no reason before moving on to suggest that because the announcement of the friendly was made so close to kick off, the fans were still loudly booing that statement and didn't actually hear the Italian anthem being played – a suggestion made by many others over the years who were there. They did perhaps stretch credulity a little by stating that the majority of those invading the pitch had merely been seeking autographs but they ended with the exhortation to forget any grievances and, 'to shake hands in good-will so that friendship and the true spirit of sport may prevail'.

Of course, the IFA had been worried in the immediate aftermath of the match that they could face the prospect of playing behind closed doors or at a neutral venue for the next game and they had met soon afterwards to draw up a report which no doubt attempted to argue in their favour about the problems which had occurred. They need not have worried, however, as by 13 December the Italians had already indicated their willingness to return to Belfast and when FIFA met a few days later the matter apparently wasn't even discussed. Without a doubt, this was something of a lucky escape for Northern Ireland and they were fortunate not to have incurred a penalty. Nevertheless, there was still a feeling that the nation had been let down by the events, a mood that was best summed up by Malcolm Brodie in *Ireland's Saturday Night*: 'Ireland's reputation tonight stands at zero throughout the world following those disgraceful scenes at the end of Wednesday's match with Italy. Now comes the task of rebuilding it from the debris of that disastrous day.'

SECOND TIME LUCKY

Following the Battle of Windsor, when it became clear that Northern Ireland and Italy would need to reschedule their qualifying game to a time after the Portugal game, the Portuguese made an appeal that their own game against Italy should also be moved in order that it might still be the final game of the group. The Italians, however, turned down this request on the grounds that there was no precedent for maintaining a certain order of play and the game went ahead as scheduled on 22 December in Milan.

The game was played in atrocious conditions with fog once more the culprit. It's hard to understand why the game wasn't abandoned – the visibility was awful and it was nearly impossible to see from one end of the pitch to the other. With all qualifying games for the 1958 World Cup to be completed, in theory, by 8 January, and with Italy already having to reschedule the Northern Ireland game, it's certainly fortunate that the game did go ahead. It resulted in a 3-0 victory for the home side.

On the face of it, it didn't seem a helpful result for Northern Ireland but it was. When Northern Ireland had walked out at

Windsor Park a few weeks earlier they had to beat Italy, but because Portugal also still had a chance of qualifying if they beat Italy, a Northern Ireland win might not have been enough to ensure qualification. With Portugal now out of the running, the situation was clearer for Northern Ireland whose game against Italy would now be the final group game. A win at Windsor Park in January and they could book their passage to Sweden.

The game was scheduled for Wednesday 15 January, a week later than the qualifying games were meant to finish but it was allowed by FIFA in light of the unforeseen circumstances of the first attempt to stage the tie. This time Mr Zsolt and his Hungarian linesmen arrived three days before the match with a much-simplified route from Hungary that involved only two flights instead of four.

The Italians also arrived in Belfast on the Sunday and their touchdown at Nutts Corner airport alone demonstrated that this was to be a game played in an entirely different atmosphere. Meeting the team and Italian FA delegates on the tarmac were representatives from the IFA, including Drennan, and ninety-three-year-old president, Joe McBride, the oldest head of any football association in the world. Dr Barassi, McBride's equivalent in the FIGC, announced to the waiting press that he was certain that Italy would receive a sporting welcome 'both on and off the field'. However, the surest sign that the recent past had been laid to rest was not the appearance of the IFA officials, who might be expected to have turned out in any event, but that of two hundred Irish supporters who had made their own way independently to the airport, located some distance from Belfast, to greet the Italians. Back in Italy, the captain who had been at the centre of so much controversy the month before, Ferrario, had been dubbed 'the Belfast Gladiator' and the waiting Irish fans acknowledged his new title, shouting 'Here comes the Gladiator!' as he made his way down the steps of the plane.

As they had done on their previous visit, the Italians were happy to go shopping in Belfast and pose for photographs in between training sessions. Irish linen was much sought-after – Italian players told reporters that it made a fine gift for wives or girlfriends and that it was much more expensive at home. The Irish, meanwhile, had assembled under Doherty and Morgan at their base in Portstewart. However, not all of them had arrived yet. McParland was taking part in an FA Cup replay for Aston Villa and both Harry Gregg and Jackie Blanchflower were potentially needed for European Cup duty for Manchester United at Old Trafford against Red Star Belgrade.

However, all the players were determined to get back to Belfast in time by hook or by crook. McParland recalls his own journey: 'We were playing Stoke in the Cup and we had a draw and another draw and then the third game was on a Monday in Wolverhampton to be followed by a Wednesday game in Belfast. So I had to play in that game, I played in a load of games on the trot – Saturday, Wednesday, Saturday, Monday, and then it was the World Cup match. I played in the game at Wolverhampton and we lost that, then I was taken immediately to Heysham by car, on to the boat and over to Ireland.'

For the two Manchester United players, their match was the first leg of an all-important European Cup quarter-final. Jackie Blanchflower had lost his place in the United team to Mark Jones a while before and when Jones, who was a doubt for the game against Red Star, was passed fit to play, Blanchflower was cleared to travel to Portstewart. For Gregg, however, it looked as if there was to be no release. He had signed for Manchester United just weeks beforehand, after the first Belfast game, and he was now the most expensive goalkeeper in footballing history. His presence at the match with Red Star was essential and there seemed to be no hope of Manchester United passing up on his services. In the end a compromise was worked out. Matt Busby said that if Gregg came through the match with Red

Star without injury he would be given special dispensation to travel to Northern Ireland to play in the Italy game a night later. It would be very physically demanding for Gregg to play in two matches of such vital importance on consecutive days, but permission was given and Gregg was up for the challenge to help with the qualification dream.

As to the rest of the Northern Ireland team, there were a few changes to be made. Dick Keith at fullback had picked up an injury but fortunately this was one of the few areas where Northern Ireland had a replacement of equal ability in the shape of Leicester City's Willie Cunningham. Up front, they were boosted by the news that Billy Simpson, their most effective centre forward, was available again and he stepped back into the team at the expense of Billy McAdams. Another centre forward that arrived on to the scene just as McAdams was bowing out was the young Derek Dougan of Portsmouth. He was named as a reserve and brought into the fold to bond with the rest of the team following comments from his club manager that his young starlet was good enough to make the transition to international level.

The Italians, on the other hand, were forced into a number of changes they would rather not have made. Cervato and Chiappello, each of whom had been major causes of on-field ugliness in the first game, were both injured. Cervato had scored the cheeky and slightly unsportsmanlike goal in Rome and Italy would rue his absence for this crunch tie, although the match was perhaps more likely to pass off peaceably without these two. Up front Bean had been dropped after a poor performance in the December game. A further absence due to injury was their important playmaker, Guido Gratton, who had had a tooth removed and was running a fever. He was replaced by yet another naturalised Italian, Dino Da Costa, originally a Brazilian, who added a fourth nationality to the Italian team.

As before, there was a buzz of excitement about the game

throughout Northern Ireland, but this time the interest was also present throughout the rest of the UK, resulting in the BBC offering a substantial fee to take a live feed of the game (minus the opening ten minutes!) to show across the BBC network and to relay on to Italy and the continent.

Doherty was now preparing his team for their moment of destiny. The night before the game he took them out to a local cinema – a viewing of their epic victory over England from a few months before was on the bill by way of motivation. However, one sideshow to the impending international that certainly wasn't helping with Doherty's preparation was his position as manager of Doncaster Rovers. In the weeks leading up to the showdown with the Italians, Doherty had become embroiled in a different sort of face-off in the Doncaster boardroom. One of the directors of the club, Hubert Bates, had spoken out against Doherty's team selections and was generally undermining his position. Matters came to a head during a series of boardroom meetings that were reported widely in the press. Doherty had the backing of the rest of the board but no apology was forthcoming from Bates and when the board then asked Bates to resign he refused to do so. The matter ended up dragging on right up to the international match and beyond when, despite having the backing of the majority of those running the club, Doherty decided he had had enough and resigned. While all this unnecessary aggravation was most unwelcome in the build-up to Doherty's biggest ever game as a manager, it's quite possible that the chance to get away from it all to Portstewart with a group of players with whom he had bonded well was a relief – an opportunity to escape from the pressures in South Yorkshire.

As for the players, they felt a mixture of confidence and trepidation. 'We thought we'd win,' remembers Billy Bingham. 'There was a feeling in the camp and also Peter Doherty had a great rapport with players to get them going, he had that certain something. He was a great motivator. And the Irish had that wee bit of fight in them.' Morgan would no doubt have been working his magic with the team too but for Jimmy McIlroy the task was still a daunting one against a team packed with footballing superstars. 'In those days our attitude was, "We're only a little team, we're playing the big boys." So we were probably more relaxed going into each match than the Italians would have been or any of the top teams. I think we surprised ourselves. I think the night before we played Italy I can remember being in bed thinking, "Crikey. I hope we don't get trounced tomorrow."'

With everything set for the biggest game in Northern Ireland's history, fate − and fog − once more intervened. Harry Gregg had come through his encounter against Red Star Belgrade fit and well, and had been granted permission to make his way to Ringway Airport in Manchester to fly to Belfast, but the IFA must have had a feeling of déjà vu when he reported that he was stuck at the airport, unable to take off due to fog. Originally he had been due to take the Heysham ferry the night before but he had been unable to make it in time after the game, so he had had to resort to plan B, which was to fly over on the morning of the match. For three anxious hours Gregg waited for the news that he was cleared for flight, but eventually all hope was lost. 'When it became obvious that even the fastest jet couldn't make Belfast in time to get me to the match, I gave up. A newspaper photographer had a bright idea when he suggested taking me to his home to watch the match on TV. At least, I thought, I could watch my team-mates, even if I could not take part in the game myself. The next morning I realised something else − that bright photographer had a minor scoop to himself. The pictures he had taken of me watching the match on TV were published in the newspaper for which he worked.'

Gregg was out of the contest but all was not lost. The position of goalkeeper was another of the few in which they had some decent cover in the shape of Portsmouth's Norman Uprichard. Uprichard remembers how he was informed of his big moment:

'Before the match we had been training just outside Coleraine on the coast and were on the coach driving to Belfast. We stopped at Halls Hotel at Antrim for lunch before ... Peter Doherty told me at about midday that Harry was fogbound at Manchester. Peter confirmed that I was playing, just as I was looking forward to a nice big meal. I settled for tea and toast instead, as usual before a game, and went out starving.'

The crowds meanwhile were beginning to make their way towards the ground in their thousands for another capacity attendance. Such was the demand in Belfast for transport to the game that the IFA was forced to liaise with the local authorities in advance to help supporters get to the ground. Billy Drennan, the IFA Secretary, recalled in a TV interview, 'There weren't as many motor cars on the road then and we arranged with the tramway company so that a tram left the City Hall from 12.30 until 2.30 at two-minute intervals to take the spectators to Windsor Park.'

As the teams arrived and the stadium filled up, Northern Ireland and Doherty focussed their minds on the task ahead. They knew that they must win – whereas for the Italians a draw would be enough. Ironically, if they had accepted the local referee, Tommy Mitchell, in the last match they would already have qualified with the draw they required. Now they had to do it again and without some of their best players. However, their manager, Alfredo Foni, was a man who had won the World Cup himself in 1938 and he could still call upon a glittering array of talent for the Italian squad, including Ghiggia and Schiaffino. In addition, there was a huge incentive for the Italian players. While the Northern Ireland players would be picking up their usual £50 international appearance fee, the Italians – who had been on a £100 per man bonus for the December game, in addition to their normal fees – were now estimated to be on a bonus of anywhere between £500 and £800 per man for either a win or a draw, a staggering amount of money for one game.

In the days leading up to the match there was much talk from officials from both teams about how they expected the occasion to be a sporting one. The programme notes for the match made no mention at all of the fracas in December. Instead they described Italy and Northern Ireland as footballing friends and hoped that they would remain so for many years to come. The Irish supporters knew that the eyes of the world were on them and that there could be no repetition of the scenes from 1957. Even so, security was tightened at the ground this time and there was a much larger RUC presence as well as more stewards.

Fears that any of this security would be needed were soon banished as the teams took to the field to rousing cheers.

The teams lining up that day were:

NORTHERN IRELAND: Uprichard; Cunningham; McMichael; D. Blanchflower; J. Blanchflower; Peacock; Bingham; Cush; Simpson; McIlroy; McParland

ITALY: Bugatti; Vincenzi; Carradi; Invernezzi; Ferrario; Segato; Ghiggia; Schiaffino; Pivatelli; Montuori; Da Costa

A total silence descended across the stands when the Italian national anthem was played and the Italian press enthusiastically applauded at the finish to show their appreciation of the Irish fans. The game kicked off and the cynical and vicious tackling of the first game was entirely absent, although Peter McParland recalled that the match was nevertheless robust and challenging.

The Italians were quickly out of the blocks and a speculative lob from the brilliant Schiaffino was the first test for the home team. However, Northern Ireland soon found their way into the game with McParland shooting wide. A flowing contest developed, with Schiaffino also going wide for Italy, then McIlroy for Northern Ireland, followed by Da Costa cracking a shot into the side netting. First blood was drawn by Northern

Ireland when a move started by McParland saw Peacock threading the ball through for McIlroy who beat Bugatti from all of twenty-five yards to slam the ball into the roof of the net to the delight of the capacity crowd. McIlroy took obvious delight in a fabulous goal: 'Within fourteen minutes I had scored the first goal, a real pile-driver, the sort of screaming shot that goes in, perhaps, once in a season. No better occasion could have been reserved for that one.'

For the first time in the three matches they had played with Italy, Northern Ireland found themselves in the lead and it allowed them to play with a new level of confidence. They started to take control of the game. First, Billy Simpson went in, seeing his close range shot turned over the bar by Bugatti. Then, a superb pass from Danny Blanchflower unlocked the Italian defence to set Wilbur Cush clear and he struck low to the left side of the goal. Bugatti pulled off a fine save but the ball spilled back out and Cush, who had followed after his shot, made sure of it the second time to put Northern Ireland two goals up and send the fans into what must have seemed like fantasy land.

Of course, the Italians remained a threat but Uprichard was having a fine game and he pulled off a series of saves, stopping a couple of balls from Pivatelli in particular. It was the Irish though who remained the most constant menace, their front five causing continual problems for the Italian back line. In particular, the central triangle of their attacking line did most damage, with McIlroy, Cush and Simpson interchanging positions and Simpson often playing deep, just ahead of the midfield, then darting forward to confuse the Italian defence. When the whistle blew for half-time Northern Ireland walked off the pitch to tremendous and well-deserved applause. The game looked to be in their pocket.

Northern Ireland were a slightly different team in the second half, perhaps resting too much on their laurels and believing the job to be already done. Of course, a win was far from being in the bag. Italy had talent in spades and could quickly turn the game around. Also, Italy did not need to win, as their manager Foni would have reminded his team at half-time – two goals would be enough to scrape them a draw and the one point they needed for qualification. Sensing that Northern Ireland had relaxed a little, the Italians were quick to seize this opportunity to claw their way back into the game.

A move started by the ever-dangerous Ghiggia saw the ball passed to Montuori who came inside and crossed the ball into the Irish penalty area. Then disaster struck. Uprichard, such a composed figure throughout the first half, fumbled the cross and the ball spilled out of his grasp under a challenge from Da Costa. Uprichard scrabbled on the ground to win the ball back but it was Da Costa's boot that made the telling touch and the ball squirmed its way into Northern Ireland's net. It was now 2-1 and all the Italians needed to do to book their flights to Sweden was to score one more goal. Fifty-seven minutes had been played and Northern Ireland knew that they were facing half an hour of constant bombardment from the Italians. As he makes clear in his book *Right Inside Soccer*, McIlroy was well aware that the game now rested on a knife-edge – 'Individually the Italian players were brilliant, particularly the forwards, and despite our heartening lead, many an Irish heart stopped its beat when Italy's forward line had possession of the ball.'

The game was to turn again, however, in the sixty-eighth minute, and this time back in favour of Northern Ireland as Hungarian referee Zsolt took centre stage. With the first play-off infamous for the extreme leniency shown by local referee Tommy Mitchell towards some very dangerous fouls, it is possible that Zsolt over-compensated in this match. By all accounts, the game had been played in a good spirit. If some of the challenges had been firm and hard it was only because the potential prize on offer to both teams was so important. When Alf McMichael made a strong but perfectly legal challenge on

Ghiggia, the Uruguayan responded by clipping the Irishman with a backheel. In the modern game such behaviour would result in a red card, a three-game suspension and a lot of negative press. In 1958, however, it would only have been judged as rash and might perhaps have provoked some retaliation as the match progressed, but few would have seen it as being particularly worthy of punishment. Zsolt had other ideas though and when he made the decision to send Ghiggia off, it was clear that Italy were paying the price of their sins from the previous game.

Alf McMichael, who had been on the receiving end of the backheel, appealed to Zsolt to reverse his decision, even though Ghiggia was perhaps the single most dangerous man on the pitch, capable of creating the moves from which Italy might yet destroy the Irish World Cup dream. As McParland says, 'Zsolt proved he was one of the world's top referees. His understanding with the linesman was perfect, and he interpreted the advantage rule better than anyone else I'd seen. On the other hand, I thought his decision to send Ghiggia off the field was a harsh one, but Italy's moustachioed right winger was caught red-handed – red-booted if you like. Alf tried to appeal for Ghiggia, but the referee shooed him away. "Judging from the expression on his face, I thought he was going to send me off as well if I didn't shut up," Alf told me.'

With Ghiggia gone the odds now once more favoured a Northern Irish win but the remaining twenty-two minutes continued to see chances come and go at either end. Northern Ireland were forced to dig deep into their reserves of willpower, fired up by the passion and hunger of the Windsor Park fans. 'It was all hands to the pump,' McParland remembers. 'We battled and fought and scrapped and we were trying to get the third goal to put them right out of it. We didn't care what the Italians thought, we went in and had a go at them. We had Wilbur Cush, the pocket battleship as they called him then. Wilbur was in the midst of it all getting stuck in. He was a big, big man at Belfast that day. For a little man he was big in stature for the way he knocked people around and tackled. We gave them as good as we were taking and the crowd were terrific. Once we got in the lead and they could sense, oh, we're going to win this game you know, they got in behind us and they really pushed us along. I was on my knees with about half an hour to go and they inspired me to keep going and to fight on to the end.'

With the finishing line in sight, Northern Ireland really began to reassert themselves and started creating more dangerous chances as the clock ticked down. At one point, they might possibly have had a penalty when Invernizzi seemed to handle the ball in the penalty area. Shortly afterwards, Billy Simpson put the ball in the net but it was ruled offside in what was certainly a marginal decision. McIlroy and Simpson both had chances in the closing stages of the game and McParland and McIlroy again brought great saves from Bugatti within the final four minutes. And then the agony was over. Zsolt blew for full time and Northern Ireland knew that their precious two points were safe. They were going to the World Cup.

'Those last fifteen minutes were the longest I have ever known. Yet, somehow, we held on until the final whistle put us out of our misery,' recalls McIlroy. 'Feeling I was living the greatest moment of my life, I straightaway turned a cartwheel on muddy Windsor Park. Suddenly I looked at Ferrario's face: it was contorted in agony. The famous Italian centre half, victim of a savage assault on his only previous visit to Belfast, was leaving the pitch, this time in tears.'

Bingham too remembers feeling elated. 'It was fantastic. We gave it everything and we didn't expect that we would win. I suppose most of the players thought if we got a draw it would be great. And you could prepare yourself for a loss because this was a very good team we were playing. But we just got stuck in, that Irish mentality of having a go and not lying down, kept coming through. Italy were one of the best teams in Europe then and of course back home they would get some stick, wouldn't they? A country of one and a quarter million beating the team, it wouldn't go down well, no. The Italians liked to win. And generally they did.'

Doherty's tactics had triumphed on the day and the *Belfast Telegraph* was quick to point out the debt the country owed to his astute management of the team. Malcolm Brodie singled out several of the players for special mention. 'Bertie Peacock has rarely had a better international. The same could be said for Jackie Blanchflower, who was cool, calm and deliberate in everything he did. Last month he played Gastone Bean out of the Italian side. It looks like Pivatelli will go the same way.'

Most telling of all, though, was the reaction of the Italian press. Just one month earlier they had been calling for all manner of sanctions against the Northern Ireland team, now they sang their praises and proclaimed that their own side had been beaten fair and square. *Il Giorno* reported that Italy had been 'distracted and outclassed by the dynamic Irish players' while *Il Messaggero* colourfully described how the Italian team had been 'roasted like thrushes on the Irish spit'. *Gazzetta dello Sport* praised Jackie Blanchflower and the back line while also adding that 'Italy was honestly eliminated from the World Cup tournament by a team which dominated the field completely from the twelfth minute of play to the end.' Such praise was the surest sign that the Northern Ireland victory was well deserved.

The defeated Italian team were due to fly out of the country the day after the match but once more fog intervened. The entire Italian team were left stranded in Belfast, licking their wounds. Zsolt was also stranded but didn't seem too concerned – he was photographed happily reading a report of the game in the *Belfast Telegraph*. The Italians, however, were less keen to hang around and took a train to Dublin in the hope of being able to fly from there. Even then their misery was not at an end, as McParland recalls. 'The Italian crowd weren't happy with them and they had to change the airport that they were due to arrive at in Italy because a crowd was waiting on them with rotten fruit.' As for the small band of Italian supporters native to Northern Ireland, McParland jokes: 'The only support they had was all the chip shops and ice cream shops. They were all supporting them, especially in Newry. They had blue and white scarves and all the colours in the window. I kid on and say that there was no fish and chips in Newry for two weeks after that, they went into mourning after we beat them.'

Brimming with pride, Peter Doherty told the *Irish News* that there was more to come from his side. 'Nobody gave us a chance of reaching Sweden. Now nobody will give us a chance of doing well there. But this team has been together for four or five years and is a happy family and has not yet reached its peak.' He was right. But internal conflict within the IFA would soon create a question mark over whether Northern Ireland could continue in the World Cup, and tragedy was just around the corner.

NEVER ON A SUNDAY

The IFA may have been happy to turn its back on the tradition of losing matches, but the issue of playing on a Sunday was harder to resolve. Unfortunately for the Northern Ireland team, Article 32, Clause 2 of the IFA constitution forbade the playing of football on the Sabbath and many people agreed with this. Matches were almost certain to be scheduled on Sundays during the World Cup and having the IFA rule waived or changed wasn't ever going to be a possibility. The voting structure of the IFA meant that all the leagues under its jurisdiction got a vote. As a result amateur football clubs, which made up the vast majority of the clubs playing in Northern Ireland, had the majority of the votes. Of these clubs, a significant number were from church leagues and they were opposed to Sunday football. This meant that while the IFA top brass very much wanted Northern Ireland to play at the World Cup, and most of the top club sides from the Irish League would have backed this stance, the clear majority of voters were fundamentally and implacably opposed to playing on a Sunday.

This situation was something of an embarrassment for the

IFA who were faced with either having to withdraw from the tournament or asking FIFA if they could be exempted from playing their matches on Sunday, meaning that the scheduling of the tournament would have to be changed to accommodate them. Given that FIFA's answer would almost certainly be no, this option was virtually a withdrawal in itself.

The clash between the FIFA schedules and the IFA constitution had been raised as an issue before Northern Ireland qualified for the World Cup and had been discussed in the local press. Until qualification the IFA said that they were sure it wasn't going to be a problem. It's hard to know if they were guilty of wishful thinking, of sticking their heads in the sand, or were just thinking that Northern Ireland wouldn't qualify anyway. There was even a suggestion that the IFA had acted unscrupulously in entering the competition and Danny Blanchflower reflected on this just a few years later. 'It was argued that we should not have entered the competition knowing that our rules would prevent us carrying it through. Someone claimed that our Association had taken part with the intention of making money from the preliminary ties; never expecting to overcome Italy and Portugal to qualify – but the team had let them down!' Whether or not there was any truth in this, the fact remained that Northern Ireland's unexpected qualification posed massive problems for the IFA and presented the possibility of national humiliation in the footballing world.

In modern football we are used to the organisers' clever manipulation of fixtures and spreading games across the schedules to extract maximum television revenues. Premier League games are now played right across the weekend and into Monday night, rather than at the traditional time of 3 p.m. on a Saturday, to allow more money to be made from televised matches. World Cup games are shown one at a time with the exception of the final group games where two matches are played at once to stop teams gaining an advantage from knowing the outcome of the other match. In the 1950s things were very different, though, with the matches from all four groups of four teams taking place simultaneously. This meant that very few matches from the World Cup were seen live by the public at home and it also provided Northern Ireland with an even bigger challenge in their struggle to find a way through the Sunday playing issue. The chance of an entire swathe of group games being moved to a Saturday to accommodate Northern Ireland was close to nil and even getting just Northern Ireland's game moved to a different day seemed extremely unlikely.

Reluctant even to ask the question of FIFA, the IFA gambled instead on being able to sort out the issue internally. On the face of it, their chances appeared slim to none. Not only did the Churches League and their allies command a large block vote, but a change in the rules to remove the Sunday clause from the constitution would require a three-quarter majority. The less-than-conciliatory attitude of the anti-Sunday brigade made things even more difficult, with one prominent voter, an undertaker by trade, proclaiming, 'Ireland will only play on Sundays over my dead body.' The voter in question was William Wilton, Vice President of the IFA!

The players, of course, suffered more than anyone during all this behind-the-scenes wrangling and they were very much aware even as they walked off the field in triumph after defeating Italy that there would be problems ahead. Jimmy McIlroy recalls the immediate post-match conversations: 'As I was being congratulated in the dressing room by an IFA official, I asked him: "Is all this effort going to be wasted? Have we qualified for the World Cup simply to withdraw?" He made a pledge: "You boys have done your bit out there on the field. Now we'll carry on the fight in the legislation chamber." What a sad commentary on Irish football that such a fight should even have been necessary.'

The IFA only beginning the fight to overturn the constitution after the Italy game gives weight to the accusation that the IFA had primarily entered the competition for financial benefit. It's much more likely, though, that they had simply been putting off the battle, hardly believing that it would be necessary. The press, however, had been warning about the situation as far back as the previous spring when Portugal had beaten Italy to increase Northern Ireland's chances. On 27 May 1957, the *Belfast Telegraph* led with the headline, 'Northern Ireland may have to scratch from World Cup'. Now that the matter needed to be addressed, another *Belfast Telegraph* headline suggested that the IFA could even be fined for having wasted FIFA time by taking part.

While it seemed highly unlikely that any of the players would want to forfeit their trip to Sweden because of the issue over Sunday playing, the anti-Sunday voters and their allies lobbied them nevertheless. Peter McParland remembers being sucked into the debate: 'I remember getting a letter and it was from a Lord's Day Observant person and I think there was the name of a well-known Irish politician on it but I didn't look at it enough. I rolled it up and threw it away. I wasn't for that. But as we were playing that season, going towards the World Cup, we were meeting each other, the players were playing against each other in England and that was the first conversation. The first thing they would say was look, this is a once in a lifetime situation, we're not standing any of this nonsense. We were in a situation whereby lots of people around the world didn't know where Northern Ireland was and we had a chance to go out there and put Northern Ireland on the map. So why should we lie down to people? The players had their own minds. Of all eleven, there wasn't one player in the group who said I'm not playing on a Sunday.'

One member of the team, Bertie Peacock, even found himself unable to avoid the issue while attending church. As he recalled later, 'It was our work and if we had to play on a Sunday we just had to play on a Sunday. My minister said, "Bertie, you'll hardly go to the World Cup." I said, "Sir, if it's my work I'll be going," and he just laughed at me. He probably knew it was a chance in a lifetime. If you want to play in the World Cup you have to play on their terms.'

While the IFA were late to wake up to the problems facing them, the matter had been raised privately in the voting chambers in May 1957. At an IFA Annual General Meeting held in Derry/Londonderry a member named Michael McColgan made a brave move to have the Sunday rule overturned due to the possibility, faint as it then was, of Northern Ireland playing in Sweden. The result was an absolute landslide victory for the Sabbath contingent with an overwhelming vote of 89-7 against the motion. The seventy-six representatives of the Churches League at the meeting all voted against the proposal. Anecdotal evidence from the time suggests that the Churches League bussed their representatives to the meeting to ensure that the ban remained intact. The result did not augur well for the more progressive elements within the IFA.

And yet, both at grassroots and at senior levels within Irish football, there was a clear belief that Northern Ireland should take up their place at the World Cup. Even people who were opposed to relaxing the ban on Sunday football within Northern Ireland could see the benefits of presenting their nation to the world in the competition. Some people put forward the view that Sunday football outside Northern Ireland didn't count, that it was possible to uphold the rules regarding the Sabbath and still take part in the World Cup as it was held elsewhere. Indeed, this point was raised in the press in relation to Scotland and Wales – both teams were taking part in Sweden and didn't play Sunday football domestically. There had actually been a convention between the home nations in the 1940s on this very subject – only Northern Ireland had subsequently maintained the complete ban on Sunday football both inside and outside its jurisdiction.

A meeting of supporters held at this time endorsed the view

that Northern Ireland should attend, while a meeting of the amateur clubs drew the same conclusion. Senior clubs were said to be of the same opinion. However, at a meeting convened between them, representatives shied away from making a statement, feeling that they had no mandate from their clubs to vote on the issue. Arguably this was evidence of the fact that the boards of many of the individual clubs contained a number of people bitterly opposed to Sunday football.

Within Northern Ireland the local press was overwhelmingly in favour of the trip to Sweden going ahead. Malcolm Brodie didn't mince his words in *Ireland's Saturday Night*: 'If we have to withdraw then let us hide our heads in shame, let us forget about being a world soccer power.' He also recounted that several of the players had approached an IFA Council member after the Italy game to ask him about the situation. When the Council member said that the rules stated they couldn't go, one of the players hit back by suggesting that if they weren't allowed to go to Sweden then the players wouldn't play against Wales in their forthcoming final Home Championship game. Such was the publicity surrounding the debate that the BBC broadcast a radio programme, *Your Questions*, on the subject from the Whitla Hall in Belfast with various speakers giving their opinion on the matter. Danny Blanchflower was also interviewed on the subject on the radio in January 1958, when he made it clear that he believed that the IFA had delayed tackling the issue of Sunday playing: 'I don't think the Irish officials wanted to think about it at the time. They rather felt inclined to cross the bridges when they came to them.'

With the eyes of the world on Northern Ireland a decision was needed and quickly – the draw for the World Cup was due to take place on 8 February. In the end, the matter was taken up at a meeting of the IFA Council. Players, fans and all those within the game and the IFA who were in favour of Northern Ireland flying the flag for their country breathed a sigh of relief as common sense prevailed and the Council voted in favour of attending the World Cup by twenty votes to eight. It wasn't a straightforward victory – the vote only went the way it did on the grounds that Northern Ireland might be financially punished for withdrawing as they had entered the competition knowing about the issue. There were also conditions attached, chiefly that the IFA would be expected formally to request that FIFA exempt the team from Sunday matches. Nevertheless, after the threat of withdrawal hanging in the air for so long, the stipulation seemed like a price worth paying.

The impossible task of changing the IFA constitution had been sidestepped by the Council decision. However, it was clear that there were some people who were still very unhappy about the matter. The eight members of the Council who voted against the motion insisted on having their names recorded, including the IFA Vice President, William Wilton. The Presbyterian Church condemned the move as 'a retrograde step, bound to have a detrimental influence on the life of the community. This is bound to bring discredit upon the Province.' The Royal Black Institution also voiced their disapproval, stating that they were 'profoundly disappointed that the Northern Ireland soccer legislators countenanced such an unprecedented and retrogressive step' and that any future examples of Sunday football would 'meet with the strongest possible opposition from the Institution'.

With the matter seemingly resolved, the Northern Ireland team focussed on the official draw on 8 February. But tragedy was about to strike. Manchester United had been playing the second leg of their European Cup quarter final against Red Star Belgrade in Yugoslavia. They drew 3-3, a result good enough to send them through to meet AC Milan in the semi-finals. However, having received very little help from the Football League, who had been opposed to United taking part in European competition and hadn't been prepared to rearrange their fixtures, the club had chartered a special plane to get them home in time to fulfil their next domestic game. Northern Ireland players Harry Gregg and Jackie Blanchflower were part of the squad.

The plane landed for refuelling in Munich on the afternoon of 6 February. The pilot made two attempts to take off but both were aborted due to technical problems. The players were told to disembark and to return to the departure lounge. There was some debate as to whether to postpone the take-off until the following day but the captain decided to try again. It was now snowing and when the players were recalled to the plane fifteen minutes later there was a covering of slush on the runway, adding to the apprehension of several of the players. The technical problems meant that a longer run-up to take-off was required but the runway was of a sufficient length and the authorities did not anticipate any problems. However, as the speed of the plane fluctuated on the slush-covered ground the aircraft, now committed to an attempt to take off, didn't lift off in time. It crashed through the perimeter fence of the airport and smashed against a house, losing its left wing in the process. The right side of the fuselage hit a shed filled with fuel, which then exploded, while the left side of the cockpit thudded into a tree. The tail of the plane had also been ripped off along the way. The co-pilot, Captain Rayment, was trapped in the cockpit and urged Captain Thain to get himself out. When Thain did so, he discovered flames perilously close to the right wing and the fuel supply, which could have spelled disaster for the surviving passengers. Heroically, he re-entered the plane to retrieve two hand-held fire extinguishers to try and contain the fire.

Many of the passengers were killed instantly. Others were injured and close to death. Harry Gregg regained consciousness – he felt blood running down his face and initially thought that he was dead: 'I was afraid to touch the top of my head because I felt that the objects which had hit it must have sheared off my scalp.' Finding that his seat belt was no longer there he stumbled towards a hole in the plane and into the disaster zone outside. Parts of the plane littered the ground and Thain was fighting the flames. He shouted to Gregg to get clear in case the plane blew up but Gregg heard a baby crying and turned back to search through the wreckage. He found the baby girl unharmed and her distraught mother and was able to help them both out of the wreckage to safety.

Gregg was surrounded by his teammates: dead, dying, unconscious or struggling with injury. He caught sight of his old schoolboy international friend, the young man Matt Busby had sent to meet him at the train station as he arrived to join Manchester United, Jackie Blanchflower. Gregg described Blanchflower's injured right arm as being almost severed and Blanchflower said he thought he had broken his back. Gregg tried to reassure him that he was all right, and used his tie to fit a tight tourniquet round Blanchflower's arm to try and arrest the flow of blood, possibly saving his life.

Of the players, only Gregg and Bill Foulkes were in any fit state to help. A van arrived and Gregg and Foulkes lifted Blanchflower and Johnny Berry into the back before it sped off to a Munich hospital. Northern Ireland's two players survived but so many of the rest of the team didn't. Of the forty-four people on board seventeen died either instantly or at the site of the crash. Three others died afterwards: Frank Swift, an ex-goalkeeper of Manchester City who had been covering United in Europe in his capacity as a journalist; Captain Kenneth Rayment died of brain injuries several weeks later in hospital; and Duncan Edwards, possibly the finest young player in English football at the time, who died in hospital fifteen days after the crash.

Of the twenty people who died, two were aircraft crew, eight were journalists who had been covering the game against Red Star Belgrade, two were civilian passengers and eight were Manchester United players. The dead from United included club captain, Roger Byrne, and their England international striker, Tommy Taylor. The famous Bobby Charlton was among those who were badly injured. Two players never played again due to their injuries, bringing to ten the total number of players Manchester United lost from their squad. The team manager, Matt Busby, almost joined the fatalities list, spending two months in hospital where he was twice read the last rites, before he was well enough to leave.

As news of the disaster broke, the footballing world went into mourning, especially in Britain where there was shock and heartbreak at the deaths of so many young men who had graced playing fields up and down the country. It was a sombre IFA secretary Billy Drennan who flew the following day to the World Cup draw in Sweden alongside representatives from England, Scotland and Wales. England had just lost some of their best players, with the fate of others still unsure, while Northern Ireland was facing the possibility of losing the services of Blanchflower, even though he had survived, and who knew what effect the crash and its aftermath would have on Harry Gregg?

The draw could hardly have been worse for Northern Ireland. Awaiting them in Sweden would be Czechoslovakia, an extremely capable team who for many were the dark horse of the tournament; Argentina, the South American champions; and West Germany, the reigning World Champions. This was a 'Group of Death' for Northern Ireland – their qualifying group, which had seen them compete against Portugal and Italy, had been hard, but this was going to be much much tougher. As Bingham recalls, 'The thoughts were that that was one of the hardest draws you could have and the second thought was that, being the fighters we were, we could rise to it.'

Confidence was high in the Northern Ireland camp following their achievements against Italy. Jimmy McIlroy remembers the players in buoyant form: 'The tougher the opposition the better this Irish team played. I know it sounds big-headed but we didn't fear any other country in the universe.' Peter Doherty was even more upbeat. He told the *Northern Whig*, 'We are afraid of nothing. The Irish have a great fighting spirit and I have every confidence in the ability of our team to win through to the next stage. We do not mind taking on Germany or the Argentine. Better to meet them early on than later.'

Drennan was forced to go through the embarrassing process of asking FIFA to exempt Northern Ireland from playing on Sundays at the tournament, as stipulated in the agreement that had been reached at the IFA Council meeting. Unsurprisingly, the request was denied, and Northern Ireland discovered that not only would their opening match against Czechoslovakia be a Sunday game, but so too would their match against West Germany.

Back home in Northern Ireland, news of the Sunday fixtures gained as many headlines as the draw itself. Now that Northern Ireland was actually going to play on a Sunday, the protestors redoubled their efforts to prevent the matches from going ahead. On 10 February – only four days after the Munich air disaster – a Methodist group convened and made public a request for the IFA to advise its players not to play on Sundays. Three days later, on 13 February, the Churches League met in Belfast's YMCA. They hoped to call an Extraordinary General Meeting of the IFA at which they knew their bloc vote would prevail. They still considered that the article in the constitution should take precedence over the IFA Council decision and they were, rather ominously, now making noises about taking out an injunction to prevent the team from playing. On 16 February the campaigners upped the ante even further by holding a large rally in the Assembly Hall. As well as being fronted by the Very Reverend Dr A.F. Moody, a former moderator of the Presbyterian Church, the party of speakers included the Vice President of the IFA,

William Wilton.

This was a nightmare for the IFA and all the progressive elements within it. Against the background of the horrific Munich Air Disaster, and with one of their brave players who had helped them to qualify for Sweden lying crippled in hospital, lucky to be alive, the IFA's Vice President was now in open rebellion against the majority of the Council. On 20 February the Churches League formally requested that the IFA abide by the regulations in their own constitution or face further action. The matter went to an IFA Emergency Committee. While the committee could not ignore the threat of litigation – after all, the protestors were completely in the right in terms of the IFA constitution – it remained firmly behind the decision that the team should go to Sweden, albeit in the knowledge that, somehow, they were going to have to find a way of persuading the protestors to back down.

The breakthrough came just over three weeks later when the IFA and the Churches League reached a compromise that allowed them both to claim some kind of victory. In a joint statement, the Churches League agreed to the Northern Ireland team taking its place in Sweden and the IFA agreed that 'no team under its jurisdiction shall again enter or be permitted to enter for any competition, or play in any international matches, in which the team would be required to play on a Sunday.' With Sunday games very likely to take place at all future World Cups, this essentially meant that Northern Ireland would never again be allowed to enter the competition and, in effect, removed the team from all future international competition outside of the Home Internationals.

There was one further concession to the Churches League, one that probably went unnoticed by many people – the Northern Ireland youth team, which had been due to play in a European tournament in Luxembourg at Easter, was forced to withdraw. With no assurance from the organisers that matches wouldn't be played on Sundays, the Churches League had demanded their withdrawal and the IFA had been forced to comply. It was a bitter blow to the teenagers and their families, especially given that the tournament was only a month away and preparations for the trip were advanced. This was the sacrifice that the IFA had to make to secure the World Cup for the senior team.

Clearly, the ban on entering any future tournaments that the Churches League had insisted on would be utterly unacceptable to the IFA going forward and they almost certainly agreed to it thinking that they would be able to find a way around it before the next World Cup. For now at least, the battle was over. However, the frustration and antagonism that the whole fracas had generated was not so quick to disappear. Jimmy McIlroy is, to this day, critical of the role the Churches League played in events during the early months of 1958. 'Looking back now, I think what a silly decision. I suppose it wouldn't have happened in any other country except Northern Ireland.' Closer to the time, his views in his autobiography were even more scathing: 'The majority of senior clubs want us to play on Sundays. The majority of players want to play on Sundays. The majority of spectators want us to play on Sundays. Above all, the people running our international side want it. Hundreds of insignificant clubs voted against it. That is why ... all major decisions ought to be taken by senior clubs. The opinions of the amateur leagues should be recorded ... and ignored! Such men are millstones to Irish international prestige.'

Such feelings had, however, to be set to one side. The focus now was Sweden and preparing Northern Ireland to take on some of the world's elite teams and that seemed like a daunting task.

ONWARDS TO SWEDEN

Northern Ireland's preparations for Sweden coincided with the culmination of that season's British Championship and their match against Wales in Cardiff in April. Since the team's last game against Italy in January, two of their very best players had been victims of a horrific plane crash that had taken the lives of many of their friends. Jackie Blanchflower had only left hospital in mid-March so it was out of the question that he would be able to play against Wales. As for Gregg, he was proving to be as indomitable off the pitch as he was on it. In spite of the awful scenes he had witnessed during the crash and its aftermath, and the mental toll that must have taken on him, he was back playing for Manchester United when they played their first game after the disaster – less than two weeks later.

With half of their team dead as a result of the crash and even those who had survived facing a long journey back from injury, Manchester United were effectively unable to continue as a footballing power that season. Except for Harry Gregg and Bill Foulkes they had no team. It is to the credit of other teams in the English League as well as a mark of the respect felt for

Manchester United and a recognition of the scale of the tragedy that deals were cut quickly to sell and loan players to United so that they could put together a team for the rest of the season. The new team's first fixture was a Fifth Round FA Cup match at Old Trafford against Sheffield Wednesday on 19 February. It speaks volumes for the character of both Gregg and Foulkes that they were able to play in the game at all, and the fact that Harry Gregg kept a clean sheet in a 3-0 victory is remarkable. As far as Northern Ireland went, Gregg was back and the team could count on him as always.

In many ways, the Northern Ireland team that Gregg was a part of in Wales that April was the quintessential line-up of players from that period. With the obvious exception of Jackie Blanchflower, this was the strongest team, featuring all of the most famous names associated with qualifying and the subsequent World Cup. Simpson had by now made the forward position his own and was backed up by McIlroy and Cush as the inside forward line. McParland and Bingham dominated in the outside positions and Danny Blanchflower and Peacock patrolled the midfield as the halfbacks. Gregg stood resolutely in goal and in front of him were Alf McMichael and the two men who had recently vied for the remaining fullback position – Cunningham and Keith. With Jackie Blanchflower out of the team, both men could be accommodated in the starting line-up, with Keith moving into the centre back position from his favoured right-back role.

In spite of the terrific line-up, the result was a draw. Knowing that they had to win to be absolutely sure of winning the title, the Irish were rather nervous and cagey throughout the game, perhaps unused to the pressure of being favourites for once. However, in the sixty-fifth minute Cush beat his way past two Welshmen to cross the ball for Simpson to head it home. For the next twenty minutes Northern Ireland were on the brink of making history. Then five minutes from the end, a mistake from

McIlroy allowed the Welsh to gain possession of the ball. There seemed to be little to fear as the ball was moved up the field and then tamely hit into the Irish box by Hewitt. Unluckily for Northern Ireland, it was deflected into the net by Dick Keith's hand with an unsighted Gregg left flat-footed in surprise. The game ended a 1-1 draw.

There was still some slight hope for Northern Ireland – Scotland and England had yet to play the final game of the tournament and if they finished all square then Northern Ireland could still lift the title. The English prevailed, however, and the result meant the title was shared by Northern Ireland and England. It was undoubtedly a disappointment for Northern Ireland and they were perhaps undeserving of the volley of criticism fired in their direction by Malcolm Brodie in the *Belfast Telegraph* who went through the team and took them to task both individually and collectively. McParland was his main focus and he claimed that it was time he was left out of the team. Bingham, Peacock, McIlroy and Keith were also in the firing line in an uncharitable article that didn't seem to factor in that Northern Ireland had lost Blanchflower to serious injury and that the last few months had been a rollercoaster of emotions for them. Only a few years before, a draw away to Wales would have been considered a fine result and worthy of praise. Perhaps the piece was a sign of just how far Northern Ireland had travelled in such a short time.

Despite his dissatisfaction with the team's performance against Wales, he was quick to acknowledge the challenges for the team in their preparations for the World Cup. In the run-up to the competition, most qualifying teams played an intensive series of friendlies to test and prepare them. For Northern Ireland, this just wasn't an option, as they could not afford any risk of injury for their preferred starting line-up. They had almost certainly already lost one star player and their options for replacing another were limited. Brodie himself pointed out just before the game with Wales: 'The blunt truth is that we have so few players of the correct calibre available to step into the national team. Every country is nominating lists of up to forty players from which their World Cup party will be chosen. No matter how you tried you couldn't get anything like that number from Northern Ireland without plunging into the depths of mediocrity. You would be lucky if you reached the twenty mark.'

It is true that Northern Ireland could never have named a forty-man initial squad, but the final twenty-two-man selection should have been within their grasp. In the end, though, Northern Ireland chose only seventeen players, forgoing the right to pick another five players as allowed by the rules. The official line was that they didn't have any more players capable of doing themselves justice at World Cup level. However, selecting such a small pool of players seemed like a wilful hampering of their own preparations for the tournament – surely any sort of player was preferable to no player in the event of injury or some other eventuality. Given a tight schedule of three group games in the opening week, tiredness and injury were actually quite likely, so it seems even more perverse that the Irish would hinder their own chances in this way.

McParland remembers that the limited squad was very much to his advantage. 'I had a bit of a stinker in that game [against Wales] and it was the last game before the team would be picked to go to the World Cup. I was rooming with Willie Cunningham and I said to Willie at the end, after we had a drink and went to bed, "I haven't done myself any good tonight for making the World Cup team, you know." And Willie said to me, "We've only got seventeen players, you've nothing to worry about!"'

Doherty had actually utilised several players over the previous seasons who did not make the final squad, so the notion of there not being enough players of quality does not adequately explain the small selection. Players like Billy McAdams, Eddie McMorran and Jimmy Jones had all been in action for Northern Ireland within the last twelve months and all would have been useful members of the squad. McAdams had been deemed good enough to play in the first home game against Italy just a few months before in December 1957, a must-win game with qualification at stake, but was not even considered for the squad that went to Sweden. One wonders if money came into it. Bringing five players fewer may have made the trip cheaper, especially when the trip already involved the backroom staff of Doherty and Morgan as well as the selectors and IFA officials.

While Northern Ireland took the smallest squad to the tournament, there were other nations who also didn't take the full complement, with some surprising names among them. The FIFA lists credit England with a twenty-two man squad but only twenty players actually made the trip, with two left at home as reserves. Likewise, and most bizarrely, the World Champions, West Germany, named a full squad but only took eighteen players.

The Northern Ireland team was made up of the eleven players who had played against Wales, and six back-up players. Unsurprisingly, Norman Uprichard and Tommy Casey, who had been in and out of the first team for years, were included, as was Sam McCrory, who had scored one of the goals in the victory over England the previous autumn. He had recently fallen out of favour with the selectors following a poor showing when he played for the Irish League Select XI against the British Army, but was brought back in for the World Cup, given that many of the other attacking players had not been selected.

The remaining three players were more of a surprise. Fay Coyle hadn't impressed on previous outings for Northern Ireland and he hadn't been called upon since a lacklustre performance against Portugal in the opening qualification game. However, the selectors were somehow convinced that he deserved a place ahead of people who had previously scored at international level. Two uncapped players made up the numbers – Grimsby Town's Jackie Scott, who was playing domestic football for a mid-table

Second Division team, and the teenage Derek Dougan, who had been making a name for himself at Portsmouth that season. Dougan had been brought into the squad as twelfth man for the win over Italy in January. McParland recalls being particularly impressed with Dougan when Aston Villa played Portsmouth. 'I was changing in the dressing room after the game and next thing he's [Dougan] standing beside me. He'd come into our dressing room and I'd only ever seen him on the field. So I said to him, "You're just after giving the best centre half in the league a chasing there. Keep that up and you'll be a player." Jimmy Dugdale was our best player and he used to eat all the centre forwards – Lofthouse, Tommy Taylor of Manchester United, all these great players, but Derek Dougan ran him a bit ragged.'

The trio of McAdams, McMorran and Jones, who had all scored for their national team and, in the case of the first two, were used to playing at a high level in England, must have been particularly disappointed not to make the squad, especially given the calibre of some of those who did.

Northern Ireland did in fact name a squad of twenty-two players, despite never considering taking more than seventeen. The five additional players who were named raise even more questions. They were the uncapped twenty-year-old Sammy Chapman of Portsmouth, a trio of uncapped players from the Irish League (Roy Rea of Glenavon, Tommy Hamill of Linfield and Bobby Trainor of Coleraine) and the veteran defender, Len Graham, who had just finished bottom of the Second Division with Doncaster Rovers and who hadn't been involved with the international team since 1955. The inclusion of three uncapped Irish League players certainly makes a mockery of the non-inclusion of Jimmy Jones who was just about to become top scorer in the Irish League for the sixth season in a row. And while McMorran was an older player who was slipping down the divisions, the same could certainly have been said of Len Graham, not to mention Sam McCrory.

In the end, Jackie Blanchflower did not make the journey to Sweden, a real blow to the players. McParland remembers the impact it had on the team: 'Jackie was a big loss because he'd been an outstanding player for us at that particular time and Manchester United were working off him because of how well he did for us. From originally being a middle of the park man he went in and played centre back and did a big job. I'd seen him up at Manchester before when he was recovering and he just couldn't get himself into shape again to play football, so it was most unfortunate. But most unfortunate for us because we had few players and he was one of our main men at the back. And we lost him. So we had to shuffle around to get someone to take his place.' As it turned out, Blanchflower never played professional football again.

Harry Gregg was probably Jackie's closest friend in the Northern Ireland set-up. He was his team-mate at Manchester United and had known him from when Blanchflower played as a schoolboy at internationals. 'Jackie was a lovely person and sadly, because of what happened with the accident, he never played again and he was a great loss to Northern Ireland. I know what happened to his arm, I saw it. I know what happened to his legs at the time, I saw it. But I said to him, "Blanchy, you could have played again." And he said, "Aye, Greggy, but I couldn't have played as well as I did play." That was the answer.'

Saddened as he was by the absense of Blanchflower, Gregg continued to perform at the highest level for Manchester United. At one point after the Munich Air Disaster it seemed as though the team would, almost impossibly, continue where they had left off. United had reached the semi-finals of the European Cup on their fateful trip to Belgrade and now had to fulfil their obligation to play that game against the Italian giants, Milan. Amazingly, United managed to win the first leg 2-1 to set up the possibility of reaching a dream final against Real Madrid. It wasn't to be though and Milan took the second leg 4-0 and the tie 5–2 on aggregate.

In the First Division, United's challenge for a third successive title, a feat only achieved twice before quickly faded as they slumped down to ninth place. However, in the prestigious FA Cup, it looked just possible that United could achieve something of a fairy-tale ending to their tragic season as they navigated their way through round after round to reach their second successive Wembley final with a chance to avenge the sense of injustice that had followed their defeat the year before by Aston Villa.

For the Manchester United and Northern Ireland keeper Harry Gregg there were still other issues to mull over. The battle against the Churches League had been won by the IFA but Gregg was still wrestling with his conscience over the matter. He had been brought up in a house that observed Sunday as a day of worship, and while he was in training camp in Blackpool preparing for the FA Cup Final he became restless and anxious: 'I didn't tell anyone but I went to a telephone book and got a telephone. I looked for a Church of England minister and rang him up and asked could I come and see him. He said of course I could and I went along and sat and talked and I remember ever so well him saying, "If a child were dying would you think that God would think it was wrong a doctor should save the child?" The question answered itself and it was a great, great burden off my back.'

United played Bolton Wanderers in the FA Cup final a few days later and there was to be no happy ending after all. Bolton and their inspirational player Nat Lofthouse had clearly not read the script the nation had written, with a near repeat of the year before. This year it was Lofthouse as the centre forward who charged in on goalkeeper Gregg to flatten him and knock him into the goal in the process of scoring Bolton's decisive second goal in their 2–0 victory – causing controversy to rage for the second year running.

Gregg picked himself up from the heartache of Wembley and concentrated instead on the job at hand in Sweden. The English domestic season was over and preparation began in earnest. Normally, the domestic fixtures list forced the Irish players to squeeze national training into the few days before internationals, but now they were able to spend longer together than they ever had before. However, they had to train without their talismanic manager who couldn't meet up with the team until they gathered in London before travelling on to Sweden. Doherty, who had taken over as manager of Bristol City during the season, was on a pre-arranged end of season tour with the club and was unavailable. Nowadays, players enjoy a well-deserved rest following the exertions of the season, then meet back at their club several weeks later for light training and then possibly go on tours to play friendlies and prepare themselves to get match-fit for the new season. In this period, however, teams would immediately embark on a tour at the end of the season as a way of winding down. It seems unthinkable that Doherty wasn't available to look after the training of his squad but he was employed by Northern Ireland on a part-time basis only, and so was obliged to find additional employment – employment that now stopped him from being involved with the national team when they needed him most.

Doherty was not alone in missing the initial training. Gregg was seeing out the end of Manchester United's European Cup run in Milan while Newcastle's McMichael and Keith, Cunningham of Leicester City, McIlroy of Burnley, Peacock of Celtic and McParland of Aston Villa were all committed to club touring and friendlies. McCrory of Southend United and Scott of Grimsby Town were also unavailable for the same reason. Today, the World Cup is the centrepiece of the whole footballing calendar with schedules worked out for years in advance to avoid any clashes with it. Nothing can stand in the way of World Cup organisation and squads assembling to train for it. In 1958 an end of season tour by Grimsby Town took precedence.

A number of players from the squad were nevertheless available to come together at Windsor Park in mid May for training under the supervision of Danny Blanchflower and Gerry Morgan. Dougan, Uprichard, Bingham, Cush and Casey were able to make the start and Simpson was available the following day after his final game for Rangers before the summer break was played that night. For the players involved in tours there would be no problem keeping match-fit, although injuries were obviously a concern for the team. For the players in Belfast it was all about keeping themselves in good condition before travelling to London at the end of May to rendezvous with most of the rest of the team and then flying out to Sweden. McMichael and Keith, however, were unable to make even this get-together and would meet the squad once they had finally finished their business with Newcastle in Europe.

On 2 June, when the majority of the squad finally met up in London to make the onward trip to Sweden, the spirit in the camp was good, and confidence and humour were in strong supply. The squad posed happily on the steps of the plane and the press was happy to report some of the antics of Gerry Morgan. Apparently he had taken a stand on a soapbox at the famous Speaker's Corner in Hyde Park and entertained passers-by with his famous comic horse racing commentary. And when one player announced that all you heard about now in the papers was 'de Gaulle, de Gaulle' – the famous French general and politician who was about to be swept to power in crisis-hit France – Morgan responded that the Irish would have a new motto for the World Cup of 'de goal, de goal'.

With the Munich crash still fresh in his mind, Harry Gregg declined to travel by plane and made the journey to Sweden by sea and land. An IFA official, Joe Beckett, offered to accompany him, though this seemingly generous offer from Beckett left something of a sour taste for Gregg: 'I went out by ferry and overland to Sweden. The gentleman who took me out was batman to Lady Glentoran and he was kind enough to do that. But he immediately got on an aeroplane back to Northern Ireland after dropping me off in case he'd be tainted by the fact that we had to play Sunday football and because he didn't want any part in it.'

McMichael and Keith were the last two members of the squad to make their way to Sweden, and it was a nerve-wracking trip. Following the conclusion of Newcastle's tour in Romania, the team discovered that there weren't enough seats for all of the players on their flight home. One would have expected that, given their World Cup commitments, the two Irishmen would have automatically been given two of the seats, but instead, lots were drawn. Fortunately, McMichael and Keith secured places but six of their Newcastle team-mates were left behind in Bucharest. There followed a terrifying flight through a thunderstorm over Czechoslovakia followed by changes in Prague, Brussels, Amsterdam and Copenhagen before they finally arrived in Gothenburg and made the winding road-trip to Tylösand.

Braving storms both real and metaphorical, Northern Ireland had reached Sweden. They were ready to take their place in the world footballing elite and quickly set about turning this out of the way corner of Scandinavia into a part of Ireland. However, even as the complete squad trained together for the first time, further disaster had already hit the team.

A SWEDISH HOME FROM HOME

The Northern Ireland base of Tylösand was a seaside resort on what is known as the Swedish Riviera, just a short drive from the town of Halmstad. It was the perfect base for the team as their first two fixtures were to be played there. The securing of the Tylösand base was a triumph for the IFA. Billy Drennan had been quick to secure it after the World Cup draw in February. Hearing that the Czechs were also interested, he made arrangements to fly out to Tylösand as quickly as possible but his plane was delayed for four hours by bad weather. However, the Czechs were faring even worse on the twisting and turning roads and ended up being hampered by snowdrifts. By the time the continental suitors arrived, Drennan had already concluded the deal.

Being based in Tylösand was one of the best things to happen to Northern Ireland. Very quickly, the team felt at home there, largely because the locals gave them such a warm welcome. As Malcolm Brodie recalled over fifty years later, 'The camaraderie was tremendous and the ability of the fans to be a part of it. Tylösand was like a part of Northern Ireland.' With access to a terrific training centre, the team thrived, as Peter McParland remembers: 'The camp that we had was absolutely marvellous, better than most of the teams had. Some of the press boys had come to see us and said you're way better than England or Wales, and Scotland had a bit of trouble I think. We were enjoying being out there and the people in Halmstad took us as their team. When we had time off we were in the little town shopping and looking around and they were inviting us in, giving us tea and cakes, and enjoying us being there. That was a nice experience for us and it was a lift to be amongst those people. With it being a seaside resort, we were even allowed out for an hour to sit in the sun and then back in. We had everything well organised.'

Billy Bingham has fond memories of the great relationship the players developed with the locals: 'We met some of them and had them in for tea and all sorts of things and charmed them in our sweet Irish way … I think they liked us because we were underdogs. We were fighters, we wouldn't go down without a battle.'

The Irish charm offensive, led by the mercurial Gerry Morgan, ensured that Northern Ireland had a large degree of 'home' support for their two opening games. This was important since there were few fans from Northern Ireland who could afford to make the journey to Sweden. England, by virtue of being a much larger nation, could rely on a greater number of fans making the trip. They could also count on there being more ex-pats living in Sweden who would try and get to their games.

A small number of Northern Ireland fans, however, did travel to Sweden and they certainly made an impression on the team and helped to make the Irish players feel at home. Micky McColgan and Leslie Nicholl famously made the entire trip by moped and boat, stopping off initially in Manchester to meet Jackie Blanchflower and to wish him well with his recovery, before travelling across to Europe and up to Scandinavia. When they arrived in Tylösand, they made their way to the hotel of the Northern Ireland team and set up camp on the lawn, as Peter McParland remembers: 'They had a little tent there and the boys used to go into this tent and have a cup of tea and they used to call it Dave's Inn. We had a cup of tea there in the morning and then we'd go to training.'

The two fans quickly made an impression, as Danny Blanchflower recounted: 'Tylösand is one of Sweden's sophisticated resorts and the hotel one of its better houses and it didn't seem right to pitch tents on the lawn. When the hotel manager marched forth to engage the campers we expected to see them bowled out. But the rascals invited him into their abodes, gave him a cup of Primus-brewed tea, charmed him with the blarney and had him eating out of their hands. It got to the stage where he was sending them off on match days with special buttonhole carnations.' The manager eventually gave McColgan and Nicholl a room in the hotel, though the Primus stove went with them and Dave's Inn continued to be a drop-in centre for the players.

The friendship between the players and the fans often showed itself in practical jokes, including one ambitious prank by Gregg and Cush on McColgan, recounted here by Gregg: 'One night we got Micky McColgan out and Cush says let's go and do his room. So we put the bed out the window and up a tree, and we rolled the carpets up. We took every single piece of furniture we could find, dumped it, and went away and waited, and eventually, waiting for the riot, heard Micky come in. We were away hiding in another room and waited ten or fifteen minutes, complete silence. We thought he'd maybe snuffed it or something. Then we went and knocked the door and a voice says, 'Come in, you whores' and there he was, sitting in the middle, on the floorboards, with a Primus stove – we'd missed it – and a kettle on it. He was brilliant, he took it all.'

Not surprisingly, Peter Doherty had been concerned that

Gregg would still be fragile after the Munich crash. He decided that instead of having him share a room with a player who might keep him awake at night talking and joking, that he would have him share with Gerry Morgan who was older and more responsible. The move backfired – Gerry had a habit of pacing the floor at night, sometimes until 4 a.m., sharing his wit as he did so – and Gregg's sleep was disturbed more than ever: 'If I didn't have bad nerves before I roomed with him I had bad nerves after I roomed with him.'

Another famous pair of room-mates from the campaign were two players from east Belfast, Derek Dougan and Billy Bingham, an odd couple who were nicknamed 'the long and the short'. If the players ever got bored or conversation began to slow there was always one sure-fire method of restoring high spirits, as Gregg recalls, 'All anyone had to say was, "Do you think Doug is faster than Bingy?" The two of them would have been running for the next two days. Or they'd say, "Do you think Bingy's a better dancer than Derek?" or "Do you think Bingy's a better singer?" That was us entertained for the next two or three weeks because you had the two of them either singing or dancing or trying to beat each other at Snakes and Ladders. Unbelievable. They were our entertainment.'

The team also gained a dedicated new fan and friend in Bengt Jonasson, a thirteen-year-old schoolboy from Halmstad. 'He was a wee boy who came to the training ground,' recounts McParland. 'He was probably the one who we noticed most of all there with us. He was getting the ball and throwing it back and Gerry took him under his wing.' Harry Gregg was particularly fond of young Bengt: 'He was always round our camp and he took a shine to me and became friendly with me. I'll always remember that boy. He went everywhere with us. In the end he went on the coach with us to training and things like that.'

Jonasson was there because he had read in his local paper that the Northern Ireland team would be staying very close to his hometown of Halmstad so he decided to go and check them out while they were training. Even today, he has very clear memories of the team's arrival: 'I had read about Harry Gregg and the accident in Munich so I very much wanted to meet him and have his autograph. I went down to the place where they stayed and I remained there from morning till evening and finally I met the players and begged for their autographs. They were very polite and gave them to me and after that I came to the hotel every morning to see them training and practising.'

A great bond developed between Bengt and the players, especially Gregg and Morgan, helped by the young man's excellent grasp of English, and before long he was eagerly offering his services as unofficial interpreter for the squad. 'I helped them shopping in Halmstad. The ones serving them didn't understand English so I helped them. Also, when they had spare time they liked to play golf and I was a keen golfer, I had started to play a couple of years before, so I knew where the golf was and I could help them to organise tee-times and so on.' Bengt eventually became the team's unofficial mascot: 'I went with them on the bus and they decided to keep me as a mascot for the team and I was lucky to be sitting on the players' bench watching all the games. At one stage they even asked me to take part in the tactical meetings they had at the hotel so I knew about their tactics and how they were supposed to play the teams.' The team thought that Bengt brought them luck and they took him everywhere with them.

In many ways, the scene was set for a great campaign for Northern Ireland. However, in the background, the team were dealing with a sledgehammer blow to their chances. At their very first training session disaster struck for centre forward Billy Simpson: 'I was just running ... there was no tackling or anything and it was a pulled muscle. Just, all of a sudden, the left thigh pulled.' It seemed innocuous enough but it was deemed serious enough for Simpson to sit out most of the rest of that day's training and to seek treatment from Gerry Morgan. Peter McParland saw what happened that day and knew that it would have serious consequences for the team: 'It was obvious straight away – that's Billy finished in the game and that was … a real knock-back you know, he was our main centre forward, a boy who was getting the goals for us and he was out now, so that was tough to take.'

An injury to Simpson was a real blow for Northern Ireland. The troublesome centre forward berth in the team had been difficult to fill and Simpson's absence would require a major rethink of the Irish tactics. The *Belfast Telegraph* initially played down the news, quoting Gerry Morgan as saying, 'It's not serious' as he used an infrared heat lamp to treat Simpson. Simpson himself was quoted as saying, 'I have full freedom of movement but when I kick a ball a sharp pain grips me.' The team doctor Dr George Scarlett remained hopeful that Simpson would recover for the opening game. In fact, the *Belfast Telegraph* seemed more concerned that Willie Cunningham had been struck down by a fever, something that would have been disastrous to the Irish back line, already rejigged in the absence of Jackie Blanchflower. With Cunningham confined to bed and Simpson's injury giving concern, the team had plenty to think about: 'In those days they hadn't the same facilities for looking after players,' says Simpson. 'Nowadays they have everything to look after the players but in those days it was different. The treatment that they gave you then isn't up to today's standards. They did the best they could really, but it was a pulled muscle. They'd say go out there and forget about it. You can't forget about a pulled muscle.'

Simpson's injury took place on the Tuesday before the tournament and was a daily issue in the press as it became clear that Simpson's chances of being able to play were receding. By Friday, Simpson was still unable to return even to light training, though he pleaded with the selectors to be kept in the frame for another day. In the end it was only delaying the inevitable and on Saturday Simpson was officially ruled out. Although there was still hope that he might make enough of a recovery to play later in the tournament, it was not to be. He had worked hard alongside Doherty and the players and shared the team spirit and camaraderie and he had seen that team become a force to be reckoned with, a force that could take on and beat old foes such as England and battle through the qualifying rounds, but Simpson's World Cup was over and he spent the rest of the competition on the sidelines.

If Northern Ireland's decision to bring only seventeen players to the tournament instead of the permitted twenty-two had originally seemed naive, now – with Simpson out of the team and Cunningham still recovering from a fever – it appeared positively suicidal. Northern Ireland were at a disadvantage before a ball had even been kicked and now needed to come up with a new plan of action on the eve of one of the biggest matches in their history.

THE DREAM START

With Billy Simpson out of the game against Czechoslovakia, Peter Doherty and the three selectors who had come to Sweden had the problem of choosing his replacement. They had four options: to recall Fay Coyle who had not been impressive in recent outings; to hand an international debut to the young Derek Dougan; to bring Peter McParland in from the wing to the centre; or to gamble on the Iron Man, Tommy Casey, normally a midfielder. All these options were less than ideal and it speaks volumes about the lack of confidence in these alternatives that Doherty and the selectors waited until the day before the game before admitting that Simpson was unfit to play. In the end it was to be the teenage Dougan who got the nod, with the advantage that if Northern Ireland wasn't entirely sure of what he would deliver on the pitch then neither were their opponents.

That desire to know as much as possible about your opponent made Doherty and Blanchflower head to Denmark to see the Czechs play their final preparation game against a Danish Select XI in Copenhagen. It was a hundred–mile round trip by car and ferry but it was a worthwhile exercise. Doherty left both impressed and hopeful, telling reporters, 'The Czechs are fast, have wonderful ball control, but they can be so easily upset.'

Much has been made of the importance of this spying trip but at the time, the focus was on the fact the Irish had left things until the last minute. In its report of the journey to Copenhagen, the *Belfast Telegraph* scolded the IFA for having made no effort until then to see any group opponent's matches. Cost was undoubtedly one of the reasons – the IFA had already been publicly shamed in *Ireland's Saturday Night* for reducing Doherty's expenses for the Wembley match the previous autumn. However, sending Doherty or an official to watch a few matches would have cost little compared to the money the team stood to make from the tournament and the failure to see this is indicative of the attitude prevalent in the IFA at the time.

Northern Ireland's match with Czechoslovakia took place on 8 June. Of course, the day of the match was a Sunday, and perhaps as a show of goodwill, the team, a mixture of Catholics and Protestants, attended a service in a tiny Tylösand church before boarding their coach. As Blanchflower remembered, 'We sang the hymn "Fight the Good Fight" and listened to a sermon on "Faith moving mountains". It was all, I felt, a well-aimed blow against the anti-Sunday-soccer brigade back home in Northern Ireland.'

As the Irish coach departed for the riverside setting of the Örjans Vall stadium, Doherty and Morgan were working their magic, encouraging the players and boosting their morale. Doherty's final words to the press the day before must have bolstered the confidence of his team: 'We have everything to win and nothing to lose. Nobody believes in us but remember this – we have defeated England and beaten Italy. We have a team which is working smoother as a unit than perhaps any other World Cup nation.' There was no question about this. While the Irish had shown some organisational naivety, the team were a tight-playing unit, who were bound in friendship and prepared to work hard for each other.

In facing Czechoslovakia, it was clear that the Northern Ireland players would need to draw on all of that determination and commitment. As the *Northern Whig* correspondent Hamilton C. McDowell reported on the eve of the match, 'The Czechs are one of the best teams in the tournament and might well win it.' This view was 'based on the fact that the Czechs went to the Argentine and lost by only a goal to the South Americans. However Jack Scott (Grimsby Town) said that his team lost by only 1-0 to Dukla which supplies eight men to the Czech national side and if Ireland is not a better team that Grimsby then I will eat my hat.' This humour and bravado buoyed everyone's spirits but there was still no getting away from the fact that Northern Ireland were highly unfancied, their tournament odds of 33-1 contrasting sharply with those of 7-1 for the Czechs who were fourth favourites out of the field of sixteen.

Peter McParland has vivid memories of Northern Ireland's arrival at the Örjans Vall stadium. 'When we got to the ground that day we were in front of the Czechs and as we were going in they were arriving at the ground. It was a communist country then, you know, and the curtains were pulled over in the coach, like the Iron Curtain, but we were showing off to the Swedish people coming in and waving.' He also recalls the swell of good spirits on board the coach. 'When we got within striking distance of the ground we all went into "When Irish Eyes Are Smiling" and that was a big thing. We were driving up to the stadium and singing our heads off and that was a real inspirational thing.'

Fortunately, Willie Cunningham was well enough to play as centre half in the team, though it's worth noting that he had never played in this position before. A natural right back, he was selected to take over this important lynchpin role. Another right back, Dick Keith, had stepped into the role following the serious injury to Jackie Blanchflower but he had not impressed and now reverted to his normal position.

Doherty's tactics for the game were simple – to try and frustrate the Czechs. He knew that they liked to control games through their silky passing and possession. Doherty felt that Northern Ireland's best chance of getting something from the game was to sit deep, leaving Dougan and Cush alone up front, with McParland and Bingham pulling back even more than normal on the wings and Peacock sitting in front of the defence, on the front line of the anticipated Czech movements. It was hoped that Northern Ireland could keep the game very tight and defensive and still be able to spring forward with fast counter attacks when the need arose.

Around 11,000 spectators turned out for the Northern Ireland and Czechoslovakia match, a relatively small number by today's standards but not an unusually low number for the time, especially at a fairly small stadium such as Örjans Vall. (The scramble for World Cup tickets that we are familiar with today is a relatively new phenomenon – even in 1966, tickets were still available on the day of the World Cup final in which England, the host nation, played.)

The teams that day were:

NORTHERN IRELAND: Gregg; Keith; McMichael; Blanchflower; Cunningham; Peacock; Bingham; Cush; Dougan; McIlroy; McParland

CZECHOSLOVAKIA: Dolejší; Mráz; Novák; Pluskal; Řadek; Masopust; Hovorka; Dvořák; Borovička; Hertl; Kraus

Recently discovered footage gives a real sense of the struggle that the match was for Northern Ireland. Peter McParland had already said that, 'they gave us a going over for the first ten minutes, they really got at us and the ball was flying across our goalmouth, we were under pressure and Harry was doing his nut, but we survived those ten minutes and if they had got a goal it could have ruined our World Cup, but they didn't.' However, the footage shows what none of the match reports mentioned, which is that the Czechs came very close to scoring in the opening seconds of the game. A quick and slick move from the kick off ended with the ball flashing just wide of the Irish net from a header. How different the Irish story would have been had that ball found its way inside the post. Instead, Northern Ireland steeled themselves to face the challenge and dug deep into their reserves of courage and teamwork.

Doherty had identified Dvořák as the Czech danger man and it was Peacock's job to keep him under control, a job he stuck at resolutely. Having weathered those difficult first ten minutes, Northern Ireland became more and more comfortable with keeping the Czechs at bay. They now found the confidence to launch attacks, primarily through Blanchflower providing long passes upfield for Cush to latch on to. Cush's terrier-like work rate was already proving troublesome for the Czech defence and his low centre of gravity and strong build meant that he was a difficult man to knock off the ball once he had it. It was becoming clear that Cush might well hold the key to Irish hopes in the match.

The breakthrough came in the twenty-first minute when Northern Ireland won a corner. The ball was played short to McParland who then tried to weave his way past the Czech defence to get a cross in. A Czech defender tackled McParland and succeeded in clearing the ball, but it was found by Jimmy McIlroy who immediately lofted the ball into the box where Wilbur Cush, unquestionably the smallest man on the pitch, headed the ball firmly into the Czech net. Against all odds, Northern Ireland had taken the lead.

The confidence the goal bred in the Northern Irish team was huge and McParland almost scored again a minute later from a Cush free kick. Derek Dougan also had two chances before the half-time whistle but wasted them both. Although they'd had a good first half, there was a feeling that something wasn't right, that the team wasn't performing at its best. By all accounts, Dougan had struggled to find any form in the opening forty-five minutes, perhaps shackled by the specific game plan that Doherty had put together. For the second half it was agreed that Dougan could revert to what he did best, which was to roam freely, finding space for himself and making runs of his own choosing. Bingham would take over Dougan's position.

As the game got back under way, Northern Ireland grew in confidence – Peacock continued to neutralise many of the Czech moves, Blanchflower came into the game more and more, Cush and Bingham worked to cause a great deal of trouble for the Czechs, and Dougan was presenting a growing threat to their opponents. McParland recollects, 'Danny took control of the middle. We were playing control football and kept our nose in front in comfort in that game.' As the second half progressed, the Czechs became increasingly desperate and threw themselves at Northern Ireland with increasing abandon.

It has been well documented that Harry Gregg was heroic during the World Cup and that his body took a considerable degree of punishment and the newly discovered footage of this match shows Gregg taking a particularly hard hit as he dives into a fifty-fifty challenge on the ground near his goal. You can clearly see the Czech player's foot, studs up, colliding with Gregg's shoulder. Not for Gregg, though, the timewasting antics of many modern footballers – he merely winces with pain, gets up and continues with the play.

If the first ten minutes of the game had been torrid for Northern Ireland, the final ten were even more so. But Northern Ireland had the measure of this Czech side by now and the Czechs, who probably started the game supremely confident of a victory, were also reluctantly beginning to understand the determination of their opponents and the strength of their resolute defence. Despite the Czechs notching up an incredible seven free kicks on the edge of Northern Ireland's penalty area in a frantic five-minute spell, there were to be no more goals and the final whistle drew applause from the Swedish fans for 'their team' and ovations for Wilbur Cush.

Suddenly, anything seemed possible. In that moment, to be a Northern Ireland player in the green shirt, seeking out comrades for handshakes and celebratory hugs, was to understand that there was now no limit to what they could achieve. They were up against mighty teams but each team had its weakness and Northern Ireland had exploited the Czech vulnerabilities and played with heart, soul and togetherness. No one gave them a chance against England or Italy and no one had given them a chance in this group, but they were already turning expectations on their heads. As Gregg says today, with no small degree of emotion, 'We believed. But very few else believed. They thought, wee Northern Ireland has qualified for the World Cup; they'll be home next week. *We* didn't believe that.'

For Bingham there is a certain relish in winning against all odds, when you've been cast as the underdog. 'Winning's great of course. But when you're not expected to win, it's even greater. They were a respected team, Czechoslovakia, and they'd had some good results and when you win these games it gives you a lift, it gives you a feeling of "we can do this".'

After the match a proud Doherty proclaimed that the match had been 'a triumph for our tactics. We knew that the Czech inside right, Dvořák, was very dangerous with his sweeping shots so we put Peacock on him. The rest, Blanchflower had to take. Everyone was fine, but I want to pay a special tribute to Peacock – he was the best player in the game.' For Blanchflower, 'this was one time when the artisan beat the artist'.

The press, both in Northern Ireland and Sweden, were full of praise of Northern Ireland who had torn up the form books so early in the tournament, and who received particular plaudits for being the only one of the nations from the UK – who had all qualified for the only time in World Cup history – to register a win in their opening fixture. The press agreed with Doherty on the subject of Peacock and singled him out for the highest praise. Malcolm Brodie in the *Belfast Telegraph* reported that 'his tackling was fierce and fair, his passing the acme of accuracy and his general distribution left nothing to be desired. A five star performance and one which has made him the talk of Halmstad.' *Dagens Nyheter* in Stockholm, in an piece entitled 'Fantastic Harry Gregg chops down the Czechs', also gave credit to Peacock, calling him, 'a little black ant who dominated his side of the field and completely throttled Dvořák so much that that he went over to the other side of the field in an attempt to get room to move, but there was no escaping Peacock who pounced on him like a hawk.'

Dagens Nyheter also highlighted the great work by Cush and Bingham, noting that they 'steamrollered the Czech defence into mistakes with their tremendous bursts'. The local *Hallandsposten* in Halmstad also praised the diminutive duo, pointing out that 'the clever and fast right wing of Cush and Bingham mesmerised the Czechs', while they also applauded the 'shrewd Irish tactics … formulated by Peter Doherty and Danny Blanchflower.' Dougan received a mixed report but certainly the *Northern Whig* felt that he had grown as the game had progressed and that he was deserving of another outing against Argentina.

Northern Ireland were worthy of all the plaudits that came their way and were rewarded with a night out to celebrate their success. In terms of the professional standards of modern football, this may seem like a strange thing to do at a tournament but, as Bertie Peacock explains, it was all part of the management techniques employed by Doherty: 'Peter had a way with him. When you worked hard and you had done a good job and you were finished that evening you got an evening out but you also had to report at eleven the next morning at the training ground.'

Blanchflower records the night out after the Czech match in his autobiography: 'We celebrated by taking over the local nightclub and having a big party. Our supporters substituted for the band and everyone had a riotous time.' The next morning, perhaps feeling more than a little groggy, the team was afforded the major honour of being granted a civic reception in Halmstad. For a foreign team to be given this recognition – and after only one game – was a marker of how much the people of Halmstad had warmed to the Irish. Bingham recalls being 'greeted by a large crowd. Already we were being recognised in the streets, and the feeling was growing that we were "their" team.'

In the aftermath of their Czech win, Northern Ireland were famously described by one foreign journalist as 'the jokers in the pack' at the World Cup – no one had expected too much of them but they had arrived with a bang and the footballing world was waking up to the potential of this happy-go-lucky and hard-working team. But the players had little time to rest on their laurels – their match against the South American champions, Argentina, was just three days away.

MIGHTY ARGENTINA

One of the main challenges that faced Northern Ireland in their game with Argentina was that Billy Simpson was still not fit to play. Again, a decision had to be made as to who would replace him. While Dougan had won some qualified praise from the press after the first game, that had largely been founded on his performance in the second half. As late as Tuesday, the day before the Argentina match, the decision had still not been made as to whether Dougan would retain the position of centre forward. The three selectors were torn between keeping him, replacing him with Fay Coyle, or even bringing in Tommy Casey – the rumour was that it seemed very likely that Dougan would be left out. The players thought that this was harsh, especially given that the alternatives were either a player who had never really done a great job before or using a midfielder out of position. When the announcement came on Wednesday morning it confirmed that Dougan had indeed been set aside and that Fay Coyle, a player who had only managed three appearances all season for Nottingham Forest, would play. Billy Bingham believes Dougan should have been given another chance. 'Quite apart from my own firm belief that it is nearly always a bad policy to change a winning team, it seemed hard luck on Dougan, who more than atoned for his bad first-half display against the Czechs by what he did after the interval.'

Quite what the selectors had expected from a nineteen-year-old – who had travelled to Sweden probably not expecting to play and who had been thrust into making a debut at the World Cup against a highly fancied team – is anyone's guess. Given how much Dougan had improved as the game went on it seems inexplicable that he wasn't given another chance, especially given the paucity of alternatives. Traditionally, the selectors hadn't allowed players much time to get a feel for this position in the team and one bad performance was usually enough to get them the axe. The decision to leave so many centre forwards at home when there was still room for them in the squad now, more than ever, seemed like complete folly.

Peter McParland still feels the same as he did in 1958 about the decision not to use Derek Dougan. 'I personally would have kept Dougan in the team. He was a nineteen-year-old boy out there with us. And he was keen to do things. Maybe another game with Dougan and he'd have shone but he couldn't get it going in the one game. I know Derek was upset over that because I was fairly friendly with Derek up until he died. That was one of his things, the World Cup. "I didn't get a big enough chance," he told me.'

Dougan's time would come and he remains a cult football figure from the 1960s and '70s, but the World Cup in 1958 had come just too soon for him. He went on to write many books about football and was someone with forthright and strong opinions about both the administration and playing of football, which he expressed in his newspaper columns. He was instrumental in campaigning for increased player rights as chairman of the Professional Footballers' Association between 1970 and 1978, and became chairman of Wolverhampton

Wanderers for several years in the 1980s. However, his time at the World Cup in Sweden is not mentioned in his writings beyond the most passing of references. It was only in 2006, just before his untimely death, that he spoke out about the subject by controversially stating that the real reason for him being dropped was that Coyle's ex-club Coleraine stood to benefit by 'two or three thousand pounds' from Forest if he was picked and that '[the selectors] weren't bothered about winning the World Cup or reaching the next round.' It's impossible to tell if Dougan's comments, quoted in Steve Gordos and David Harrison's *The Doog*, are accurate or if such a payment was due but it is worth pointing out that one of the selectors happened to be the chairman of Coleraine. One thing that is sure is that Dougan considered himself hard done by, a fact illustrated by his remark in the same book: 'The Derek Dougan of ten years later would have challenged Doherty, confronted him and said, "I'm going to strip and go out and play and you can do what you want."'

Apart from Billy Simpson being out, Northern Ireland were at full strength, with Bingham having overcome a slight knock in the Czech game. Their second match was again scheduled at the Örjans Vall stadium in Halmstad. Newcastle United legend Jackie Milburn was out in Sweden with the Northern Ireland team, picking up coaching skills from the tournament and also doing some spying for them. Since all the group games took place simultaneously, managers and players were unable to check out opponents in person. Jackie Milburn was the member of the Northern Ireland party assigned to miss the Czech game and to go instead to watch Argentina as they took on the reigning champions West Germany in their opening game.

Milburn's report would have both alarmed and given hope to Doherty. Argentina were among the most skilful operators in the entire competition – they opened the scoring against West Germany and seemed in control of the game with a degree of passing skill far in excess even of the Czechs. However, the Germans had clawed their way back into the game and eventually ran out comfortable 3-1 winners as the South Americans descended into bickering among themselves. The result offered Northern Ireland some hope that they too might take victory over the Argentinians. Despite the obvious dangers of going up against a team filled with such talent, it was possible that the tactics that had been employed so successfully against the Czechs could be used to get under Argentina's skin and disrupt the flow of their game. Milburn also reported that the six and a half foot 'centre half, Néstor Rossi, is the biggest man I have ever seen, dominating the centre of the field. There is no possible chance of getting through the middle and it is obvious that all attacking moves will depend on the speed and thrust of the wingers, McParland and Bingham.'

More puzzling was the comment from Milburn and his fellow spy, the Irish selector Sammy Walker, that the Argentinians appeared to be playing out of position and operating in the wrong areas of the pitch. This was something completely beyond Walker's and Milburn's ken – the Argentinians weren't playing in the wrong areas of the pitch, they were simply ripping up the conventional ideas of football tactics and rewriting them. The accepted tactics employed by all teams in the 1950s was the WM formation, so called because it appeared to spell out those letters when you placed the player positions on to a map of the pitch. Each shirt number corresponded to a particular area of the field of play. What Milburn and Walker didn't know was that the Argentinians had changed to a new 4-2-4 formation. It wasn't an Argentinian idea but, at this stage, it was uncommon enough to totally perplex even a wise old footballing head such as Milburn.

Another concern was Argentina's intimidating record in recent tournament play. In the previous year's Copa America (the South American international championship), Argentina had finished even ahead of Brazil, who were highly fancied for the

At the training ground in Tylösand. Left to right:
Bingham, McParland, Dougan, Uprichard.

Wilbur Cush relaxing on the beach at
Tylösand.

The squad prepare their tactics for the forthcoming games at the World Cup.

The opening ceremony of the 1958 World Cup at the Ullevi Stadium in Göteborg.

Wilbur Cush heads home Northern Ireland's first ever World Cup goal against Czechoslovakia.

Gregg, Cush and Morgan leave the pitch with the satisfaction of a job well done against Czechoslovakia.

Gregg, McMichael, Blanchflower and Peacock all look on helplessly as Menendez scores for Argentina.

McParland celebrates with Cush after scoring to take the lead against the World Champions, West Germany.

FUSSBALL-WELTMEISTERSCHAFT

Gregg making one of the saves against West Germany which would earn him the Goalkeeper of the Tournament title.

FOTBOLL-VM I SVERGE

McParland and Bingham celebrate as they leave the pitch after the play-off game against Czechoslovakia.

BENGT JONASSON

The injured Harry Gregg outside the team hotel hoping that he can cast aside his walking stick in time for the game against France.

Jimmy McIlroy in action against France in the World Cup quarter-final.

The team's famous young mascot, Bengt Jonasson, with Gerry Morgan.

Bengt conducts the band at Windsor Park before the England game in October 1958.

Northern Ireland's returning heroes take to the field against England in their first game after the World Cup.

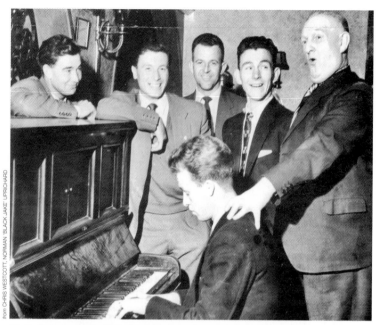

Billy Bingham plays piano as Gerry Morgan entertains the team watched by Jackie Blanchflower, Jimmy McIlroy, Norman Uprichard and Bertie Peacock.

Harry Gregg, Bengt Jonasson and Peter McParland reunited for the first time in fifty-six years for the *Spirit of '58* documentary in June 2014.

World Cup in Sweden. What was less well known, though, was the sheer scale of Argentina's achievement. They hadn't just won – they had systematically crushed, destroyed and annihilated the opposition. The final round of the tournament was a seven-team group with each team playing against their six rivals. Argentina's results were astonishing. Opening with an 8-2 destruction of Colombia they went on to win 3-0 against Ecuador; 4-0 against 1950 World Champions Uruguay; 6-2 against Chile; and 3-0 against their fierce rivals Brazil. Their only defeat came in the final dead rubber game of the tournament when they had already been crowned champions.

Even more worrying was the fact that the World Cup was Argentina's real priority, which they had been working towards methodically since 1955. Thirty players had been brought together that year with the express goal of winning the Jules Rimet trophy. Since then the squad had been whittled down to the very finest players. Argentina employed a strict no-alcohol regime and they had reportedly had a ton of beef and five hundred chickens sent to Sweden from their homeland to keep their muscular players well fed. Having lost their first game it was now win or bust for the team. Defeat by Northern Ireland would be an ignominious end to their dream of winning the World Cup. Their manager, Guillermo Stábile, described their performance against the Germans as 'absolutely pathetic' and, as he went on to make clear, the Northern Ireland game was the perfect chance to reignite their World Cup prospects: 'We must resign ourselves to the result. Tomorrow we will come with fresh power against Ireland.'

Argentina were at some disadvantage, however. Four of their best forwards, who had helped them to their superb Copa America triumph, were unavailable to them for the World Cup. Sivori, Maschio, Grillo and Angelillo had all signed for European teams and, although the Argentinian football authorities wanted them to come to the World Cup, the players' union had objected, stating that only those players loyally based in Argentina should be available for selection. Nevertheless, even with some of their best players removed, this was still an Argentinian side to fear.

While the Argentinians came to terms with their poor performance and had three serious injury doubts following their first game, the Northern Ireland players spent the days after their opening match in celebratory mood, even more so because it was Wilbur Cush's twenty-ninth birthday the day before the Argentina game, a fact which brought Cush a significant amount of media attention. Cush was hopeful of a win against Argentina, telling the press, 'A win tomorrow will let us have a nice enjoyable game on Sunday so we'll certainly go flat out.' An Irish victory would almost certainly take Northern Ireland into the next round of the competition if Czechoslovakia failed to beat West Germany. One person who thought that Northern Ireland stood a good chance was the English match official Arthur Ellis, who had almost stood in as a replacement referee at the Battle of Belfast the previous November, and who was out officiating at the World Cup. In the wake of Northern Ireland's opening win he had told the *Irish News*, 'Nobody believed me when I said the Irish team is Britain's best. They have a wonderful team and fighting spirit, Gregg is fantastic and Blanchflower is in the top rank of world players.' High praise indeed, but now the time had come for Northern Ireland once more to prove themselves worthy of it.

As the teams walked out on to the pitch on Wednesday 11 June before a crowd of over 14,000, Blanchflower knew that he was setting a new record as the most capped Northern Ireland player, although the quality of the opposition meant that there was precious little time to celebrate overturning Elisha Scott's tally of thirty-one caps. Up front, one can only imagine what Fay Coyle must have been thinking as he moved into position and came up against the six foot six inch bulwark of Argentina's defence, Néstor Rossi.

The teams that lined up that day were:

NORTHERN IRELAND: Gregg; Keith; McMichael;
Blanchflower; Cunningham; Peacock; Bingham; Cush;
Coyle; McIlroy; McParland

ARGENTINA: Carizzo; Dellacha;Vairo; Lombardo;
Varacka; Corbatta;Avio; Menéndez; Labruna; Boggio

As the match got underway it was, surprisingly, Northern
Ireland who took the upper hand. Just as they had found it
hard to get going at the start of the Czech game, so Argentina
were caught cold in this second group match. Remembering
Milburn's advice that the best, and perhaps only, method of
successfully attacking Argentina was down the wings, Northern
Ireland concentrated all their efforts into the flanks with
Blanchflower controlling the passes out wide from the centre.
After just four minutes their bustling and energetic play was
rewarded when Blanchflower back-heeled a ball to Bingham
who whipped in a cross that Peter McParland headed past the
Argentinian goalkeeper, Carrizo. The game had barely started
and Northern Ireland were one up against one of the top nations
in the world. For the small but noisy band of supporters from
Northern Ireland inside the stadium, it must have seemed like
some kind of dream.

And yet it was a dream that kept giving. Instead of the goal
bringing Argentina to their senses and forcing them to reorganise
and get back into the game, they continued to be mesmerised
by the speed of the Irish play. Just six minutes later McParland
shot wide when he had a good chance to double the lead – it
seemed as though Northern Ireland would surely add to their
score before long. Bingham went close with a free kick over
the bar and Cush also had a shot from a free kick but Northern
Ireland couldn't quite make their superiority count. Meanwhile,
when Argentina did present any sort of threat, Harry Gregg was

there to snuff it out with a save or a lunge to the ground to pluck the ball from an attacker's feet. One *Irish News* journalist estimated that Northern Ireland had 90 per cent of the play during the opening thirty minutes. However, football can often be cruel to those who fail to capitalise upon their ascendancy while it lasts.

For some unfathomable reason, Northern Ireland began to abandon their hugely successful tactics around the half-hour mark. The pacey and frantic wing play gave way to long through balls from the centre, which were easily picked up by the giant Rossi. These bad tactical decisions gave the ball away more and more to Argentina and, at the same time, the accuracy of Northern Ireland's passes began to falter. The tide began to turn against the men in green as Argentina grasped the unexpected lifeline that had been thrown to them. In theory, this should have been the kind of game in which Blanchflower thrived, acting as a conductor in the middle of the park and channelling all the moves through himself to the danger zones out on the wings. Instead, this most intelligent and tactically aware of footballers inexplicably lost confidence in what he was doing and reverted to a simpler form of football, one at which Argentina quickly showed their superiority.

As Argentina pressed forward, it was left to Gregg to try and keep his team in the game, a challenge to which he seemed equal. However, when the ball bounced and hit Dick Keith on the hand and a penalty was awarded to Argentina, it gave Gregg little chance. Peter McParland remembered the infamous Latin temperament being on display during the taking of the penalty. 'As Corbatta walked up to take the kick their inside right flung himself to the ground, refusing to look!' The ball crashed into the net, sparking wild scenes from the South Americans, as McParland recalled. 'The Argentinians just went crazy. With the rest of the team dancing in the middle of the field, Corbatta set off on a cook's tour of the stadium, waving to the crowd.'

It was a body blow to Northern Ireland and Gregg was later forced to make two more flying saves to stop a complete collapse. Yet it all could have been very different if Northern Ireland had only managed to take the opportunity presented to them shortly afterwards. A brilliant move started by Alf McMichael saw the ball move first to Blanchflower, then to McIlroy before McParland sent it across to the centre to present an easy chance for Fay Coyle from just six yards out. However, the man the selectors had gambled on blew his big chance and shot wide with the goal at his mercy. Conceding a goal was a demoralising way to finish the first half, but missing an easy chance to restore the lead must have heaped further misery on the players.

Northern Ireland had not only squandered a lead but they seemed to have lost their way in the game entirely. Even more worryingly, for such a tight team who loved each other's company, they were getting sucked into squabbles as the frustration began to tell. A bad pass from Blanchflower had at one stage threatened danger and Gregg had had to rush out and rescue the situation. He was not shy in telling his captain what he thought. Gregg laughs as he recounts the argument with Blanchflower. 'My words of choice were not too pleasant and I was giving it something terrible. This is typical Danny, he says, "How dare you address me in that manner?" We go into the dressing room at half-time and of course the great Peter is there and Danny's still giving it back to me. "You are a hooligan. How dare you?"'

Matches can often be turned around at half-time but this one, having turned once already, was heading in only one direction. Northern Ireland's efforts were game enough and their players were still committed, but the skill and showmanship of the Argentinians now began to tell as they turned on the style for the second half. It took only ten minutes for them to take the lead with Menendez knocking the ball past the oncoming Gregg. From that point there only ever seemed like one winner. Just five minutes later, it was all done and dusted as Avio headed home a Corbatta cross to make it 3-1. For the rest of the game, it was all too easy for Argentina and they entertained their supporters with footballing flair. 'The soccer scientists toyed with us, teased us, and despite having only three goals to show for their superiority, did a fine job of taking the mickey out of Ireland,' remembers McIlroy. 'Once on top, the game was great fun for Argentina. They even dispossessed their own team-mates as they turned on the exhibition stuff.'

Northern Ireland finished the game with two good chances but McParland's header went over and Cush shot inches wide. However, the Argentinian victory was a fair reflection of the gulf between the teams for most of the match, as Peter McParland admits: 'They gave us the runaround for most of that game. They were a good side and they took us apart.' For Bingham there was no argument with the scoreline and looking back he is frank about the result: 'I thought we had a poor game against them. They were just better on the day.'

In press coverage after the match, it was Coyle who came in for a savaging, with the *Northern Whig* perhaps the most outspoken: 'Coyle was a rank failure at centre forward. His incredible miss just before the interval could well have turned the tide of the game.' However, some positives were still to be found as the inevitable post-mortems began. Jimmy McIlroy was judged to have had one of his best games for Northern Ireland for some time and McParland's game drew a lot of praise, as did Gregg's heroics in goal, which had succeeded in stopping the scoreline from becoming embarrassing. It was perhaps Peacock, though, who drew the most column inches of support for another tireless and combative effort. The Swedish press seemed baffled that Northern Ireland had so radically changed their game plan when they had seemed to be in control; as was Malcolm Brodie who summed up the issue succinctly: 'Sunday's match against Czechoslovakia was won with correct tactics. Last night we lost because of wrong ones.'

In the space of a few days Northern Ireland had gone from conquering heroes to demoralised players who had been outclassed and who now had only a faint chance of going through from the groups. In fact, it seemed likely that the only way Northern Ireland could qualify was by beating the World Champions in their final game. In a rather mean-spirited statement, which ignored that Northern Ireland had run his team ragged for the opening third of the game, the Argentinian manager, Stábile, mocked Northern Ireland's prospects in their next game: 'You have no chance of beating the Germans for you have not got the technique or the forwards.'

There was a more magnanimous performance from Peter Doherty who paid credit to the victors while having reservations about their chances of success against Czechoslovakia. 'The Argentinians deserved their success but if we had got that other goal just before half-time I think they would have folded up. Their two goals came from close in. They are wonderful ball players, but they are certainly not as good a team as the Czechs.'

After such a defeat, it must have been tempting to simply head back to camp and mope. But that was not Northern Ireland's style and they responded to the defeat quite differently, as Danny Blanchflower points out: 'We admitted their superiority by holding another party at the local club – this time to drown our sorrows. The Swedes were delighted with our attitude.' As Harry Gregg points out, 'There was little chance of the downbeat mood remaining for long. In addition to the wisecracking Gerry Morgan, we had Mickey McColgan for company.' With the help of Morgan, the good humour of the fans, and a flow of drink and friendship, Irish spirits were soon reviving. Northern Ireland had suffered a setback but they were still in with a chance of qualifying, even if they had to beat the World Champions to do it.

UP AGAINST THE CHAMPIONS

On 11 June West Germany drew 2-2 in their game with Czechoslovakia, meaning that there was still everything to play for – any of the four teams in the group could still qualify for the next round. The Germans were favourites to go through, having come through the first two games unbeaten – all they needed was a draw. Argentina was fancied to join them, with the expectation that they would beat the Czechs and that Northern Ireland would fail to beat West Germany. However, the Czechs knew that if they could find their form against the South Americans and if the Germans beat Northern Ireland, then they could still make it into the final eight of the tournament. For Northern Ireland, the road ahead was difficult but their aim was clear: beat the World Champions. Results from the other matches would impact on whether they would get to the next stage, but beating the Germans was their starting point.

Bizarre as it might seem, the rules around what happened if teams in the same group finished level on points still hadn't been decided as the final round of group games began. It seems unthinkable that FIFA could start the World Cup with uncertainty around the rules, especially given that there had been dissatisfaction regarding the way the groups had been decided at the previous World Cup in 1954 where many odd rules regarding the format of the tournament had been introduced and then permanently dropped. FIFA were keen to adopt a goal average method in instances of a tie (a slight variation on the modern goal difference) but the Swedish hosts were arguing for a play-off. FIFA were clear on the disadvantages of play-offs – extra games would need to be organised and the teams involved would be more tired and at a distinct disadvantage if they progressed to the next round to play against a team that hadn't had to squeeze in an additional match. However, ticket sales had been disappointing for the tournament and the Swedes felt that there was a chance of several groups requiring play-offs, which would generate extra ticket sales. A few days before the final group games it appeared that FIFA had opted for goal average and the press duly reported the story. But the story turned out to be an inaccurate leak and FIFA adopted a play-off option under pressure from the Swedish FA, with goal average being the deciding factor if three or four teams finished equal – it would be impossible to schedule more than a single play-off game per group. These issues were of interest to Northern Ireland because a tie on points was a distinct possibility in their group and so the ruling could have a significant impact on them.

It's unlikely that such matters were at the forefront of Peter Doherty's mind as he worked on motivating and encouraging his team after their defeat by Argentina, and faced – for a third time – the issue of who should fill the troublesome centre forward role. Billy Simpson was at this stage taking part in light training but it was obvious to anyone who watched the training matches between the two halves of the squad that he was a mere passenger in proceedings, with no possibility at all of being match-fit. Coyle was no longer even in the running after his failure against Argentina, and neither was Dougan, whose poor first-half against the Czechs was still being rather harshly held against him. In effect, this left Northern Ireland now with just fourteen players to choose from – twelve outfield players for ten outfield positions. Given the extreme lack of options it was clear that Northern Ireland were going to have to experiment.

One possibility was to play McParland in the centre forward role. He was having a good World Cup, had notched up a goal against Argentina and was no stranger to scoring at the highest level, as evidenced by his two goals in the previous year's FA Cup Final. He was big and strong, as well as agile, and he presented a powerful aerial threat – qualities of a good centre forward. However, to play McParland in this position would mean losing all the positives he had been providing by playing down the left wing. When things had been going well against Argentina in that famous first half hour it had been the twin prongs of attack provided by McParland and Bingham down the outside channels that had been the cornerstone of the success. Essentially, Northern Ireland needed two Peter McParlands, one on the wing and one in the centre.

The other option was to bring in Tommy Casey as a makeshift centre forward. This had actually been Doherty's preferred option for the Argentina game, but he was overruled by the three selectors, one of whom hadn't even seen Northern Ireland's opening fixture. Naturally a wing half, Casey had played upfront before for Northern Ireland, as inside forward against Portugal at Windsor Park the previous year. However, the move was largely judged to have been a failure, and he reverted to his normal midfielder position during the match. If Casey couldn't succeed as an inside forward, then what hope was there of him being successful as a centre forward? On the other hand, Casey was said to be eager to take on the task, judging that this might be his only opportunity of serving his nation at the World Cup since Bertie Peacock and Danny Blanchflower were both playing in midfield. Casey was also on the transfer list at his club,

Newcastle United, surplus to requirements, so a good showing in Sweden would make him more attractive to other clubs. In the end, they opted for Casey, playing a midfielder as their striker in their crunch must-win game against the World Champions, their third different centre forward in three matches.

The rest of the team remained unchanged, with Jimmy McIlroy and Willie Cunningham both able to shake off some minor knocks and niggles and Harry Gregg, who had taken a significant degree of punishment from Argentina and Czechoslovakia, also judged fit and able to participate. However, if Malcolm Brodie of the *Belfast Telegraph* had had his way there would have been one radical change to the team. Danny Blanchflower had been having a decidedly muted World Cup and many felt that he had let the Argentinians off the hook in the second game by abandoning his tactics. In his usual forthright way, Brodie said what many others would probably have shied away from thinking. 'To be candid, his displays in the last two matches merit his exclusion, but such a step might perhaps be too drastic in a game on which too much depends. Come on, now, Danny! What about another of those performances which have earned you the tag of one of the world's greatest wing-halves? Pull up those socks, get those sleeves rolled up, too. Or else your international future could be in jeopardy.' The chances of Blanchflower, the captain, being dropped were non-existent and Brodie's comments were more of a rallying cry to him – his stature and experience were needed more than ever in a game of this magnitude.

Unlike Northern Ireland's first two games, this final group game was being hosted in Malmö, some sixty miles away from the Irish base in Tylösand. Up to this point, Northern Ireland had been used to having the support of the vast majority of the fans at their matches. However, this would not be the case for their forthcoming match as a massive ten thousand supporters had travelled to Sweden to support West Germany. Game, set and match to the Germans on the support front? Not quite.

Northern Ireland may well have had pitifully few supporters from back home but a heart-warming statistic estimates that up to eight thousand of the citizens of Halmstad made the journey down the winding coastal roads to the tip of Sweden in order to continue their support for their adopted team.

On Sunday 15 June Northern Ireland boarded their coach for Malmö Stadion. With them were young Bengt Jonasson and four of the supporters who had become particularly close to the players – McColgan and Nicholl, hosts of Dave's Inn, along with Billy Malcolmson and Jack Mahood. They left Tylösand at 10 a.m. and arrived at the Hotel Arkaden in Malmö in the afternoon and had a pre-match meal of poached eggs and toast at 5 p.m. They also attended a church service in Malmö, perhaps in part to make up for the fact that they were playing another match on a Sunday.

The team seemed to be in good spirits and Blanchflower was in an optimistic mood when he spoke to the press: 'We have a chance. When we played the Czechs we came up against new techniques and the same against Argentina. We learnt a lot from those matches and I doubt if the same problems will be presented by the Germans. Their game is like that played in the British Isles. We should not have to search for the answers as if in the dark as we did when the Argentinians got their tail up. We are going to give them a fight. We have been in similar circumstances before and come out intact.'

Blanchflower's assessment was certainly true. The German game was built on speedy wing play, robust challenges and hard work – almost identical to Ireland's own. However, West Germany were the World Champions and the team took that confidence and prestige into every match they played. Only three players had survived the four years since the 'Miracle of Berne', when the Germans had beaten what everyone considered to be the finest team on earth, Hungary, at the Swiss World Cup. West Germany had been annihilated by Hungary 8-2 in one of the group games but they had steadily improved as the tournament had progressed and pulled off what seemed to be the impossible by beating Hungary in the final. The man who had scored two of the goals in that 3-2 win, Helmut Rahn, was still very much their danger man and he was expected to give the veteran fullback, Alf McMichael, a lot of hard work down the wing. Their captain, Fritz Walter, and the impressive inside left, Hans Schäfer, were the other two survivors, but a host of new talent had been added to the team, including the young Uwe Seeler, making the first of his four successive World Cup campaigns between 1958 and 1970.

Northern Ireland were, however, ready to meet the huge challenge that the Germans represented. 'I just felt that we'd reached the stage where we were going out on to the field believing that we were every bit as good as the opposition and there was no reason why we shouldn't win,' remembers Jimmy McIlroy. McParland agrees: 'We had a good bunch of players, top men, and it was a challenge to go out against the Germans and do our stuff. We enjoyed the challenge.' For Billy Bingham it was important that Northern Ireland did not allow themselves to be overawed by their opponents: 'I think what you had to do was try and bolster the players, lift them up a little bit in as much to say, we have a chance. You couldn't go negative. You couldn't say, this is West Germany and we'll defend and we'll do this. More, we've got a chance, but we have to be solid, we have to work as a team unit today probably more than in other games.'

One thing that is certain is that it was not a nervous Northern Ireland taking the field against the champions. It is the mark of truly great teams that they perform when the cards are stacked against them – merely completing wins against inferior opposition is no true measure of sporting greatness. As the Northern Ireland team walked out there is every indication that they felt fate's hand on their shoulder and were very much equal to the task before them. After all, this was a team used to being underdogs. They had had to battle for every success of the last few years, against expectations, and always with an incredibly small pool of talent to call on. The very fact that they were on the pitch at all was testament to all that they had overcome already. So they now had to do it all again against the World Champions? Well, it was simply time to dig in and get on with it, the same as usual. These men were used to fighting their way out of tight corners and they were ready to do so again.

Stepping out in the Malmö Stadion, which had been purpose-built for the World Cup to an odd diamond-shaped design, Northern Ireland were met by 21,990 fans, their largest audience of the tournament. Two VIPs were among their number – Lord Wakehurst, the Governor of Northern Ireland, and King Gustaf of Sweden who made his way on to the pitch to walk along the two team line-ups and shake the players' hands following the national anthems. As if the occasion wasn't intimidating enough, there was also the small fact that this match had been selected to be the live match of all the games being simultaneously played that day and would therefore be watched by a combined audience of hundreds of millions worldwide. It was a sobering thought that more people would be watching Northern Ireland play that match than had ever watched them play in all their previous matches put together. Any slip-ups would be witnessed live by a global audience.

Blanchflower won the coin toss and elected to change the ends that the two teams had naturally gravitated towards on taking the field. Tommy Casey and Jimmy McIlroy gathered in the centre circle and moments later kicked off the biggest match in Northern Ireland's history.

The line-up that day was:

NORTHERN IRELAND: Gregg; Keith; McMichael; Blanchflower; Cunningham; Peacock; Bingham; Cush; Casey; McIlroy; McParland

WEST GERMANY: Herkenrath; Stollenwork; Juskowiak; Eckel; Erhardt; Szymaniak; Rahn; Walter; Seeler; Schäfer; Klodt

The German onslaught began at once and, as expected, they tested the Irish defence by going down the wings. Disaster struck for Northern Ireland in the fifth minute – Gregg, who had already pulled off a number of fine saves, twisted his right ankle and was limping badly. It was clear that the injury was serious. In the modern game there would be little possibility of a player remaining on the pitch with the limitation of movement that Gregg was experiencing, especially with almost the full match still to be played – it would risk further and long-term injury to continue. But no substitutes were allowed in 1958, so the options were to go down to ten men or to put someone else in goal and move Gregg outfield into a passenger position where he wouldn't have to do too much moving. None of these things happened. Instead Gregg heroically played on, not even receiving any treatment until half-time. Such was the pain that kicking the ball was impossible and for the remainder of the game Gregg had to ask one of his defenders to take his goal kicks.

A wounded animal can often be the one that strikes out the most fiercely and so it proved to be with the injured Gregg. He refused to allow himself to become a target or to lose heart. Instead, he propelled himself superhumanly into the fray and into legend itself. Almost spurred on by his injury, it was as if he felt he was playing on borrowed time and must attempt every save and hurl himself in front of every ball. As the match progressed, Gregg reached new heights of excellence, attempting things that most goalkeepers wouldn't even dream of. Uwe Seeler was a man who on any other day might have scored a hatful of goals, not because the Northern Ireland defence was weak, but simply because he was part of a very good team indeed and because he was a brilliant young player who was able to shoot accurately and often. That day, however, Gregg was equal to anything Seeler sent his way. It was almost a personal duel – two great players determined to gain advantage over the other. The early rounds certainly all went to Gregg and he pulled off two marvellous saves in the first half.

Though the Northern Ireland players had been deflated when they saw that Gregg had sustained a serious injury, they drew inspiration and fire from his full-throttled surge back into the white heat of the game. They carried Gregg's spirit into their tackles and play. Peacock continued where he had left off in previous games, busying himself all over the pitch and rushing in with crunching tackles. Bingham and McParland continually teased and probed the German defensive lines, with Bingham causing all sorts of trouble for his opposing fullback Juskowiak and pulling the German line out of shape.

Around the eighteen-minute mark Juskowiak went in for a loose ball challenge with Tommy Casey and the Iron Man was badly injured. However, he managed to push the ball to McIlroy and play continued, with the ball being moved to the German box. The German goalkeeper, Herkenrath, was forced to come out and challenge Wilbur Cush. Then the ball fell to Bingham and was swiftly returned to the danger area near the champions' goalmouth to be met by Peter McParland who thumped the ball home into the net. Northern Ireland were in the lead.

McParland's second goal of the tournament was made possible by Northern Ireland's rather unorthodox choice of centre forward. Casey had been playing quite deep, and had been much further back than a centre forward normally would be. 'It gave me the chance where I thought that I'd try and get into the middle a bit more,' remembers McParland. 'If Peter Doherty had said to me, right, we're going to play you at centre forward now I would have told him what the trainer of Aston Villa told me. He always said, "You're a good centre forward when you're playing outside left. When you're playing centre forward you're marked out of the game." And I felt that. Any time I was playing centre forward I felt that I was marked tight but they couldn't pick me up when I was coming from the left side. And Danny Blanchflower was looking for me to come in on balls he would play in.' Necessity often leads to new ideas and so it was here – the problem at centre forward now proved to be Northern Ireland's strength.

Celebrations at taking the lead were tempered by the fact that Casey, who had started the move that led to the goal, was forced to leave the field of play to seek treatment. Morgan supported the limping Casey as he left the pitch, with a very worried Doherty close by as he assessed the situation. Not only had his opponent's studs raked down Casey's unprotected shin, which was now bleeding heavily, but he had also gone over on his ankle during the challenge. Still, what were two injuries for a man made of iron? Casey received four stitches to his badly gashed shin and had his ankle strapped up, then returned to play on. However, in his absence and with the Northern Ireland team down to ten men, the Germans struck back.

Helmut Rahn had already proved dangerous down the flank in the early stages of the game and now, just two minutes after Northern Ireland had taken the lead, he raced through and chipped the ball over Gregg to score an equaliser. Gregg had seemed invincible but here was evidence that he was not. Even with Casey continuing to play, it was clear that Northern Ireland were down to only nine fully fit players.

It was time for Northern Ireland to dig in and they did. McMichael now had the measure of Rahn and his early successes down that side of the pitch began to dry up. Gregg picked himself up from the disappointment of conceding the goal and continued where he had left off. All around the pitch the Northern Ireland players worked tirelessly to contain the German threat and to create their own chances. As the half-time whistle sounded it was an incredibly even contest and more goals could have been scored if Dick Keith hadn't cleared off his own line or if shots from McIlroy and McParland had found their target. One particular moment of magic saw McIlroy dribbling in from the wing and dancing through several challenges, to push the ball to Peacock whose shot was deflected over the bar for a corner.

Doherty took advantage of the break to order his team to change their boots, feeling that the ones they had been wearing weren't gripping well enough on the surface as several players had slipped on the grass. There were two exceptions to this – Gregg and Casey, who were both carrying ankle injuries. Gregg was worried that his foot would swell if he took off his boot and he had a novel piece of advice for Gerry Morgan who was treating him. 'I said, "Gerry, don't take my boot off." "What do you mean, son?" I said, "Don't take my boot off because my leg will blow up. Just strap the boot and all on to me." I remember Gerry strapping my foot up, boot and all, and he said, "They'll think I'm daft!"'

As play got back underway, both teams continued to test each other and both looked equally capable of scoring. Gregg pulled off a number of fine saves, often finding himself in the thick of bruising encounters as he flung his body around the penalty area, regardless of punishment from the German forwards. A German radio commentator was heard to say that he was like a ghost, making impossible saves. Gregg recorded his memories of his performance in his autobiography, *Harry's Game*: 'Fortunately, this was to be one of those days for me when I hit top form. It was one of those occasions when you felt unbeatable. I remember one moment when the ball was floated across, just outside the box, and I took my cap off in mid-flight to head the ball just before Uwe Seeler.' The cap in question had been given to Gregg by a work colleague years before when he was an apprentice joiner and he had resisted all attempts by sportswear companies to replace it. After the crash in Munich he had rescued it from the plane wreckage and it was still acting as a talisman for him now as he put in the performance of his career.

Despite the German pressure, Northern Ireland created a chance at the other end. From the resulting corner Cush crossed the ball to Bingham in the centre of the box who headed it down and out towards the far post. Standing six yards out and totally unmarked was Peter McParland who had time enough when he saw the ball approach to steady and position himself to crack it hard into the German net and restore Northern Ireland's lead.

If Northern Ireland could hold on to their lead, they would go through to the next stage and West Germany would go home. However, West Germany knew that a simple equaliser would reverse the positions in the group and they came at the Northern Irish defence with renewed determination. From a corner they thought they had scored to save their World Cup hopes but the referee immediately blew his whistle for a foul on Gregg and Northern Ireland breathed a sigh of relief.

For eighteen minutes Northern Ireland held strong and fast, with the prospect of a German exit from the tournament growing and nerves among their fans increasing. However, in the seventy-eighth minute, West Germany suddenly conjured up a moment of magic. Schäfer played the ball through to Seeler who shot from twenty yards out, and his powerful strike rocketed unerringly across Gregg's goal and into the top corner of the net as he hurled himself through the air, his arms outstretched in a desperate bid to save it. West Germany were level and now it was Northern Ireland who were in trouble.

For a while the Germans looked like the team most likely to add to the scoreline but, as the clock ticked down, Northern Ireland began to reassert themselves in search of a winning goal. McParland headed over the bar from a good chance and the Germans started to play a more cagey game. They seemed to settle for what they had rather than search for another goal and risk conceding one in the process. At one point, instead of simply knocking the ball out of play on the wing to thwart a Northern Ireland move, they booted the ball out of the stadium over the low stand, to audible boos from some sections of the crowd for such blatant time-wasting tactics.

In the final two minutes of the game Northern Ireland made one last determined attack on the German goal. With Wilbur Cush in the thick of things and making a nuisance of himself to the West German defence, the ball was played in and the German defenders scrambled the ball out of the box only for it to be played swiftly back in again. The Germans were looking jittery under the constant pressure as cross after cross was launched goalwards. In the end, the ball just wouldn't fall Northern Ireland's way inside the box and when West Germany were finally able to clear their lines they also found, to their immense relief, that the referee had blown the final whistle. They were through, but it had been a close-run thing.

Northern Ireland had failed to gain the victory they had wanted but there was no shame in the draw they had earned that day. They had gone toe to toe with the champions in an incredibly even contest and had provided a great match not only for those gathered in the Malmö stadium, but for the many millions watching around the globe. It looked like Northern Ireland's World Cup journey was over but they could be immensely proud of their performance. However, there was to be one more dramatic twist, as Jimmy McIlroy recalls. 'As we trudged off the field, we were convinced the only job now left for Northern Ireland in Sweden was the packing of bags for the return journey home. Suddenly, a few of the supporters who had travelled with our team rushed on to the Malmö pitch shouting "We're still in. Czechoslovakia have beaten Argentina 6-1."'

Peter Doherty had called it correctly when he said that the Czechs were the better team and they proved it in a demolition of the South American champions. Although everyone recognised the Czechs as an excellent team, the margin of victory was unexpectedly crushing and Argentina were now bottom of the group. With West Germany going through unbeaten on four points, that left Northern Ireland and Czechoslovakia tied on three points apiece. Fortunately for Northern Ireland, the plan to use goal average had been abandoned – the margin of the Czech win against Argentina would have seen them cruise into the next round. Instead, Northern Ireland now faced a play-off in two days time and another opportunity to keep their World Cup dreams alive.

The mood was celebratory in the dressing room as the players drank in the credit being poured on them and relished the thought of continuing their campaign with at least one more game. Lord Wakehurst visited the team and Gregg fondly recalls the occasion: 'People from the government were coming in to toast Northern Ireland when they found out somebody had drunk all the whiskey. I still laugh when I think of Gerry getting a bottle out of the skip and filling it up with black tea – it was black tea they were toasting with!'

The reaction of the Irish press was one of absolute delight. Malcolm Brodie stayed up all night savouring the glory of it all, as he reported the next day: 'Five hours have gone since I left the ultra modern Malmö stadium and the excitement of that classical and tough 2-2 Northern Ireland–West Germany battle. Dawn is breaking in this land of the midnight sun, but still my heart pounds with the excitement and the tension of it all. A night which will live in memory for all time; a night when our small country with its limitation of top players made its mark on the football world.' He went on: 'It was not so much the quality of their football which impressed me, but rather the fighting, determined manner in which they played. They tackled first time, they chased every ball and they never gave up until the final whistle, which the time-wasting Germans were so glad to see.'

Cush, Bingham, McIlroy and McParland were all singled out for particular praise in the press but it had truly been a team effort with McMichael and Keith limiting Rahn and Clodt on the wings and Cunningham standing firm in the middle of the defensive line. The *Northern Whig* was impressed by Peacock, judging the 'little black ant' to have been 'once again our best half-back', and was full of admiration for Cush's 'unquenchable spirit'. However, there was no doubt which player was taking most of the headlines – Harry Gregg, who was dubbed 'The Miracle Man of Malmö'.

Hamilton C. McDowell of the *Northern Whig* suggested that Gregg had been praised too much for his performance in the first two games, which was perhaps unfair, but he was full of admiration for his playing in the German game: 'Gregg has been getting a big press from the Swedish newspapers, some of it based on hero worship and sentiment rather than on cool judgement. But if they give Harry all the stars in the journalistic sky with four-inch deep headlines tomorrow morning I say in all sincerity that he will be getting his due.' Of the other injured hero, Tommy Casey, he said, 'Tommy should get the purple heart. He earned his wound above and beyond the call of duty.'

Peter Doherty's assessment of his team was simple and to the point: 'They did us proud and never gave in.' He knew, though, that they had another mountain to climb in two days. With key players Gregg and Casey suffering from serious injuries and Billy Simpson still out, Doherty had his work cut out to develop tactics that would thwart a resurgent Czechoslovakia.

MAGIC IN MALMÖ

Northern Ireland's continued participation at the World Cup was a great achievement but the injuries sustained by Gregg and Casey were a heavy price to pay. The team doctor, Dr G.S. Scarlett told the press, 'Both are extremely doubtful but we cannot make any decision until tomorrow.' Gregg's performance was the talk of the World Cup and now Northern Ireland faced the prospect of losing him for a vitally important game, as well as having to find yet another player to fill in upfront for the still-injured Billy Simpson, who was now expected to be out of competitive action until August.

Both Gregg and Casey were X-rayed but nothing worse than swelling showed up. On their return to Tylösand, they began intensive treatment which involved Gerry Morgan treating them with a heat lamp for hours on end and Casey and Gregg sitting on collapsible chairs in the sea to let the cool, briny waters lap around their ankles. It was clear, though, that neither was going to recover in just two days, especially Casey who had the stitches in his gashed leg to consider. However, Casey was determined to come back and when told early on the morning of the play-off that he was out of contention he simply asked if he would be fit again to play France, their opponents-in-waiting, in the quarter-final.

For all the heroics on the pitch it was clear that there were major problems off it. While Northern Ireland could be proud of the efforts of its players who had performed like lions, the same could not be said of the IFA officials who were with them.

It seems that no thought was given to what might happen if Northern Ireland ended up in a play-off. The IFA officials had known that the game would be played in Malmö and yet had made no preparations or contingency plans for this possibility. Several long coach journeys weren't going to help players who were exhausted and struggling with injuries. They had played three intense and strenuous games in the space of eight days and several players desperately needed treatment for serious injuries that threatened to rob the team of their services for the next crucial fixture. But still, Northern Ireland were bussed back to Tylösand, arriving in the early hours of Monday morning. They then had to go all the way back for Tuesday morning when it would have made much more sense simply to have remained in Malmö.

Of course, playing so many games so close together increases the risk of injury and Northern Ireland weren't alone in having difficulties. Ten of the Czech players had injury concerns and the team had sent for a number of replacements to join them in Sweden. As their team official Karel Kolský told the press, 'We can't carry on like this. Perhaps one or two of our injured players will recover by tomorrow but we can't afford to take any risk. So we have sent home for a couple of men for safety's sake. We will leave absolutely nothing to chance and are determined to beat Ireland and advance to the quarter-finals.'

All teams were allowed to bring in replacements during the course of the tournament, so Northern Ireland could have done the same. However, the IFA made a decision not to send for any replacements – they could have called on a number of talented centre forwards who had played successfully for them in recent years but they chose not to do so. There is a sharp contrast between the Czech official who will leave nothing to chance and is determined to do all he can to secure victory for his team and the IFA, who left everything to chance and did very little at all to help their team in their hour of need.

It's hard to know what prompted what now seems like a self-defeating decision or who made the call. The smart money would be on the team of selectors who had left out several good players from the squad in the first place. The secretary, Drennan, may have been involved in the decision or it could have been made in conjunction with the IFA President or Council back in Northern Ireland. There is no discussion or reporting of the issue in the press so there are no clues there as to what drove the decision. One possibility is that it was deemed too expensive to bring over additional players. Stubbornness might also have been a factor – a reluctance to call upon players they had originally left out. Regardless of the whys and wherefores, the decision was not in the best interests of the team. The players were doing the job on the pitch but the hands of their manager, Peter Doherty, were unquestionably tied by not being allowed to make all the decisions or to have a full squad to choose from. The selectors had even had the power to over-ride his preferences on occasion for the centre forward role. Just when it seemed that the IFA couldn't do any more to hamper the team came the incredible news that one of the selectors had gone home. It is impossible to find any reason why just two of the three Irish selectors remained with the team after the initial three group games. However, it's difficult not to be drawn to the suggestion that they never expected Northern Ireland to go any further and planned accordingly. Harry Gregg had said that many people didn't expect 'wee Northern Ireland' to make any headway at all in the tournament and there is a strong sense that this view was shared by the officials who accompanied the team.

A selector going home, the refusal to send for help when players started to pick up injuries, and the nightmare travel arrangements all combined to act against Northern Ireland progressing any further. But both Doherty and the players still believed in themselves. Doherty expressed his high opinion of the Czechs to the press: 'I think this Czech side can be devastating and it will be a hard match. They are much better footballers than the Germans, though their tackling is not nearly so hard.' However, he went on to say, 'We have played better than we did against the Germans and we hope to show the Malmö public our top form against Czechoslovakia. We beat the Czechs last week, and why shouldn't we beat them this week?'

Northern Ireland would have to beat them, though, with two new players on the team. In some respects the decision of who should replace Gregg, despite his phenomenally good form, was a straightforward one. There was only one other keeper and he was a very good one at that – Norman Uprichard. He had vied with Gregg for the Number One jersey for several years and had lots of top flight and international experience. Billy Bingham was certainly in no doubt as to his abilities. 'Norman had great hands. You'd look at him and you'd say, he's not a goalkeeper. Look at his physique. He was a bit wiry and he wasn't tough. He wasn't big like Harry. Norman was light but he had fantastic hands for catching. He'd catch a ball other people wouldn't.'

Finding a replacement for the centre forward role was, as usual, a much bigger challenge. Once more Dougan and Coyle were not even considered. Taking this and injuries to a number of players into account, Northern Ireland had only two other fit outfield players to choose from – Jackie Scott of Grimsby Town from the Second Division or Sam McCrory of lowly Southend United from the Third Division (South). In the end Scott got the nod, albeit with a twist to proceedings. Scott, who played as outside left on the wing for his club, would be named as centre forward on the team sheet but, once the game got underway, he would immediately switch positions with McParland so that he took up his favoured left flank role, while the goal-scoring McParland would operate in the centre. Although this tactic was devised by Doherty and Blanchflower to confuse the Czech defence, it was somewhat undermined by Malcolm Brodie reporting on it in the *Belfast Telegraph* on the day of the match.

The Northern Ireland team made their way back to Malmö by coach, accompanied by their young mascot Bengt Jonasson. It was reported in the press that his family had postponed an operation he needed in order to allow him to see out the Northern Irish involvement in the tournament. The team arrived to a much more sparsely populated arena than the packed one they had played in front of for the titanic struggle against the Germans. Only 6,196 fans were in attendance since there had only been two days in which to generate ticket sales. At least, Northern Ireland had a good number of supporters at the ground. Along with their own loyal but tiny band of followers there were their new fans from Halmstad. There was also a large group of British sailors in town and a fair number of Irish-friendly Germans who were still in Malmö. Relations with West Germany had been strong following their engrossing contest, and the German manager and press were full of praise for the men in green. Not surprisingly then, those Germans who fancied taking in an unexpected extra game in Malmö got behind the fine sportsmen who had given them such a hard but fair match two days earlier.

Going into the game, Danny Blanchflower was certain of what Northern Ireland had to do: 'We must get on top early. We must get a quick goal and we must play the correct tactics.' It was essential that they did not fall behind because, although this was a play-off and could even go to extra time if required, Czechoslovakia would be declared the winners if there was a draw at the end of the match due to their superior goal average.

While Northern Ireland would progress by winning, the Czechs had the consolation of knowing that just a draw would be enough to send them to the quarter-finals.

The teams that took to the field that day were:

NORTHERN IRELAND: Uprichard; Keith; McMichael; Blanchflower; Cunningham; Peacock; Bingham; Cush; Scott; McIlroy; McParland

CZECHOSLOVAKIA: Dolejší; Mráz; Novák; Bubernik; Popluhár; Masopust; Dvořák; Molnár; Feureisl; Borovička; Zikán

Harry Gregg and Tommy Casey took their seats in the stands alongside some of the supporters who had become such friends with the team, and the play-off got underway. With 'games of destiny' against Italy and West Germany already under their belts in the last six months, Northern Ireland were becoming increasingly used to the pressure of these situations and were quickly into their stride, moving the ball around very nicely against one of the most accomplished passing sides in Europe. The opening phases of the match were fairly even with Bubernik and Masopust both trying long-range shots at the Northern Irish net and McParland forcing a good save from the Czech goalkeeper, Dolejší. Bingham had forced a corner for Northern Ireland but Feureisl shot just wide for the Czechs and Dvořák, still the key danger man in the team, thundered a shot into the Northern Irish wall from a free kick.

Northern Ireland had just gone very close to scoring, with Scott missing by inches following a nicely worked free kick by McIlroy and Blanchflower, when disaster struck. Just as had happened against the Germans the Northern Irish saw their keeper come out and go over badly on his ankle. This time, though, it was even worse than the injury Gregg had suffered. As Uprichard himself recalled, 'The grass at Malmö was very thick and clingy and my injury jinx came back to haunt me after just ten minutes when I twisted my left ankle very badly, which left me hobbling badly for the rest of the match.' Uprichard would ultimately get the same strapping treatment which had been applied to Gregg and Casey – foot bandaged up, boot and all – but before that Morgan improvised with a method that only he could have come up with, as Uprichard explained: 'Gerry knelt down behind the goal during the first half and poured two bottles of Irish whiskey around my ankle to try and keep the swelling down. As one of the newspapers wrote, "What a waste of a good whiskey!"' Quite what Morgan was even doing with two bottles of whiskey in his kit bag is unclear but the treatment was unorthodox even by his own eccentric standards. Nevertheless, even if it had no effect whatsoever on the ankle, it certainly added to his legendary status and had the makings of a fine story.

Northern Ireland were once more in trouble from injury during an important match at this World Cup. Uprichard was in severe discomfort every time he kicked the ball and was hobbling around even more obviously than Gregg had been in the previous game. The worry now was that the Czechs would exploit Uprichard's impaired mobility for their benefit and it didn't take long for them to do so.

With a long ball forward into the Northern Irish box there appeared to be little danger but then Dick Keith was bundled out of the way and the ball bounced through for Zikán to head it past Uprichard. Uprichard appeared almost rooted to the spot and there can be no doubt that his injury affected his ability to make any kind of save. As the Czechs wheeled away in celebration they must have thought that their place in the quarter-finals was assured. The prospects looked bleak for Northern Ireland. In all three previous games they had taken the lead first and had never experienced coming back from behind. But then, as had often been the case, the Northern Irish spirit took over. They simply picked themselves up and reapplied themselves to the task at hand. Blanchflower, playing a more attacking game now than he had at any point in the tournament, began to control the midfield alongside Peacock and chances soon came Ireland's way, with good efforts from McParland and McIlroy. Uprichard, too, lifted his game, just as Gregg had done, and came out of his box to successfully head the ball clear on one occasion. Perhaps the magic whiskey had had an effect.

As the game counted down to the half-time whistle Northern Ireland were still a goal behind and on course to be packing their bags for home the following morning. In the final minute of the first half Peacock pushed the ball out to McIlroy. McParland received the ball and played in Cush, whose quick shot was blocked by the keeper. The rebound came straight back to the Lurgan man who cracked another shot, only for the keeper to block again. Once more the ball came straight back to Cush but this time he was in the process of falling over, although it didn't stop him getting his leg to the ball and loosing off another shot. For a third time the keeper saved from point blank range but this time his luck ran out – the ball broke to the side and Peter McParland was waiting and shot the ball past him into the net. Of course, as it stood, Northern Ireland were still going out but they had got back level in the game and now just needed one goal. They also knew that conceding a goal just seconds before the half-time whistle would have demoralised the Czechs.

As the teams took their places back on the pitch for the second half, Northern Ireland discovered that their run of bad luck with injuries was far from over. As Uprichard recalled, 'The Czechs threw everybody forward at the start of the second half and I went in for a mad dive again, collided with Jan Dvořák, and felt my left hand just go limp. It was broken.' If Uprichard's first-half injury had sounded alarm bells for Northern Ireland then this was surely the bell of doom – you might ask a keeper to limp on with only one good leg, but to play with a broken hand into the bargain was utter madness. Uprichard should have been taken straight to hospital but if Northern Ireland were to stand any chance in the match and the tournament he had to play on, and that is what he did.

'Somehow I was heading them out,' said Uprichard years later, 'catching them with one hand or putting them round the post.' McParland jokes about the injury now, over fifty years later. 'We called him "The Clutching Hand" after it because his hand was a bit funny and he was grabbing the ball with one and clutching with the other one to hold on to it. But again, with the old Irish spirit that Norman had, from Lurgan, he did the job.' Uprichard showed bravery in spades that evening as he hurled himself at the feet of oncoming attackers. Nevertheless, there is only so much such a badly injured player can do by himself. Fortunately, Uprichard had a little bit of help – the Northern Ireland back line tried to protect their keeper from as many attacks as they could, and none more so than Willie Cunningham. He had never played at centre half before the tournament but now he was playing the game of his life to protect Uprichard. One passage of play ended with him acrobatically diving in, leg raised high, to stop the ball getting through to Uprichard and to hook it away to safety.

Although every Czech attack still spelled potential disaster, Northern Ireland now began to dominate proceedings and pushed forward in search of the goal that could save their World Cup. McIlroy had a shot saved, then Northern Ireland launched six successive attacks before winning a free kick, which forced Dolejší into action again. Faced with this wave of attacks, it seemed as though the Czechs made the decision to hang on for a draw rather than leaving themselves exposed by trying for another goal. They became scrappy and descended into shirt pulling and obstruction to try to break down Northern Ireland's attacks. Kicking the ball out of play became a favourite delaying tactic. Scott and McIlroy had chances with shots and

Billy Bingham even had the keeper beaten, only for his header to bounce off the crossbar. The Czechs were now desperately hanging on – Hamilton C. McDowell in the *Northern Whig* even went as far as to accuse them of diving: 'The Czechs were playing for time and were even falling down to try and waste precious minutes; they acted all through the second half like temperamental and spoilt prima donnas.'

Despite the Czechs' reluctance to throw too much into attacking they did still have the occasional chance and it was in the eightieth minute that Uprichard rushed out to save a Borovička shot and in the process became involved in the third act of Northern Ireland's injury tragedy. Having already damaged his own ankle ligaments during the match, Uprichard collided with Bertie Peacock and damaged his team-mate's knee ligaments. The impressive wing half, who had been the bedrock of all that was good in Northern Ireland's play at this World Cup, was now forced off the field. Peacock did return to the game – with Northern Ireland desperate for a goal he had little choice – but he was no longer able to withstand the heat of the midfield and was moved out to the left wing. Peacock's injury necessitated a number of other positional changes throughout the team with Scott moving into inside left and Cush dropping back to left half. However, Peacock kept going and he was soon involved in a move from which McIlroy shot just wide.

As the full-time whistle blew it was a tired Northern Ireland team that made its way to the centre circle. A brief tactical discussion was allowed before extra time began. Northern Ireland had been the better team in the second half and their bravery, skill, spirit and hard work had not been rewarded with the goal they deserved. They had two injured players with many others carrying slight injuries. As for Uprichard, he genuinely believed that he couldn't continue for another thirty minutes of play. 'I showed my swollen hand to Peter Doherty and suggested McParland go into goal. Peter said, "Better not, Norman. I am confident you can hold them out with just one arm and one leg."' Doherty's words had been meant to inspire Uprichard but there was also the fact that he could not afford to lose McParland, who was the only natural choice of outfield player to take his place. As the scorer of four of the five Northern Ireland goals so far in the tournament, he was required at the other end of the field.

Having given everything, the Northern Ireland team was practically on its knees and it was down to their manager and captain to try and rekindle their spirit: 'I remember the scene as we paused on the field before the extra time,' recounted Blanchflower. 'Bertie Peacock was hurt and Norman Uprichard's hand was limp and useless. Peter Doherty and I tried to revive the boys with words of encouragement. "They are more tired than we are, so keep plodding away" was the line we took.'

Perhaps spurred on by their comments, Bingham attempted to play some mind games with the Czechs: 'I gathered them [the players] all together and I said we're going to stretch our legs and do stretches and so forth. It was loosening them up a wee bit because they were a bit tight but I also thought it might worry the Czechs. I was saying, do whatever stretches you want and they were doing all sorts of things and I said, "They don't like that, keep doing it." It was to say to them, you're going to have a hard time because this is a fit team. A wee bit of psychology.'

Amazingly, Northern Ireland lifted themselves once more as extra time began and the Czechs began to look increasingly weary. In the ninth minute of extra time Northern Ireland won a free kick over towards the wing and Blanchflower prepared to pump the ball towards the box in search of McParland. It was the moment Northern Ireland had waited so patiently for and it is burned into Peter McParland's memory: 'Danny was putting the ball down and he was saying to himself, I must get this ball to Peter. I was in the middle, dropped off to the far post and it came right in front of me in the air and I volleyed it. It was a hell of a volley to keep down you know and I got right over the top of it and smashed it in the back of the net from an angle.'

It was a wonderfully taken goal and it moved Northern Ireland back into the lead and potentially on towards the quarter-finals. Blanchflower remembered the importance of the moment and how the free kick was 'one of the most accurate I have ever placed. I was ragged and tired as I went to take it. I recall urging myself that I must concentrate all the more and try and get it to McParland, which was one of our tactics at the time. With great deliberation I took the kick and it went away ever so sweetly right to the spot I had intended.'

The goal sparked wild celebrations among the Irish fans and journalists in the stands, who broke into 'When Irish Eyes Are Smiling'. As the players celebrated, McParland remembers being given some good advice from a wise team-mate: 'I was jumping out of my skin after scoring a goal. Jimmy McIlroy said, "Hey, stand here for a minute and waste a bit of time." That's what he said to me. I never thought of it but Jimmy was the old head. Let's stand here and waste a bit of time because we're in the lead now, you know.'

For the Czechs the goal was an utter calamity. They had led for most of the game and had been up against an injured keeper for most of the match as well, who had then proceeded to get himself even more seriously injured. And now they had squandered that glorious position. Moments later, though, Czechoslovakia had even more problems, when they found themselves down to ten men.

Following a Czech foul on Cunningham, a group of players had gathered while he received some treatment from Gerry Morgan. Suddenly, a fracas broke out following an incident between Bubernik, one of the star Czech players that day, and the referee, Monsieur Gigue. The referee was left with no choice but to send Bubernik off. As McParland recalls, 'Most people assumed that the Czech had said something to Monsieur

Gigue. Actually [Gigue] sent him packing for spitting in his face. "It wasn't intentional," was Bubernik's excuse. "I was spitting just as the referee was passing me." Those few drops of saliva virtually sealed the game.' This moment of madness from Bubernik made Czechoslovakia's job even more difficult. The Czechs may have been only a goal away from claiming the draw they required but to do it with ten men and against the run of play now seemed beyond them.

As if the events on the field weren't exciting enough there was now drama for the hundreds of thousands of Irish supporters listening to the match on the radio back home. An estimated audience of a quarter of a million people in Northern Ireland had tuned into the BBC Home Service for live commentary of the match. However, because the match had gone into extra time and exceeded its scheduled broadcast slot, listeners who had been sitting on the edge of their seats were horrified to hear the match fading out to be replaced with the planned BBC news programme. Since listeners in the north of England shared the same wavelength, the BBC had decided to go ahead with the scheduled news broadcast, leaving Northern Ireland listeners on tenterhooks. The *Belfast News-Letter* reported that switchboards at the BBC were jammed with angry complaints and one annoyed fan managed to get through to the Northern Ireland sports editor, Charles Freer. The fan was unimpressed by his explanation of the policy of broadcasting the news and responded with, 'News, catch yourself on man. If Northern Ireland has beaten Czechoslovakia this evening 'twill be the biggest news since the Relief of Mafeking.'

In the second half of extra time, Northern Ireland thought they had sealed the win for sure when Peacock slipped the ball into the net from a Jackie Scott pass. However, having initially given the goal, the referee then changed his mind after consulting with his linesman, who believed that Scott had been offside. It was a shame that Peacock wasn't able to crown his immaculate performances in Sweden with this goal – few players had performed so consistently or worked so hard throughout Northern Ireland's four matches.

As the match entered its final minutes, Czechoslovakia threw caution to the wind – even their goalkeeper advanced forty-five yards up the pitch to punt the ball forward in desperation. However, the Irish backline had never looked more solid. For journalist Malcolm Brodie, who was in the crowd that day, the tension was almost too much to bear and he couldn't watch any more until the whistle blew for full time: 'The late Harry Cavan and I stood with our backs to the pitch, we couldn't watch those final three minutes, and whenever we won I had a feeling that this was the pinnacle of Irish football. No longer were we just another nation.'

Brodie is on the money here. There were those who thought that Northern Ireland had reached the furthest heights imaginable by drawing with West Germany and matching them stride for stride, but this game raised the team to an even higher peak. Not only were the Czechs as good as West Germany, not only had they thrashed Argentina 6-1 just two days earlier, but Northern Ireland's performance represented the ultimate in heart and passion. Struggling with even worse injuries than they had had against the Germans, their qualification seemed miraculous. But this wasn't a lucky win against a better team with a backs-to-the-wall performance. This was Northern Ireland, with only nine fit men, outclassing, outrunning and outperforming world-class opponents in every area on the field. This was the perfect demonstration of organisation, teamwork and belief, and was a fully deserved victory for them after a punishing match and a draining schedule – it was Northern Ireland's fourth game in ten days, and it had been their best.

Ecstatic and relishing the moment, the Northern Ireland supporters danced and sang in the stands as the players lined up and saluted them. Only a tiny band had followed the team to

Sweden but to have been in the stand on that evening was to have witnessed the most astonishing result in the nation's history and the fans drank in every second of it. As Jimmy McIlroy noted, 'The scene was indescribable as Ireland's supporters, many of whom had lost their voices after singing for the entire two hours of the game, mobbed the players.' It was a moment to savour for the players, too, as Blanchflower recorded in his autobiography. 'That night after the final whistle I looked up to the stands and saw the small group of Irish supporters and officials dancing with one another up in the gangways. It was our proudest night.'

Norman Uprichard remembers that emotions were running high for Peter Doherty too. When they went back to the dressing room after the match 'Peter Doherty lifted a lemonade bottle and cracked it against the massage table. The noise and singing momentarily stopped. His voice was loaded with emotion and words almost failed him. With tears in his eyes he managed to utter, "Well done, lads. You were magnificent."'

The press reaction was, of course, ecstatic and is perhaps best summed up by the report in the *Northern Whig*: 'If you are the possessor of a fighting Irish heart you can perform wonders – and the Northern Ireland team has done just that. The draw with the mighty West Germans on Sunday was the greatest ever result by an Irish team. But tonight's result was almost as good – not because the football reached the same heights, but because it was achieved in such circumstances. The big fellows from the Prague country were up against little men who never quit. The Irish hammered them into the ground with courage and skill. If the lads in green had scored two more goals they would have fully deserved their surplus.'

Every player in the team was singled out for praise but Northern Ireland's great strength was that they were much more than the sum of their parts Not only had individual players played magnificently but they had played together and for one another. Their admirers even included the West German manager, Sepp Herberger, who said, 'Only a man who has ever been in so tough and decisive a match can appreciate what it means to be one goal down and still catch up and win. [The Irish are] the cleanest team we have fought in this tournament so far. They are tough tacklers and rough fighters but they never go beyond the rules.'

Brodie, a critic of Blanchflower early in the tournament, now toasted the captain's fine performance: 'I must give credit to Danny Blanchflower, who, after a series of sub-standard performances, turned in a classical display. His captaincy, too, was magnificent.' It had been suggested that one of the reasons why Blanchflower had been having such a subdued tournament was because he was sitting much deeper on the pitch than normal in order to give additional support to Willie Cunningham at centre half, given that the defender was new to the role. However, Cunningham had settled into the role − his performance had become increasingly assured over the course of the tournament, with the West Germany match his finest yet. Now that Blanchflower no longer needed to shield him, he had been able to move forward and play his more natural attacking game against the Czechs.

Given the superhuman effort from all eleven players, it seems unfair to single out any of them but it would be difficult not to give a special mention to Norman Uprichard, whose performance was described by Peter Doherty as 'one of the most courageous things I have seen in a football match'. Uprichard recognised the match as one of his finest. However, he was quick to point out that he was very much part of a group effort: 'Our team spirit was always in evidence, it was such a courageous effort, and, overall, we played some excellent football and fully deserved to win.'

Looking back on that famous night, McParland is also quick to point out the fighting qualities of the team. 'We were carrying a bit of fatigue but what stood us in good stead was that we were good players who were able to carry ourselves … We could play football, we could keep the ball and we had that Irish spirit as well. We had that thing, which was inspired by Peter, that we could go out and battle and scrap. When we went into that Czechoslovakia game we had to fight and battle there because they had come from hammering the Argentinians and that's no mean feat. We took them on in that game and hung in there with them.'

Northern Ireland were into the last eight of the World Cup where they would play France. England had been eliminated in a play-off and now joined Scotland on the journey home. However, Wales had beaten Hungary to secure a dream match against Brazil, who had been lighting up the tournament with their dazzling skill. A Northern Ireland victory against France would mean a likely semi-final encounter against the young Pelé and his fellow Brazilians. But that was for another day.

The story of Northern Ireland's victory over Czechoslovakia would not be complete without the now legendary words of Danny Blanchflower, who borrowed a line that was first used by Gerry Morgan. Speaking to a camera crew after the game, he joked with the interviewer: 'Well, our tactics have always been to equalise before the other team scores. I think they scored first and then we equalised, but we equalised a second time before they scored.'

THE LAST STAND

The scale of Northern Ireland's achievements in the World Cup was such that the team now began to garner recognition at a global level. When the team had entered the tournament via the qualifying groups the year before, they had done so as the smallest country in the competition. Now they were rated among the best eight nations in the world. A tidal wave of congratulatory telegrams flooded in for the team and the local postal authorities had to put on an extra delivery boy to deal with the volume of deliveries to the Tylösand hotel.

Although the game against Czechoslovakia had finished on Tuesday evening, the Northern Ireland team were delayed in Malmö until 3 a.m. on Wednesday morning as they waited for Norman Uprichard to return from a local hospital, where he had had a plaster cast applied. The coach arrived back at the hotel at around 5 a.m. Spirits had been high on the journey, with drinking and singing aplenty, but now they had to catch a few hours' sleep, get up and pack, and be out of the hotel to start another longer coach journey across Sweden to Norrköping. This 214-mile trek would eat up much of the day, a day during which injured players could and should have been getting treatment ahead of their quarter-final on Thursday evening. By contrast, the French team spent their four days before the game relaxing.

So much about the travel arrangements and organisation for the Northern Ireland team doesn't make any sense. While Gregg and Casey would certainly have been eager to be at the game against Czechoslovakia in Malmö, they should really have remained in Tylösand to continue their treatment and recovery. If they had been required for a quarter-final they could then have been sent for. Also, regardless of whether the team should have stayed in Malmö after the game against West Germany, they should most definitely have stayed there after the Czechoslovakia game. They could have celebrated their victory and still got to bed relatively early by booking into a local hotel with their belongings being sent on from Tylösand if necessary. Even if they were determined to travel back to Tylösand, there can be no case made for waiting for Uprichard until 3 a.m. An official could have waited with the goalkeeper and either come back later with him or booked into a hotel, from where they could have separately made their journey to Norrköping the following morning. As there was no possibility of Uprichard continuing to play in the tournament it seems strange that this wasn't considered.

Instead, Northern Ireland embarked on a schedule that was something akin to madness. If you were actively trying to sabotage the team's chances in the quarter-final you could hardly have come up with a better method than the one used by the IFA officials − to deprive their players of as much sleep as possible, to force them to undertake multiple long coach journeys and to make sure that the injured players got as little treatment as they could. As Danny Blanchflower reflected a few years later: 'There had been no allowance for emergency and we did not adjust to suit the demands of the moment. Foolishly we took a long coach-ride back to Tylösand that night after the tiring game. It was a tired and travel-weary team that awoke on the Thursday to face the French team in the quarter-final.' The players today certainly regret the way the situation was handled. McParland remembers, 'We had bumps and bruises, and fatigue was there as well. We travelled a hundred miles to the camp and came back hundreds of miles the next day to play the quarter-finals and that was a tough ask. We were getting treatment on the bus as they were going back.' Billy Bingham is particularly forthright: 'It was badly organised. I don't know who was responsible for that but it was badly organised and it wasn't to our benefit at all.'

Despite the continuing lack of professional organisation from the IFA it was now up to the players, inspired by Doherty, to do what they could on the pitch. As they left their adopted home of Tylösand, the staff of the hotel waved tearfully to them. Accompanying them, as always, was young Bengt. Billy Malcolmson, one of their small band of fans, was also on board and was now pressed into service as a masseur as Gerry Morgan tried to organise as much treatment as possible en route for the tired and bruised players.

Micky McColgan and Leslie Nicholl made the trip from Tylösand on their famous moped, but on the journey through the forests the front wheel jammed in one of the ruts in the road and they both fell off. Leslie fractured his scapula and Micky twisted his ankle. Even the supporters were now on the injured list.

The Wednesday evening in Norrköping was a busy one – the team hotel must have been more like a hospital as Gerry Morgan and Dr Scarlett busily attended to the wounded Northern Irish team. Of the team that had played in the epic extra-time victory against Czechoslovakia, an incredible six players had been injured to some extent. Uprichard and Peacock were the most obvious casualties and neither of them stood the slightest chance of playing against France. Added to their number, however, were Alf McMichael, (bruised thigh and leg), Willie Cunningham (bruised foot), Wilbur Cush (bruised arm), and Peter McParland (bruised foot). With Gregg and Casey now forced to cut short their own rehabilitations and return to the team only five out of the likely starting eleven against France could be considered fully fit. Of course, even those five players – Blanchflower, Bingham, Scott, McIlroy and Keith – were burdened with fatigue, both from the gruelling extra game against the Czechs and the constant travelling.

One piece of good news was that at least the question of who to choose for the centre forward role wouldn't be an issue this time. Scott was judged to have had a reasonable game against Czechoslovakia so he kept his place, albeit with an immediate switch of positions with McParland once the game got underway. Nevertheless, this was a patched-up team that fell far short of its normal strength. Doherty had joked after the Czech game that Gregg would be back 'even if we have to carry him on to the field'. In the end, nothing could have stopped Gregg from playing, but he literally had to set aside his walking aid to do so. Plenty of photographs bear testimony to the fact that he had not been walking unassisted in the run-up to the game and at one stage he and Casey had been snapped side by side, both of them on canes. 'I'm not making excuses, I wanted to play. But I was nowhere near fit,' recalls Gregg. Northern Ireland had already played with a one-handed, one-legged goalkeeper in the tournament, now they would be playing with one who needed a walking stick.

Once again, no consideration was given to flying in any replacement players with the matter even publicly mentioned, albeit in passing, in the *Belfast Telegraph* on 16 June 1958. The IFA's insistence that no one would be added to the seventeen-player squad, even though nine of them were either out of the tournament or carrying injuries that would hamper their performance, almost defies belief. Such was the paucity of options available to Northern Ireland that there was simply no choice but to bring back players who really shouldn't have been playing. As Billy Simpson reflects, 'They just didn't have the players then to bring on. The bare team and maybe two or three reserves. That was all. They hadn't the resources. We were nearly bringing the trainer on, old Gerry Morgan.'

As match day arrived, the *Northern Whig* summed up the realistic expectations of Northern Ireland in their main sports headline, 'We shall know the best – or worst – today. But outlook black for bruised and battered Ulster side.' If Northern Ireland had qualified under normal circumstances from their group, without the need for a play-off, they could have moved camp to Norrköping the following day, which would have given them three days to rest and recover before the quarter-final. Now, however, they faced an enormous and daunting task. The feeling was that the French team, although a very talented squad, was no better than anything they had faced already, and perhaps very slightly inferior. But with the lack of rest and mounting injury woes, Northern Ireland's assignment looked almost impossible. The loss of Peacock alone, one of their most consistent star performers in the tournament, was a heavy blow indeed.

And yet the players kept on believing. Despite the knocks and bruises, morale in the camp was high. As Jimmy McIlroy reflects, 'There was a great spirit in the Irish team in those days. People might say you sound conceited but we had reached the stage where no matter who we were going out against we felt we had a chance or we would put on a good show.' The *Belfast Telegraph* reported on Wilbur Cush phoning home to his fiancée and she was able to pass on the following report: 'Wilbur told me all the players are in great heart.' Danny Blanchflower's mother was in an even more positive frame of mind: 'It's simply wonderful how well the team has done. I am confident they will now reach the final.'

One of the greatest weapons in the Irish arsenal at this stage was unquestionably the motivating drive of Peter Doherty. Like an experienced general he was now trying to lift his battle-weary troops once again. Peter McParland remembers his influence well: 'He was inspiring us and working on us and he was saying, "Come on, let's beat the French and then we'll get that circus act in the semi-final." The circus act was Brazil because Peter called them circus players.' While Brazil weren't actually in the semi-finals at this stage they were very much expected to beat Wales, who also had their own injury problems. Doherty's strategy was to shift his team's focus away from playing a quarter-final match for which they were only half-fit and towards the prize of a place in the last four of the World Cup and a semi-final match against the team who were making a case for being the best in the world at this tournament. As Gregg remembers, the players were ready for the challenge as always: 'We were up for it. In fact, we firmly believed it was our destiny to meet Pelé and the Brazilians.'

Although Northern Ireland were very much the underdogs for the game, their performances so far had made people sit up and take notice, and they were certainly capable of winning. Most people recognised that a fully fit Northern Ireland team would give the majority of nations in the tournament a fair contest. At their best, they were capable of winning the match against France. For instance, although France had the tournament's top scorer, Just Fontaine, Northern Ireland had the second-highest marksman in Peter McParland, so the French would have been as cautious of facing the man from Newry as the Irish were of the Frenchman. As Smella, the French trainer, put it: 'The Irish have a fighting spirit which can move mountains.' However, this was not Northern Ireland at their best and only their famous heart and passion might be able to see them through. Blanchflower's opinion of their chances was reported in the *Northern Whig*: 'The boys can win. They have performed miracles, but the human body can only take so much punishment.'

The priority for Northern Ireland in their game against France was to try and halt the three-pronged attack of Just Fontaine, Raymond Kopa and Roger Piantoni. The loss of Peacock in this sense was immense but the 'pocket battleship', Wilbur Cush, had been drafted back into the position of left half and they could be guaranteed of tireless effort and hard tackling from him. The returning Tommy Casey took his place at inside forward.

With a huge percentage of the population of Northern Ireland listening on the radio – the match was expected to affect voting in a by-election in East Belfast – the teams took to the pitch and lined up in front of a crowd of 11,800, including a good number from Halmstad who had come to support Northern Ireland. When Northern Ireland started out in their first qualifying game against Portugal over a year earlier they could not have imagined that they would make it to the quarter-finals or have the possibility of playing Brazil in a fairy-tale semi-final.

The teams on that historic day were:

NORTHERN IRELAND: Gregg; Keith; McMichael; Blanchflower; Cunningham; Cush; Bingham; Casey; Scott; McIlroy; McParland

FRANCE: Abbes; Kaelbel; Lerond; Penverne; Jonquet; Marcel; Wiśniewski; Fontaine; Kopa; Piantoni; Vincent

As the game kicked off on a wet pitch it was Northern Ireland who were first out of the trenches with Bingham and McIlroy combining to send in a cross but it was easily dealt with by the French keeper, Abbes. Now France came forward and Fontaine tested the Irish defence, dancing past three players before crossing the ball – Gregg had to come out and make a dive to grab the ball from a French boot. Injured or not, it seemed that Gregg was continuing exactly in the same vein of form that he had shown against the Germans.

France were soon calling Gregg into action again. A powerful shot from Marcel thundered towards the Northern Irish goal and Gregg had to dive to save it. The loose ball fell to Vincent but once more Gregg dived to gather it safely from his feet. At this stage, Northern Ireland was still very much in contention. Bingham, in particular, seemed very lively down the wing with Blanchflower and McIlroy also doing what they could to orchestrate chances and the latter going very close with a shot that Abbes was forced to parry. There was even a penalty appeal for Northern Ireland thirteen minutes in when Jackie Scott was brought down in the box, but the Spanish referee waved play on.

The surviving footage of the game shows Gregg pulling off save after save during the next period of play. Every ball that was sent in high was plucked from the air or punched away. Every cross or pass sent in low was smothered by a dive. At one stage, Fontaine managed finally to beat him to the ball but his header ended up hitting the crossbar to bounce back into the penalty area from where it was then blasted over. Wilbur Cush was in the thick of battle at this point, throwing everything he had into last-ditch tackles. As the English journalist Ian Wooldridge of the *News Chronicle* pointed out, however, Northern Ireland were very much in the game and as the first half wore on they started to come more and more to the fore: 'McParland and McIlroy – flashing deep into French territory as a double spearhead – had me out of my seat half a dozen times with their shots and headers.' Jim Platt in the *Irish News* reported a similarly positive story, singling out Blanchflower, who was 'playing magnificently and in a quarter of an hour he sent through at least twenty fine passes.'

It was in the thirty-sixth minute that a great opportunity was presented to the Irish. The ball was floated in perfectly to the French box and Peter McParland managed to get the better of his marker and rose majestically into the air. His header struck true and the ball travelled goalwards. This was the moment the Irish fans had been praying for. As McParland remembers, 'I banged a header in and the keeper didn't know what day it was. It hit his arm, over the top. And that was at point blank in the six-yard box where I hammered it. I think that might have lifted us a wee bit.' It's a wonderful understatement – Northern Ireland were already tackling and harrying as if their lives depended on it.

Incredibly, Northern Ireland had gained ascendancy in the game as it headed towards half-time. Despite McMichael suffering from a slight handicap to his movement following the previous game, the three-man Irish defence was standing firm. In front of them, Blanchflower and Cush were working as hard as they had ever done and distributing the ball out to the wings whenever they could. Bingham was playing well out there and had nipped in at one stage for a shot that had flashed just wide of the post. Although their most glorious opportunity had been saved by a fine reaction from Abbes, they must have been looking forward to resting their tired limbs and getting another of those famous pep talks from Doherty and a few laughs from Gerry Morgan. Sadly, it was at this point, just two minutes short of holding out against the French for the whole first half, that disaster struck.

A French attack into the Northern Ireland box seemed to have petered out when the ball ricocheted off Dick Keith and bounced to the left. Unfortunately, the French inside right, Wiśniewski had continued a run into the area and he now found himself unmarked as the ball fell directly into his path. He still had a lot of work to do though as he was at an incredibly acute angle to the Northern Irish goal and Gregg was already alert to the danger and rushing out to face him. With Gregg just inches from making another famous diving save, Wiśniewski produced a sublime finish, lofting the ball delicately over Gregg and somehow making the angle into the Irish net. It was a truly fabulous piece of finishing but it was desperately hard luck on Northern Ireland. For forty-three minutes this battered group of Irishmen had gone toe to toe with one of the World Cup's flair teams only to concede just minutes away from the chance to rest and regroup.

Northern Ireland didn't let their heads go down. They immediately responded with two good attacks in the dwindling seconds of the first half, but any momentum they were able to build up was abruptly halted by the referee's whistle for half-time. As they came out for the second half, Northern Ireland still had fight left in them. They continued to press for an opening to bring themselves back on level terms. Bingham worked hard to put in a great cross, which only needed a touch from a player in the box to turn it into the net, and Cush provided a great opportunity for McIlroy from a free kick. Cush saw that McIlroy had somehow found himself completely unmarked in the centre of the penalty area. The French defence had temporarily lost concentration, hadn't noticed McIlroy, and were not ready for the kick. Cush took the kick quickly before they could sense the danger but McIlroy miscued as he turned and missed the ball completely from just eight yards out. It was a dreadful miss since the ball had seemed certain to produce the goal that would have brought the Irish back level. Nevertheless, it proves that up to the tenth minute of the second half Northern Ireland were still very much in the game.

In the fifty-fifth minute, however, the uphill task for Northern Ireland became a mountain when France doubled their lead. Gregg had already been called on to make another series of saves and he seemed to be having yet another great game. But the French knew that if they kept knocking then a goal must answer, and with fresher legs at their disposal they also knew that the Irish defence would weaken as the game went on. Their chance came when a Cush clearance from defence went straight to Penverne and then across to Fontaine who evaded his marker and hammered the ball past Gregg from the six-yard line.

Nine minutes later everyone knew it was all over. Gregg had still been making his trademark dives and the Irish were still gamely throwing themselves into tackles, albeit more sluggishly. However, the flair of the French now dominated the game and the majestic Kopa threaded a beautiful pass through the Northern Ireland defence that found Fontaine. Gregg began his run out to him but he must have done so knowing in his heart that this time there was no hope. Unmarked and with plenty of time, Fontaine stroked the ball underneath the Manchester United keeper and the score was now 3-0.

Northern Ireland were now visibly wilting. Blanchflower pulled ever deeper to try and stem the flow of the French attacks but France scored a fourth goal in the sixty-eighth minute. Piantoni ran on to a ball that had been played hard on to the right wing and just about managed to keep it in play. He then embarked on a mazy run as he forced his way past Dick Keith, entered the Irish penalty area and bore down on goal from a narrow angle. With both McMichael and Gregg trying to intersect him he lofted the ball over them and it was 4-0. It was a stunning individual goal, and with twenty-two minutes left of the game, the fear was that Northern Ireland would end up being humiliated.

The game now was beyond Northern Ireland, that much was clear, but pride kept them going far beyond what their weary bodies should have been able to produce. Footage from the closing minutes of the game shows Northern Ireland still trying to attack and throwing themselves into all manner of last-ditch stops as the French inevitably counterattacked. Some of the tackles are quite brilliant and you have to marvel at the resolve of the team. They may have conceded four goals but they were still competing as if it was 0-0 and there was everything to play for. A blocked shot denied Cush the honour of a consolation goal and the final whistle sounded to send France through to the semi-final against the Brazilians, who had just beaten Wales by a single goal. Northern Ireland's World Cup odyssey was over but they held their heads high.

McParland looks back on the game with a hint of regret: 'I think we'd reached our limits. The power and the strength had been sapped out of us in the games before and the French turned it on. They'd been sitting with their legs up for four days … I would have loved to have had four days with my feet up and then to go out there and play the French because we would have given them a game. But it wasn't to be.' There is a strong sense of an opportunity missed in McParland's remarks, and that is a view that was shared by captain, Danny Blanchflower. 'It is history now that we were heavily beaten 4-0, but had we not been handicapped by travel tiredness and injuries, I am sure Ireland could have beaten France. This is not the sour grapes verdict of a bad loser. We had practically no chance … even before the teams kicked off.'

Northern Ireland were out of the World Cup but they had given everything they could, even when the odds had been stacked against them. This was acknowledged in the praise heaped upon them in the press at home. Malcolm Brodie declared, 'That green-shirted eleven gave all they possessed, but they had reached the limits of physical endurance and in the end they left the field limp and exhausted. Their hearts were willing but their flesh weak.' There was a difference of opinion between Brodie in the *Belfast Telegraph* and Hamilton C. McDowell of the *Northern Whig* on the subject of Blanchflower, with Brodie once more quick to criticise the captain and McDowell arguing that circumstances had forced Blanchflower into a different type of role, and that in the France game, he had 'shone more brightly than in any of the other matches. He never ceased trying to rally the reeling side.' McDowell went on to praise the entire squad: 'For my money this is the best team ever to represent the country. They made Irish soccer history and to have played five games in the World Cup is something home followers should never forget. The heart was still there but the tired bodies which had taken part in the previous two games just could not respond to its promptings.'

One rather unflattering report appeared in the English press – from Desmond Hackett in the *Daily Express* – and was deservedly shot down by Blanchflower when he came to write his autobiography a few years later. 'His sniping report of our defeat by France was one of the most out-of-tune considerations I had ever read of a sporting event. His smug report was a sad and ill-informed epitaph for what had been a very gallant World Cup crusade by Northern Ireland.' Hackett had not followed Northern Ireland throughout the tournament and had only latched on to them when England had gone out, so his comments were based on a lack of knowledge of Northern Ireland's phenomenal showing in the tournament as a whole.

Nevertheless, the opinion of the Irish, Swedish and most of the English commentators was resoundingly positive in tone, despite Northern Ireland's heavy defeat. As McParland noted, 'We had achieved more than anyone had dared hope for, and in doing so we had captured the hearts of the Swedes. In that final fling against France several hundred people from Halmstad were singing Irish songs in the crowd. Even Sweden's team manager, George Raynor, admitted that we were as popular as his own team!'

Northern Ireland's participation in the tournament was over, but the drama was not, as the team were about to find out on the journey home.

HOMEWARD BOUND

Northern Ireland may have been heavily beaten in the quarter-final but they were justifiably proud of their achievements during the tournament. Before they travelled home, they celebrated their success with a banquet that was full of the usual craic, singing and all-round good humour that had so endeared them to their Swedish hosts. In his speech, the Swedish FA representative, Frank Perrsons, declared that he was delighted to have been chosen as the liaison for the Irish team and that he had 'never met a happier bunch of sportsmen and officials'. Northern Ireland could certainly leave Sweden with the knowledge that they had been a credit to their country. Blanchflower is reported in the press at the time to have told the players, 'We have gone to the limits of our ability and nobody can do more than that. I also hope that our team spirit will continue for many years to come.' Doherty, meanwhile, was keen to praise the unsung hero of the team, Gerry Morgan, whom he described as 'a first class influence on the team'. The future looked bright for Northern Ireland. They had a new legion of fans, not just among the Swedes, but also in broader European terms, and their footballing stock had increased significantly – Spain had plans to approach them for a prestige friendly, something unthinkable a few years earlier.

One person missing from the celebratory banquet was the little boy, Bengt, who was heartbroken that his newfound friends would soon be going home. Gregg set about rectifying the situation – he found the child and brought him in, hoisted upon his shoulders, to loud cheers from the players who had become his friends. 'I didn't do it for any show reason,' remembers Gregg, 'for the child had been close not only to me but to the whole party. I felt it only right that the child should be in there because he had been with us all the way through. He was very much a part of our party and accepted by everyone in the camp.'

When the final goodbye came for Bengt and the players a few days later it was almost too much for the young lad to bear: 'I was devastated by the thought of not seeing them any more. So, when they left, I was standing on the railway station and actually crying,' remembers Bengt. His attachment to the team touched the players and pressmen who were still with them and a plan was concocted to bring Bengt over to Belfast for a reunion with the Northern Ireland team at the first available opportunity.

As planning for the journey home got under way, Harry Gregg knew he had to decide whether to fly back with the rest of the team or to undertake the much longer trip by land and boat. In the end, he chose a third option: 'I'd made up my mind,' he remembers. 'I didn't want everyone to be flying around me with cameras and I didn't know what way I was going to react. I did it on the spur of the moment. Completely and totally out of the blue, away from the press, I went to Peter and said, "I want to fly home but I don't want to be hanging around." They immediately got in touch with British European Airways and I was rushed to the airport and got on a flight.'

In fact, they held the flight for Gregg – his train was late arriving in Stockholm from Norrköping, and such was the fame of the Irishman following his brilliant performances in the tournament that the airline was only too happy to wait for him. As Gregg took to the air, overcoming his fear of flying in a bid to get home to his family, Doherty spoke to the press, praising Gregg's brave decision. He stated that the World Cup had had a calming effect on Gregg after the troubled year he had endured, adding, 'He has come right back to the form which, in my opinion, makes him the world's greatest goalkeeper. It makes me particularly proud. I watched him as a boy, and afterwards was able to take him up and develop him.'

Gregg was accompanied on the trip home by the selector, Sammy Walker, and another Irish football official, Jack Gaw, of whom Gregg has fond memories: 'His profession in life was laxatives. The brand was Kest for Zest. He did speeches at dinners prior to going to the World Cup and he said, "My profession in life is I make laxatives. Billy Graham saves souls but Jack Gaw saves assholes."' The small splinter group of the Irish party made quite an impression on those around them. Gregg was feted as a hero and the captain sent complimentary drinks to the group. Stopping first in London, he arrived back at the old Nutts Corner airport outside Belfast on Friday evening for a warm reunion with his wife, which was captured by a number of photographers eager to get the first shot of the returning idol.

Gregg's decision to fly on ahead of his team-mates turned out to be a supremely fortuitous and prescient one. Danny Blanchflower had elected to stay in Sweden to fulfil media duties for the remainder of the competition, but the rest of the party were due to leave the next day. Having stayed overnight in Stockholm, the squad bade their farewells to the Swedish officials and made the journey to the airport. The plane was first delayed by over an hour by bad weather in the direction of Oslo and it was 3.45 p.m. before the plane took off. What happened next made Gregg's departure the day before one of his luckiest breaks.

Jimmy McIlroy recorded what happened in his autobiography: 'We had been airborne only a few minutes when Billy [Wilbur] Cush, sitting by my side, looked at me with a very worried expression and whispered: "There's something wrong with this plane. We're not climbing."' Cush was right, and an announcement stated that there was a mechanical fault with the plane – that it would have to return to Stockholm for repairs as the undercarriage had failed to retract after take-off. Unfortunately, they were carrying a full load of fuel and therefore they would be unable to land until they had used up over two hundred gallons. The pilot did his best to lighten the atmosphere and announced that, as it would be some time before they could land, he would take them on a sightseeing tour. 'I want to use up most of the fuel and I'm not paying for it,' he quipped. 'He may not have been paying,' remembered Norman Uprichard, 'but most of us were praying. I can recall sweat dropping from dear Gerry Morgan's nose and a large succession of gin and tonics did much to help me come to terms with whatever destiny had laid out for us.' With the plane's captain doing his best to calm passenger fears with a running commentary on the sights below, the aircraft finally landed an hour later with teams of fire engines flanking the runway in case of emergency.

'There was an immediate rush for the bar to sample the medicinal properties of the airport brandy,' recalled McIlroy. 'After two and half hours of "medicine", we again boarded the plane home. As we took off, the strains of "When Irish Eyes are Smiling" filled that plane. Some passengers must have thought we were terribly brave, but credit for our high spirits should really have been accorded to Messrs Martell and Hennessy!'

It was reported that Alf McMichael, who had come through a frightening plane journey to join his team in Sweden, was unhappy about taking to the air again but he was eventually brought round and the team were then London-bound, with the exception of Bertie Peacock, Billy Simpson and Willie

Cunningham, who were all taking a later flight to Prestwick airport in Scotland. Arriving too late for connecting flights to Northern Ireland, the team shared an extra night together at a hotel in Richmond, Surrey, before catching the first flight the next morning via Manchester to arrive back in Northern Ireland. Several of the team had travelled on to homes in England so it was a depleted squad that touched down on Irish soil early on Sunday morning. Nevertheless, players such as Wilbur Cush, Derek Dougan and Dick Keith were given a fine reception at the airport by the ninety-four-year-old President of the IFA, Joe McBride, who had been forbidden to accompany them to Sweden on doctor's orders.

Norman Uprichard remembered one final piece of penny-pinching from the IFA at this time. The players asked to keep their tracksuits from training as a memento of the tournament. 'The reply was "sorry", we couldn't have them as they were needed for a youth international coming up soon. That was a very big disappointment. We thought the least they could have done was to give us the tracksuits.' However, matters were soon rectified – perhaps after counting the profits from playing in the tournament – and the IFA gave engraved gold watches to each of the players who went to Sweden.

The Northern Ireland team returned to their everyday lives and the final matches of the World Cup were played. West Germany and France went out in the semi-finals and Brazil ultimately triumphed 5-2 over the hosts, Sweden, in a memorable final that was testament to the free-flowing skill of the Brazilians, and of Pelé in particular.

That only left the small matter of who would receive the individual honours at the World Cup, prizes that were fiercely contested and much treasured. The 'Golden Boot' winner for top scorer at the tournament was Just Fontaine who set down a mark of thirteen goals in just six games – a tally that no one has ever come close to beating. The FIFA Team of the Tournament was voted on by the gathered journalists and there was – and is – a significant amount of prestige attached to being nominated for it. It was here that Northern Ireland really made an impression. Not surprisingly, Harry Gregg was selected as goalkeeper – his performances against West Germany and France in particular had been outstanding, and his sheer bravery and tenacity in the face of injury made him the natural and very worthy winner of this position in the team. Danny Blanchflower was nominated as a midfielder, making an amazing double for the Irish. Other alternative versions of the team in the Swedish press even included a third Irishman, Peter McParland, at outside left.

This official FIFA team selection needs to be viewed in context. In 1958, the team contained six players from the all-conquering Brazilian squad, two Frenchmen, two Northern Ireland players, one Swede and no one else. The fact that Sweden, who reached the final, and had the advantage of being host nation, with all the goodwill that went with it, managed only a single player in the team – fewer than Northern Ireland – is remarkable. No other British players out of the four home nations made the selection, just two Northern Irishmen, who, when everything had been considered at the end of the tournament, were judged to have been among the finest eleven players in the world. At the 1998 World Cup in France, the official selection was increased to create a 'squad' rather than a 'team' of players and it's tempting to think that if the same policy had been in operation forty years earlier then Billy Bingham, Peter McParland and Bertie Peacock would also have made the list.

This acknowledgment of his performance by the world's pressmen is something Gregg is very proud of to this day: 'The captain of Brazil [Hilderaldo Bellini] had the most votes for personality of the World Cup and I was second. I think Pelé got eighty-four votes. Sound ridiculous? *The* Pelé, but he was only a young Pelé then.' Gregg is also happy to recall that he made friends even among the players he was duelling with. 'Uwe

Seeler and I have been friends over the years and it's nice to know that. A lovely story, though, is that the former President of the IFA was in France about ten years ago and a gentleman came up to him and said, "Can you tell me if Harry Gregg is alive or dead," and it was the French winger, Just Fontaine. That's very nice after all those fifty odd years.'

Since they had all gone separate ways after the tournament, there was no official reception for the team when they returned to Northern Ireland. Instead, it was decided that a banquet would be held to honour the team and celebrate their World Cup success. The natural date for the event was 4 October, following the Home International game against England at Windsor Park, and the first time that the team would be back together again. It also presented Malcolm Brodie with an opportunity to reunite Bengt Jonasson with the squad. Bengt remembers the invitation vividly: 'I got a letter from them asking me to come to Belfast to bring luck and to be the mascot for their match against England in the autumn in Belfast … It was probably a big decision from my parents to let a thirteen-year-old boy leave Sweden in those days. Malcolm Brodie convinced my father he would take good care of me and I got the permission from my parents to come. In London, Danny Blanchflower met me and he followed me to Belfast on the next flight. And then we were here for about one week. We had our camp up in Portstewart so we stayed there a couple of days preparing for the game. And a little bit of golf we played as well at Portrush. After the game, Belfast City had invited both teams to a gala dinner and all the people were there. I'm so happy to have all those autographs from that dinner so that's a very good memory for me. We stayed at the Grand Hotel in Belfast and I was introduced to the mayor and got a lot of presents from Belfast City.' Bengt still has all the letters that Brodie sent him regarding the trip as well as a little card booklet that was specially produced outlining his itinerary during his week-long visit.

Bengt was no mere bystander to the match proceedings at Windsor Park. The IFA gave him the role of conductor of the pre-match band, standing on a podium in the middle of the field in front of a crowd of 60,000 fans, many times more than at the largest football game he would have seen in Sweden: 'Danny Blanchflower helped me to write some words I was supposed to say to all the people and I wasn't that afraid talking to people then. I wouldn't do it today but 60,000 people watching me, thirteen years old, making a little speech and conducting the band, that was fantastic. Having that picture of myself standing there is very precious to me.' The *Belfast Telegraph* also put together a special book of photographs to commemorate Bengt's visit.

After Bengt returned to Sweden, Gregg and McParland continued to write to him and their letters are among his most treasured possessions. Meeting the players again must have seemed like an impossible dream but that did happen in 1961 when the producers of *This is Your Life* contacted Bengt, then sixteen, to come to London to appear on the Danny Blanchflower edition of the show. He has fond memories of his trip and of the occasion: 'We rehearsed for three or four days and people were coming from Canada, America and myself from Sweden. I was supposed to come into the scene first by saying something in Swedish so Danny Blanchflower should recognise the sound of that language and realise that it was me coming in. So the words were "sparka bollen in i mål, Danny" – that means "kick the ball into the goal, Danny".'

This turned out to be one of the most famous editions of *This is Your Life*, but for all the wrong reasons. Suddenly confronted by Eamonn Andrews and his big red book, Blanchflower simply turned and hurried off, considering the programme an invasion of his privacy. His refusal to feature only served to make him even more famous than he already was but it was disappointing for Bengt who had looked forward to seeing him. As Bengt recalls, though, Blanchflower did turn up for the aftershow party to meet those who had gathered together to honour him. 'He came there and he saw all of us coming from every part of the world. Well, he was so sad, Danny, about not showing. I think he regretted not showing up at that time.' Bengt would not see any of his old friends again for over fifty years, until he flew to Belfast from Sweden to take part in the *Spirit of '58* documentary in 2014 and was reunited with Harry Gregg and Peter McParland. By then, much had changed for all of them, but the spirit of that great time was still very much in evidence.

SPIRIT OF '58

The game that Bengt witnessed in Belfast was a thoroughly entertaining end-to-end thriller, with a final score of Northern Ireland 3: England 3. England may have disappointed at the World Cup but they were still a very good side indeed and considered themselves among the world elite. They faced a Northern Ireland side that was brimming with confidence. Three times Northern Ireland took the lead with goals from Wilbur Cush, Bertie Peacock and Tommy Casey, and three times England pulled back, with responses from Bobby Charlton, Tom Finney and then Charlton again. However, Northern Ireland had also hit the woodwork twice and therefore could once more claim that they had suffered bad luck against their old foes.

A 2-2 draw with Scotland followed before Northern Ireland finished that season's Home Internationals with a thumping 4-1 win over their fellow World Cup quarter-finalists, Wales, at Windsor Park in the spring. It was the biggest victory of the Doherty era so far and if goal scoring had been a stubborn problem for the Irish in the past, it now appeared to have been solved with nine goals in three games. They had even scored twice against Spain in a glamour friendly in October (albeit in a 6-2 mauling in which an under-strength Irish team faced a glittering array of Spanish superstars). The 4-1 win was enough to tie that year's British Championship with England again and one could make a very good case that during 1957/58 and 1958/59 Northern Ireland was the best team in the British Isles. During these two seasons, their head-to-head record against England was superior, and they had gone further and been much more impressive than England in the World Cup. It appeared that Northern Ireland were on the brink of lasting glory.

Sadly, it wasn't to be and continued success eluded Northern Ireland. The squad that had taken the world by storm would never be gathered together again at the same time, although that isn't perhaps that surprising as teams tended to select only twelve players for international matches in the pre-substitute era. It is a fact of football that faces change and teams evolve. Several of the players who had flown to Sweden, such as Fay Coyle, Jackie Scott and Sam McCrory, would never be selected for international duty again. Billy Simpson, Tommy Casey and Norman Uprichard would all make their final appearances during matches played in the autumn of 1958, just months after the tournament. Of the remaining eleven, only three of them would still be on international duty by the time of the next World Cup in Chile.

The biggest blow to the team at this time, however, was the loss of their inspirational trainer, Gerry Morgan who died suddenly in Belfast in the spring of 1959. His funeral brought together a tremendous array of stars from the world of football to pay tribute to a man who had been a talented footballer at club and international level but who would be remembered forever as the trainer of Linfield and Northern Ireland and as the unsung hero of his nation's successes. His unique ability to make people laugh and to put players at ease by downplaying any situation through humour were vital ingredients in turning Northern Ireland into such a close knit family of players. He had made playing for Northern Ireland fun and he was sorely missed.

The 1959/60 series of Home Internationals brought three straight defeats for Northern Ireland, a major shock at the time given that they were defending a share of the title. The bubble had burst and the 1960/61 series brought three more defeats, all of which made for depressing reading as the Irish conceded five goals in each game. They fared little better the following season with two defeats and there was only a draw against England to offer any real encouragement. However, playing against nations outside of the UK seemed to raise Northern Ireland's game and they were very much the nearly men when it came to qualifying for the next World Cup. Twice they lost to West Germany by a single goal (including one extraordinary game at Windsor Park where Billy McAdams – not selected for Sweden – scored a hat-trick in an unlucky 4-3 defeat).

Reflecting in late 1961 on Northern Ireland's slump in form Danny Blanchflower noted, with a degree of melancholy, the passing of the glory days: 'The World Cup events in Sweden were the great soccer pinnacle for the Northern Ireland team. The simple truth is that we reached a peak beyond our wildest estimation, one that was too high for us to continue to stretch for. It may take a long time for the people in Northern Ireland truly to appreciate how great those years around the "pinnacle" were.'

Blanchflower was in no doubt at all about Doherty's pivotal role in Northern Ireland's glory years. 'Peter was fortunate to have some good players in his time – players who held him in respect and worked hard for him. But they gave him that because they knew he deserved it. Back in the early 1950s when he took over we were all young, inexperienced players. He fired us with his enthusiasm. His team talks were like a compelling drug to us – every word drove us more eagerly on to the field. He breathed the very spirit of his style of play into us.' And, rather sorrowfully,

Blanchflower reflected on the lessening of Doherty's powerful influence on the players as the years passed: 'Peter could not do … for us what he did those ten years or so ago, simply because we were not the same people, the same players, that we were ten years ago. Ten years have passed by and changed him too.'

On 18 April 1962, a week after a heavy defeat to Wales, Peter Doherty tendered his resignation to the IFA. At a board meeting on 26 April, this was formally accepted. Danny Blanchflower was put in temporary charge of the team for a friendly against the Netherlands the following week but the permanent replacement was to be one of Doherty's most faithful players, Bertie Peacock. The years had taken their toll and the fine crop of young players that had come through together a decade earlier were now veterans. Some of them, such as Danny Blanchflower and Jimmy McIlroy, were still playing at the very top level and enjoying successful seasons but for many there had been a decline, signalled by them moving down the leagues or to less glamorous clubs. Some of the new players who came into the Northern Ireland squad around this time probably weren't quite equal to the older players they were replacing. There were exceptions, of course, such as the young Terry Neill, but, generally, as the team began to look less and less like the one from 1958, the quality dropped.

Individually, the team of '58 still continued to create headlines. In the season following the World Cup Billy Bingham, now playing for Luton Town, was the talk of the country – he scored in every round of the FA Cup as the little team carved their way to the final. They were unfortunately beaten by Nottingham Forest and Bingham, as the clear danger man, was marked out of the game. The following season, 1959/60, saw Jimmy McIlroy lauded as one of the greatest players in the British Isles when he played a pivotal role in taking Burnley to the league title as champions of England. The 1960/61 season saw one of the most memorable achievements by a Northern Ireland player.

Danny Blanchflower not only captained Tottenham Hotspur to the league title but added the FA Cup as well to achieve the ultimate prize in English football at that time – the Double. This was the first time in the twentieth century that a team had won the Double and until then it had been dismissed as an impossible dream. The team of that season remains the most legendary in Spurs' proud history and Blanchflower its most famous and iconic player.

It didn't end there for Blanchflower. In 1961/62 Tottenham won the FA Cup for a second successive year, meeting Jimmy McIlroy's Burnley in the final, a glamour tie between two of England's top clubs of the period. The next season brought even more silverware for Spurs when they became the first English team to win a European trophy by taking the European Cup Winners' Cup. At this highpoint Blanchflower retired, but Bingham was around to keep the flag flying for Northern Ireland. Transferred to Everton, he played an important goal-scoring role that helped the club win the English First Division in 1963.

While these veterans enjoyed an Indian summer to their careers, there was a return to the days of toil and struggle for the national team. The Doherty era was over but, for a time, the skills of a young George Best drew attention away from Northern Ireland's failure to qualify for any of the major championships over the years. Once more, they were the weakest team in the annual home championships and campaigns on bigger stages were usually undertaken with little realistic hope of success. As time passed, the memories of 1958 began to fade. A new generation of fans began to follow the team and the achievements of the 1950s moved first into legend and then flickered and disappeared altogether.

Ironically, it was a period of renewed success in the 1980s, with Billy Bingham as manager and Bertie Peacock as his assistant, that finally extinguished the nation's memories of

1958. Not only did Northern Ireland return to the World Cup in 1982, they even made it to the quarter-finals. Once again, France was their nemesis. Northern Ireland also made it into the next World Cup in Mexico in 1986. Much good-quality full-colour visual material of these appearances is available, providing a lasting reminder of Northern Ireland's involvement and that, along with the passing of time, seems to have contributed to the falling away of the story of 1958.

It is disappointing, for example, that Peter Doherty was not interviewed for the 1982 or 1986 World Cup. His experiences of the 1958 World Cup and his thoughts and opinions of Northern Ireland's chances would have been fascinating to hear. Doherty lived until 1990 and, although most football fans in Northern Ireland today are unaware of the fact, he was probably Northern Ireland's second-greatest ever player. In his own time, he was a legend and considered to be the best inside forward in the game, though sadly very little footage of his playing days has survived.

While the 1958 World Cup might have faded from collective memory, it remained important for all those who were involved – the friendships made and the sense of achievement never faded for those who were there. The players had a deep emotional connection to those great times and a number of reunions took place over the years. The last major one was in 2010 before an international game against Italy at Windsor Park when a small band met to mark the achievement of qualifying against the same country in January 1958. The individual bonds forged between the players also remained strong over the years and many of them stayed in contact with each other, sharing friendships that lasted well into old age. At the time of writing, only five of that great squad survive and for each of them, even though they all enjoyed great personal success at club level, it is the time spent with Doherty, Morgan and the Northern Ireland team that remains their fondest memory of the 1950s. The memories of Wembley, the games against Italy and the triumphs in the World

Cup are deeply engraved on the hearts and minds of those who shared in them.

'We were confident then,' remembers Billy Bingham of the mood of the team under Doherty. 'We were going out thinking we were going to win. You never thought – and this is to do with the management as well – you never thought we were going to lose. So when you get a team that's thinking that way and they're doing their stuff, you've got a winning side.' Norman Uprichard remembers the 1958 team as 'one of the finest squads in [Northern Irleand's] history, in terms of spirit and camaraderie.'

For McIlroy, the success of Northern Ireland lay in the coming together of a unique team of players, an experience that that he'd also had at club level: 'Burnley's a little town and we didn't have big money players to play with. But, for some time, we had eleven outstanding players and they made us champions of England. I class what happened to Burnley in the sixties the same thing as happened to Northern Ireland. When we finished playing in those days we came off the field as if we were walking on air or something. I feel proud because along with my team-mates we did a lot. We put Northern Ireland on the world map and that was something that really made me feel good.'

Peter McParland has much to say on the scale of the team's achievements: 'It was like winning the World Cup for us to get to the quarter-finals; it was a great feeling and I think the rest of the world in football had probably never heard of Northern Ireland before that. And if we'd listened to some people – don't kick the ball on a Sunday or whatever – if we'd listened to those people we'd have missed all that fun. For me it was the most exciting part of my career, being in that run with that Irish team in the World Cup. The regret is that I would have loved to have rested the players, to have put my feet up for four days and said, right, we'll play the French now and see if we can get to the semi-final. Probably we were the best international team in the British Isles then and it took a period of time to build up to that and we peaked then, the peak was there in the World Cup. In England or Scotland they were laughing, saying, "Oh they're going there, they'll get murdered. And look at the group they're in, they'll get slaughtered." And we didn't. We proved to everyone that we'd got something among us. It was good fun, we enjoyed doing what we did, and I'm sure maybe the people that were anti us going out there ended up saying, "Oh, good job they didn't take what we were saying serious and stay at home and pray." They were probably praying for us out there in the end.'

The 'Little Black Ant', Bertie Peacock, echoes Peter's views about 1958 being a career high. 'It was a big deal for us all, not only Bertie Peacock. It was a big deal for everyone. It was quite an achievement qualifying for the World Cup, for Northern Ireland. It was probably the highlight of my life really in football going to the World Cup.' Billy Simpson, the player who might have made a name for himself as the scorer of Northern Ireland's goals but for injury, sums up the philosophy that he shared with the team: 'I wasn't interested in money. In those days everyone fought for each other. There were no cliques in those days. Nothing where two or three players said, "Aye, he doesn't get on with him," or whatever. There was a great harmony.' Above all, there is a very strong sense from all those in the team that they had lived in extraordinary times and were blessed to have done so. As Danny Blanchflower eloquently put it some years after the World Cup: 'I appreciate that what we all did then is no longer possible now; but I remember that we did it.'

As for their great manager, he reflected on his time in charge in a 1979 interview: 'For me the good times with Ireland were while I was managing. They were fine players and they developed as a team. That was a good Irish side, and we were unlucky not to reach the 1958 World Cup Final. I shall never forget those days.'

Harry Gregg is a man to whom the past is very important, his walls bedecked with shirts, photographs and souvenirs of his illustrious playing days, and it is no surprise that he is emotional when collecting his thoughts on what it meant to be a part of this great team. 'It was, without being dramatic, a wonderful adventure. Not just for the Harry Greggs and the Dick Keiths, the Alf McMichaels and the Danny Blanchflowers, the Billy Binghams and the Tommy Caseys and all the lads. It was a great adventure for the people of Northern Ireland. I was glad I was part of it. A very small part of it. Those are wonderful memories. Nobody can take those away and that is ... seventeen of us. *Seventeen* of us. Against the rest of the world. It's not bad is it? Not bad, no. See that group of players that I was part of, lucky to be part of? There were very few that you wouldn't go to war with. Everybody likes a fairy tale, but I was part of a bloody great fairy tale.'

APPENDIX 1

Northern Ireland Internationals under Peter Doherty

The information reproduced in this appendix is taken from Malcolm Brodie's *100 Years of Irish Football* (Blackstaff, 1980).

6/10/51	20/11/51	19/3/52	4/10/52
Scotland	**England**	**Wales**	**England**
1. Uprichard	1. Uprichard	1. Uprichard	1. Uprichard
2. Graham	2. Graham	2. Graham	2. Cunningham
3. McMichael	3. McMichael	3. McMichael	3. McMichael
4. Dickson	4. Dickson	4. Blanchflower	4. Blanchflower
5. Vernon	5. Vernon	5. Dickson	5. Dickson
6. Ferris	6. McCourt	6. McCourt	6. McCourt
7. Bingham	7. Bingham	7. Bingham	7. Bingham
8. McIlroy	8. Smyth	8. D'Arcy	8. D'Arcy
9. McMorran	9. McMorran	9. McMorran	9. McMorran
10. Peacock	10. McIlroy	10. McIlroy	10. McIlroy
11. Tully	11. McKenna	11. Lockhart	11. Tully
Windsor Park	**Villa Park**	**Vetch Field**	**Windsor Park**
0–3	0–2	0–3	2–2
			Tully 2

5/11/52	11/11/52	15/4/53	3/10/53
Scotland	**France**	**Wales**	**Scotland**
1. Uprichard	1. Uprichard	1. Uprichard	1. Smyth
2. Graham	2. Graham	2. McCabe	2. Cunningham
3. McMichael	3. McMichael	3. McMichael	3. McMichael
4. Blanchflower	4. Blanchflower	4. Blanchflower	4. Blanchflower
5. Dickson	5. Dickson	5. Dickson	5. McCabe
6. McCourt	6. McCourt	6. McCourt	6. Cush
7. Bingham	7. Bingham	7. Bingham	7. Bingham
8. D'Arcy	8. D'Arcy	8. McIlroy	8. McIlroy
9. McMorran	9. McMorran	9. McMorran	9. Simpson
10. McIlroy	10. Peacock	10. D'Arcy	10. Tully
11. Tully	11. Tully	11. Tully	11. Lockhart
Hampden Park	**Stade Olympique, Paris**	**Windsor Park**	**Windsor Park**
1–1	1–3	2–3	1–3
D'Arcy	**Tully**	**McMorran 2**	**Lockhart**

11/11/53 **England**	31/3/54 **Wales**	2/10/54 **England**	3/11/54 **Scotland**
1. Smyth	1. Gregg	1. Uprichard	1. Uprichard
2. Graham	2. Graham	2. Montgomery	2. Graham
3. McMichael	3. McMichael	3. McMichael	3. Cunningham
4. Blanchflower	4. Blanchflower, D.	4. Blanchflower, D.	4. Blanchflower, D.
5. Dickson	5. Dickson	5. Dickson	5. McCavana
6. Cush	6. Peacock	6. Peacock	6. Peacock
7. Bingham	7. Bingham	7. Bingham	7. Bingham
8. McIlroy	8. Blanchflower, J.	8. Blanchflower, J.	8. Blanchflower, J.
9. Simpson	9. McAdams	9. Simpson	9. McAdams
10. McMorran	10. McIlroy	10. McIlroy	10. McIlroy
11. Lockhart	11. McParland	11. McParland	11. McParland

Goodison Park	**Racecourse**	**Windsor Park**	**Hampden Park**
1-3	**Ground**	**0-2**	**2-2**
McMorran	**2-1**		**Bingham,**
	McParland 2		**McAdams**

20/4/55 **Wales**	8/10/55 **Scotland**	2/11/55 **England**	11/4/56 **Wales**
1. Uprichard	1. Uprichard	1. Uprichard	1. Uprichard
2. Graham	2. Graham	2. Cunningham	2. Cunningham
3. McMichael	3. Cunningham	3. Graham	3. McMichael
4. Blanchflower	4. Blanchflower, D.	4. Blanchflower	4. Blanchflower, D.
5. McCleary	5. McCavana	5. McCavana	5. Blanchflower, J.
6. Casey	6. Peacock	6. Peacock	6. Casey
7. Bingham	7. Bingham	7. Bingham	7. Bingham
8. Crossan, E.	8. Blanchflower, J.	8. McIlroy	8. McIlroy
9. Walker	9. Coyle	9. Coyle	9. Jones
10. McIlroy	10. McIlroy	10. Tully	10. McMorran
11. Lockhart	11. McParland	11. McParland	11. Lockhart

Windsor Park	**Windsor Park**	**Wembley**	**Ninian Park**
2-3	**2-1**	**0-3**	**1-1**
Crossan, Walker	**J. Blanchflower,**		**Jones**
	Bingham		

| 6/10/56 | 7/11/56 | 16/1/57 | 10/4/57 |
England	Scotland	Portugal	Wales
1. Gregg	1. Gregg	1. Gregg	1. Gregg
2. Cunningham	2. Cunningham	2. Cunningham	2. Cunningham
3. McMichael	3. McMichael	3. McMichael	3. McMichael
4. Blanchflower, D.	4. Blanchflower, D.	4. Blanchflower, D.	4. Blanchflower
5. Blanchflower, J.	5. Blanchflower, J.	5. Blanchflower, J.	5. Cush
6. Casey	6. Casey	6. Casey	6. Peacock
7. Bingham	7. Bingham	7. Bingham	7. Bingham
8. McIlroy	8. McIlroy	8. McIlroy	8. McIlroy
9. Jones	9. Shields	9. Coyle	9. Jones
10. McAdams	10. Dickson	10. Cush	10. Casey
11. McParland	11. McParland	11. McParland	11. McParland

Windsor Park	**Hampden Park**	**Estádio José**	**Windsor Park**
1-1	**0-1**	**Alvalade, Lisbon**	**0-0**
McIlroy		**1-1**	
		Bingham	

| 25/4/57 | 1/5/57 | 5/10/57 | 6/11/57 |
Italy	Portugal	Scotland	England
1. Gregg	1. Gregg	1. Uprichard	1. Gregg
2. Cunningham	2. Cunningham	2. Cunningham	2. Keith
3. McMichael	3. McMichael	3. McMichael	3. McMichael
4. Blanchflower	4. Blanchflower	4. Blanchflower, D.	4. Blanchflower, D.
5. Cush	5. Cush	5. Blanchflower, J.	5. Blanchflower, J.
6. Casey	6. Casey	6. Peacock	6. Peacock
7. Bingham	7. Bingham	7. Bingham	7. Bingham
8. Simpson	8. Simpson	8. Simpson	8. McCrory
9. McMorran	9. McMorran	9. McAdams	9. Simpson
10. McIlroy	10. McIlroy	10. McIlroy	10. McIlroy
11. Peacock	11. Peacock	11. McParland	11. McParland

Stadio Olimpico,	**Windsor Park**	**Windsor Park**	**Wembley**
Rome	**3-0**	**1-1**	**3-2**
0-1	**Casey, Simpson,**	**Bingham**	**McIlroy, McCrory,**
	McIlroy		**Simpson**

4/12/57
Italy

1. Gregg
2. Keith
3. McMichael
4. Blanchflower, D.
5. Blanchflower, J.
6. Peacock
7. Bingham
8. McIlroy
9. McAdams
10. Cush
11. McParland

Windsor Park
2-2
Cush 2

15/1/58
Italy

1. Uprichard
2. Cunningham
3. McMichael
4. Blanchflower, D.
5. Blanchflower, J.
6. Peacock
7. Bingham
8. Cush
9. Simpson
10. McIlroy
11. McParland

Windsor Park
2-1
McIlroy, Cush

16/4/58
Wales

1. Gregg
2. Cunningham
3. McMichael
4. Blanchflower
5. Keith
6. Peacock
7. Bingham
8. Cush
9. Simpson
10. McIlroy
11. McParland

Ninian Park
1-1
Simpson

8/6/58
Czechoslovakia

1. Gregg
2. Keith
3. McMichael
4. Blanchflower
5. Cunningham
6. Peacock
7. Bingham
8. Cush
9. Dougan
10. McIlroy
11. McParland

Örjans Vall,
Halmstad
1-0
Cush

11/6/58'
Argentina

1. Gregg
2. Keith
3. McMichael
4. Blanchflower
5. Cunningham
6. Peacock
7. Bingham
8. Cush
9. Coyle
10. McIlroy
11. McParland

Örjans Vall,
Halmstad
1-3
McParland

15/6/58
West Germany

1. Gregg
2. Keith
3. McMichael
4. Blanchflower
5. Cunningham
6. Peacock
7. Bingham
8. Cush
9. Casey
10. McIlroy
11. McParland

Malmö Stadion
2-2
McParland 2

17/6/58
Czechoslovakia

1. Uprichard
2. Keith
3. McMichael
4. Blanchflower
5. Cunningham
6. Peacock
7. Bingham
8. Cush
9. Scott
10. McIlroy
11. McParland

Malmö Stadion
2-1 *(after extra time)*
McParland 2

19/6/58
France

1. Gregg
2. Keith
3. McMichael
4. Blanchflower
5. Cunningham
6. Cush
7. Bingham
8. Casey
9. Scott
10. McIlroy
11. McParland

Idrottspark,
Norrköping
0-4

4/10/58	15/10/58	5/11/58	22/4/59
England	Spain	Scotland	Wales
1. Gregg	1. Uprichard	1. Uprichard	1. Gregg
2. Keith	2. Keith	2. Keith	2. Keith
3. Graham	3. McMichael	3. McMichael	3. McMichael
4. Blanchflower	4. Blanchflower	4. Blanchflower	4. Blanchflower
5. Cunningham	5. Forde	5. Cunningham	5. Cunningham
6. Peacock	6. Casey	6. Peacock	6. Peacock
7. Bingham	7. Bingham	7. Bingham	7. Bingham
8. Cush	8. Cush	8. Cush	8. McIlroy
9. Casey	9. McParland	9. Simpson	9. Cush
10. McIlroy	10. McIlroy	10. McIlroy	10. Hill
11. McParland	11. Tully	11. McParland	11. McParland

Windsor Park
3-3
Cush, Peacock,
Casey

Estadio Bernabéu
Santiago, Madrid
2-6
Bingham,
McIlroy

Hampden Park
2-2
Caldow (o.g.),
McIlroy

Windsor Park
4-1
McParland 2,
Peacock, McIlroy

3/10/59	18/11/59	6/4/60	8/10/60
Scotland	England	Wales	England
1. Gregg	1. Gregg	1. Gregg	1. Gregg
2. Keith	2. Keith	2. Elder	2. Keith
3. McMichael	3. McMichael	3. McMichael	3. Elder
4. Blanchflower	4. Blanchflower	4. Blanchflower	4. Blanchflower
5. Cunningham	5. Cunningham	5. Cunningham	5. Forde
6. Peacock	6. Peacock	6. Cush	6. Peacock
7. Bingham	7. Bingham	7. Bingham	7. Bingham
8. Cush	8. Crossan, J.	8. McIlroy	8. McIlroy
9. Dougan	9. Cush	9. Lawther	9. McAdams
10. McIlroy	10. McIlroy	10. Hill	10. Dougan
11. McParland	11. McParland	11. McParland	11. McParland

Windsor Park
0-4

Wembley
1-2
Bingham

Racecourse
Ground
2-3
Bingham,
Blanchflower

Windsor Park
2-5
McAdams 2

26/10/60
West Germany

1. McClelland
2. Keith
3. Elder
4. Blanchflower
5. Forde
6. Peacock
7. Bingham
8. McIlroy
9. McAdams
10. Hill
11. McParland

Windsor Park
3-4
McAdams 3

9/11/60
Scotland

1. Gregg
2. Keith
3. Elder
4. Blanchflower
5. Forde
6. Peacock
7. Bingham
8. Bruce
9. McAdams
10. Nicholson
11. McParland

Hampden Park
2-5
Blanchflower,
McParland

12/4/61
Wales

1. McClelland
2. Keith
3. Elder
4. Blanchflower
5. Cunningham
6. Nicholson
7. Stewart
8. Dougan
9. McAdams
10. McIlroy
11. McParland

Windsor Park
1-5
Dougan

25/4/61
Italy

1. McClelland
2. Keith
3. McCullough
4. Harvey
5. Neill
6. Peacock
7. Bingham
8. Dougan
9. Lawther
10. McAdams
11. McParland

Stadio Comunale,
Bologna
2-3
Dougan,
McAdams

3/5/61
Greece

1. McClelland
2. Keith
3. Elder
4. Cush
5. Neill
6. Peacock
7. Bingham
8. McIlroy
9. McAdams
10. Dougan
11. McParland

Apostolos
Nikolaidis
Stadium, Athens
1-2
McIlroy

10/5/61
West Germany

1. McClelland
2. Keith
3. Elder
4. Blanchflower
5. Neill
6. Peacock
7. Bingham
8. Cush
9. McAdams
10. McIlroy
11. McParland

Olympiastadion,
Berlin
1-2
McIlroy

7/10/61
Scotland

1. Gregg
2. Magill
3. Elder
4. Blanchflower
5. Neill
6. Peacock
7. Wilson
8. McIlroy
9. Lawther
10. Hill
11. McLaughlin

Windsor Park
1-6
McLaughlin

17/10/61
Greece

1. Gregg
2. Magill
3. Elder
4. Blanchflower
5. Neill
6. Nicholson
7. Bingham
8. McIlroy
9. McAdams
10. Cush
11. McLaughlin

Windsor Park
2-0
McLaughlin 2

22/11/61	11/4/62
England	**Wales**
1. Hunter	1. Briggs
2. Magill	2. Keith
3. Elder	3. Cunningham
4. Blanchflower	4. Blanchflower
5. Neill	5. Neill
6. Nicholson	6. Nicholson
7. Bingham	7. Humphries
8. Barr	8. Johnston
9. McAdams	9. O'Neill
10. McIlroy	10. McLaughlin
11. McLaughlin	11. Braithwaite
Wembley	**Ninian Park**
1-1	**0-4**
McIlroy	

TOUR MATCHES

These games did not count as full internationals. Substitutes were allowed in some games; their names appear in brackets. This information is taken from *1953–54 Irish Football Yearbook*.

14/5/53	18/5/53	20/5/53	23/5/53
Liverpool	**Hamilton and District XI**	**Ontario FA**	**Manitoba FA**
1. Uprichard	1. Uprichard	1. Uprichard	1. Uprichard
2. Graham	2. Graham	2. Graham	2. Graham
3. McMichael	(Bowler)	3. McMichael	3. Ferris
4. Blanchflower	3. McMichael	4. Blanchflower	4. Neill
5. Bowler	4. Neill	5. McCabe	5. McCabe
6. McCourt	5. McCabe	6. McCourt	6. Casey
7. Scott	6. McCourt	7. Scott	7. Scott
8. Crossan, E.	7. Shiells	8. D'Arcy	8. Crossan, E.
9. McMorran	8. D'Arcy	9. Hughes	9. Hughes
10. Ferris	9. Hughes	10. McMorran	10. Blanchflower
11. Lockhart	10. Blanchflower	11. Lockhart	11. Lockhart
Ebbet's Field, New York	11. Scott (Crossan, E.)	**Municipal Stadium, Toronto**	**Osborne Stadium, Winnipeg**
0-4	**Civic Stadium, Hamilton**	**2-0**	**2-0**
	4-1	**Scott, Hughes**	**Scott, Hughes**
	Hughes, D'Arcy 2, Blanchflower		

26/5/53
Saskatchewan FA

1. Uprichard
2. Bowler
3. McMichael
4. Neill
5. Ferris
6. Casey
7. Shiells
8. Crossan, E.
9. D'Arcy
10. McMorran
11. Lockhart

**Exhibition Park,
Moose Jaw
10–0
McMorran
4, D'Arcy 2,
Crossan 2,
Lockhart, Shiells**

**30/5/53
British Columbia
FA**

1. Uprichard
2. Graham
3. McMichael
4. Blanchflower
5. McCabe
6. McCourt
7. Scott
8. Crossan, E.
9. Hughes
10. D'Arcy
    (McMorran)
11. Lockhart

**Callister Park,
Vancouver
3–1
Crossan 2,
Lockhart**

**2/6/53
Victoria FA**

1. Uprichard
2. Graham
3. McMichael
4. Blanchflower
5. McCabe
   (Bowler)
6. McCourt
7. Scott
8. Crossan, E.
9. Hughes
10. Ferris
11. Lockhart

**Royal Athletic
Park, Victoria
5–1
Hughes 2,
Crossan,
Lockhart, Ferris**

**6/6/53
British Columbia
FA**

1. Uprichard
2. Graham
3. McMichael
4. Blanchflower
5. Bowler (Neill)
6. McCourt
7. Scott
8. Crossan, E.
9. Hughes
10. McMorran
    (D'Arcy)
11. Lockhart

**Callister Park,
Vancouver
2–3
Hughes, D'Arcy**

**8/6/53
Alberta FA**

1. D'Arcy
2. Graham
3. McMichael
4. Neill
   (Blanchflower)
5. McCabe
6. Casey
7. Shiells (Scott)
8. Crossan, E.
9. McMorran
10. Ferris (Hughes)
11. Lockhart

**Clarke Stadium,
Edmonton
9–1
Hughes 4,
McMorran 3,
Crossan 2**

**13/6/53
Liverpool**

1. Uprichard
2. Graham
3. McMichael
4. Blanchflower
5. McCabe
6. McCourt
7. Scott
8. Crossan, E.
9. Hughes
10. McMorran
11. Lockhart

**Varsity Stadium,
Toronto
1–3
McMorran**

**17/6/53
Berne Young
Boys**

1. Uprichard
2. Graham
3. McMichael
4. Blanchflower
5. McCabe
6. Casey
7. Scott
8. Crossan, E.
9. Hughes
   (McMorran)
10. D'Arcy
11. Lockhart

**Delormier
Stadium,
Montreal
1–4
McMorran**

APPENDIX 2

Player Appearances

A list of all the players that Peter Doherty picked to play for Northern Ireland for the fifty matches that took place over the years that he was in charge (1951–1962). The players are listed in descending order of number of appearance.

Player	Appearances under Doherty	Total appearances	Goals under Doherty	Total goals	Dates of international career
Bingham, Billy	47	56	6	9	1951–63
Blanchflower, Danny	46	56	2		1949–62
McIlroy, Jimmy	46	55	9	10	1951–64
McMichael, Alf	35	40	-		1949–60
McParland, Peter	33	34	10		1954–62
Peacock, Bertie	31		2		1951–61
Cunningham, Willie	28	30	-		1951–62
Cush, Wilbur	24	26	5		1950–61
Gregg, Harry	23	25	-		1954–63
Keith, Dick	22	23	-		1957–62
Uprichard, Norman	18		-		1951–58
McAdams, Billy	14	15	7		1954–62
Graham, Len	12	14	-		1951–58
Blanchflower, Jackie	12		1		1954–58
Casey, Tommy	12		2		1955–58
McMorran, Eddie	11	15	3	4	1946–57
Dickson, Billy	10	12	-		1951–54
Simpson, Billy	10	12	3	5	1951–58
Elder, Alex	10	40	-	1	1960–69
Tully, Charlie	8	10	3		1948–58
Neill, Terry	7	59	-	2	1961–73
Dougan, Derek	6	43	2	8	1958–73
McCourt, Frank	6		-		1951–53
D'Arcy, Jimmy	5		1		1952–53
Lockhart, Norman	5	8	1	3	1946–56
McClelland, Jack	5	6	-		1960–66
Nicholson, Jimmy	5	41	-	6	1960–71

Player	Appearances under Doherty	Total appearances	Goals under Doherty	Total goals	Dates of international career
Coyle, Fay	4		–		1955–58
Forde, Tommy	4		–		1958–60
Hill, Jimmy	4	7	–		1959–63
McLaughlin, Jim	4	12	3	6	1961–66
McCavana, Terry	3		–		1954–55
Lawther, Ian	3	4	–		1960–62
Jones, Jimmy	3		1		1956–57
Magill, Jimmy	3	26	–		1961–66
Vernon, Jackie	2	17	–		1946–51
McCabe, Jimmy	2	6	–		1948–53
Smyth, Billy	2	4	–		1948–53
Scott, Jackie	2		–		1958
Ferris, Ray	1	3		1	1949–51
Smyth, Sammy	1	9		5	1947–51
McKenna, Johnny	1	7	–		1949–51
Montgomery, Frank	1		–		1954
McCleary, Ernie	1		–		1955
Crossan, Eddie	1	3	1		1949–55
Walker, Jimmy	1		1		1955
Shields, Jimmy	1		–		1956
Dickson, Tommy	1		–		1956
McCrory, Sammy	1		1		1957
Crossan, Johnny	1	24	–	10	1959–67
Bruce, Walter	1	2	–		1960–67
Stewart, Tommy	1		–		1961
McCullough, Billy	1	10	–		1961–66
Harvey, Martin	1	34	–	3	1961–71
Wilson, Sammy	1	12	–	7	1961–67
Hunter, Victor	1	2	–		1961–63
Barr, Hugh	1	3	–	1	1961–62
Briggs, Ronnie	1	2	–		1962–65
Humphries, Billy	1	14	–	1	1962–65
Johnston, Billy	1	2	–	1	1962–66
O'Neill. Jimmy	1		–		1962
Braithwaite, Bobby	1	10	–		1962–65